DATE DUE		

" 'But the Emperor has no clothes!' shouted the child. . . ."
(Hans-Christian Andersen, *The Emperor's New Clothes*)

SIMON LEYS

THE
CHAIRMAN'S NEW CLOTHES

Mao and the Cultural Revolution

Translated by Carol Appleyard and Patrick Goode

St. Martin's Press, New York

Copyright © Editions Champ Libre, Paris, 1971, 1972, 1975
Translation copyright © Allison & Busby 1977

All rights reserved. For information, write:
St. Martin's Press, Inc., 175 Fifth Avenue, New York, N.Y. 10010
Printed in Great Britain
Library of Congress Catalog Card Number 77-12772
ISBN 0-312-12791-X
First published in the United States of America in 1977

Library of Congress Cataloging in Publication Data

Leys, Simon.
    The Chairman's new clothes.
    Translation of Les habits neufs du président Mao.
    Includes bibliographical references and index.
    1. China—Politics and government—1949-
2. Mao, Tse-tung, 1893-1976. 3. China—Politics and
government—1949-   —Sources.   I. Title.
DS777.55.L42513   320.9'51'05   77-12772
ISBN 0-312-12791-X

Contents

千人之諾諾不如一士之諤諤
史記商君傳

Foreword

"The Communist Party or the Kuomintang — which of these two dreads criticism? The Kuomintang dreads criticism: it forbids criticism, and therefore has found it impossible to prevent collapse."

Mao Tse-tung
(*Chu-tso hsüan-tu*, Peking, 1965, vol. I, p. 506)

For generations the West has systematically ignored the revolutionary forces that have appeared in China, always preferring to support the decaying order against which these forces have risen. Thus it was that from the mid-nineteenth century onwards the West preferred to prop up the crumbling Manchu dynasty against the Taiping rebellion. As the twentieth century dawned, it set its face in hostility and scorn against those who worked to create the republican movement, and preferred, yet again, to back the fossilised Empire. It never considered Sun Yat-sen (see appendix no. 6) as anything more than a picturesque mountebank who was half dangerous and half foolish; but it was perfectly ready to take a man like Yüan Shih-k'ai seriously. It distrusted Chiang Kai-shek as long as he had all the appearances of a revolutionary, but gave him its confidence and support as soon as he had shown his true nature. Mao Tse-tung, throughout the truly revolutionary phase of his career (from the twenties until the beginning of the fifties) was, in the eyes of the West, alternately non-existent or an ogre. Contrariwise, after the outcome of the "Cultural Revolution" had exposed the archaic and reactionary nature of his power and had turned him — three-quarters of a century later — into the successor, as it were, of the old Dowager Empress Tz'u-hsi, there was a complete change of opinion in the West and people flocked to his court: politicians in or out of office, financiers, industrialists, compradores, parlour revolutionaries, worshippers in search of a god, ladies bountiful, philosophers and various kinds of tourist — all elbowing their way to pay him homage.

Quite unable (or deliberately refusing) to perceive the revolutionary ferment which has continued to work deeply through China and which nearly came out into the open during the "Cultural Revolution", this motley crowd of pilgrims was simply worshipping at the altar of *power* (or whatever presented itself as such). And so Mao's authority, having victoriously crushed the revolution and imposed gun law, was henceforth to be sacred for them; this authority alone was guaranteed to restore the credit of the tourist-politicians, to grant contracts to capitalism's travelling salesmen and to provide superannuated revolutionaries with cosy sinecures. How could they fail to worship him?

On the other hand, there are those big-hearted but small-brained dreamers of revolution who, failing to realise that revolution must be invented afresh by those who make it and that it cannot be plucked like a ripe fruit from some exotic orchard, have flung the name of Mao in their rulers' face in the same way that the philosophers of the Age of Enlightenment brandished the name of Confucius. What precisely Confucius meant was of little importance to them; the less they knew about him, the better they could adapt him to their own dreams. Our present-day philosophers seem equally unwilling to enquire into the historical truth of maoism, no doubt fearing that to meet reality face to face might harm the myth that so conveniently excuses them from having to think for themselves.

But this sort of face-to-face encounter with the evidence, however painful, cannot be easily avoided by anybody who has lived through the "Cultural Revolution" on China's doorstep and who has not been shielded from the truth by a blessed ignorance of the Chinese language. The author of this work originally had no interest in political questions and had tended to confuse maoism with the liking and admiration which China, past and present, has never ceased to inspire in him. But he was impelled — by the weight of evidence thrown up in the texts, facts and personal accounts which assailed him daily in Hong Kong throughout the years of the "Cultural Revolution" — to cry out, like the child in the fairy story, "But the Emperor has no clothes!" The pages which follow are no more than a commentary woven around this artless and irrepressible cry. They are often clumsy, one-sided and incomplete, but they speak for themselves: they are the observations of a consciousness forced out of its calm retreat at the sight of what it took to be a gigantic imposture.

In spite of the vehemence which now and again shows through his arguments, the author does not lay claim to any final certainty. He is well aware of the limits of his information, of the gaps in his study of the case and of the subjectivity of his point of view. The reader can dispute his arguments and opinions, but it will be difficult to ignore entirely the facts and documents on which the author bases his interpretation. Let those whose judgements are more weighty and whose political experience is richer weave the facts given here into whatever exegesis they may attempt to make of the "Cultural Revolution". If, by taking into account the various lines of material evidence presented here, they succeed in demonstrating that the "Cultural Revolution" was indeed both cultural and a revolution, then the author will be the first to rejoice and will most gladly withdraw his impudent conclusions.

S.L.

I
The "Cultural Revolution" in its Historical Perspective

"I must state that this history is by no means impartial. It does not maintain a wise and prudent balance between good and bad. On the contrary, it is frankly and vigorously on the side of right and truth. If a single line can be found where the author has diluted his account or his judgements out of respect for some opinion, some authority or other, let it cancel out the whole work. 'What,' you will say, 'is there only one sincere person? Are you claiming a monopoly of faithfulness?' That is not my intention. I would simply say that the more reputable people may maintain their respect for certain things and certain men, but that as judge of the world, *History's first duty is to lose its respect.*"

Michelet, Histoire de France

The "Cultural Revolution" had nothing revolutionary about it except the name, and nothing cultural about it except the initial tactical pretext. It was a power struggle waged at the top between a handful of men and behind the smokescreen of a fictitious mass movement. As things turned out, the disorder unleashed by this power struggle created a genuinely revolutionary mass current, which developed spontaneously at the grass roots in the form of army mutinies and workers' strikes on a vast scale. These had not been prescribed in the programme, and they were crushed pitilessly. Certain Western commentators insist on taking the official title literally, basing their interpretation on the concept of a "revolution" in Chinese culture, or even in Chinese civilisation (the Chinese term *wen-hua* permits this double interpretation). In the context of such an inspiring theme, any attempt to reduce this remarkable event to the mean and trivial dimension of a "power struggle" rings painfully, if not slanderously, in a Western maoist's ears. China's maoists are less squeamish: the definition of the "Cultural Revolution" as a "power struggle" (*ch'üan-li tou-cheng*) was in fact not dreamed up by the régime's enemies; it was the official definition used by Peking and was constantly repeated in editorials of the *People's Daily*, the *Liberation Army Daily* and the *Red Flag* from the beginning of 1967, when the movement was sufficiently advanced to be able to do away with the protection of the cultural smokescreen behind which it had first set out.

The idea that Mao might in fact have lost power must have been difficult for European observers to admit, from their distant observation posts. Nevertheless, it was with the aim of regaining it that he launched this struggle. What is astounding is that it should be necessary (after four years of "Cultural Revolution"!) to recall this kind of evidence to mind. In fact, in Europe and

America, there are still contemporary China experts who will minimise, cast doubt upon or deny the fact that Mao had been deprived of power. Why then should Mao have needed to scuttle the party and the régime, to bring the whole country to confusion in order to take power, if he had always held it? Worse still are those who deliberately ignore the vast mass of proof gathered through the "Cultural Revolution" both in official documents (Peking press editorials) and in unofficial documents (wall newspapers, Red Guard publications); the main accusation directed at the power-holders at all levels up to and including those at the highest level — the General Secretary of the party and the Chairman of the Republic — was precisely that they monopolised all power and exercised it in a fashion that Mao was able neither to control nor to influence. Why and how had Mao found himself in this situation?

Before answering this question, it is necessary to take a look back at the "Great Leap Forward" (1958) and even, to a certain extent, the "Hundred Flowers" movement (1957), and to highlight certain characteristic aspects of Mao's political style.

In 1958, Mao launched the "Great Leap Forward" movement which, like the "Hundred Flowers" episode of a year earlier, was not the result of a collective decision by the higher party ranks but simply and essentially a product of Mao's own visionary inspiration. The principle of the "Great Leap Forward" was to lessen China's industrial and economic underdevelopment by making use of the human resources of the whole country, galvanised by one unanimous burst of revolutionary enthusiasm which would take the place of the basic equipment which was still seriously lacking or being too slowly installed. In short, in order to catapult China into communism, Mao's dream was to replace the material factor by the spiritual; instead of electrical power (Lenin's words), revolutionary power. Here we have one of Mao's most striking idiosyncrasies, one which has found expression in numberless examples in his writings and episodes in his career: an idealistic and wilful approach to problems which is in fact that of an artist or poet, for whom reality is not a ready-made element in any situation but must be invented and fashioned to follow the demands of a purely subjective and inward vision. (In this connection, a very significant example is the importance in Mao's work[1] of the well-known anecdote, taken from Lieh Tzu, of the old man who decided to move mountains with his own two hands; official exegesis is quite right to set it out as a central theme of Mao's thought.)

Let us have no illusions about the quality of Mao's artistic creation. The fame of his poetry owes everything to his fame as a politician; if Mao had not played his particular part in history, his poetical works, which are slight and often clumsy, would not have stood out from the work of thousands of other amateur poets who flourish in each generation of Chinese scholars. Certainly the poet's inspiration meets the politician's experience to outstanding effect in the poem "Snow" (to the tune of *Ch'in yuan ch'un*) which is memorable in the same sense as "Song of the Great Wind" by Liu Pang, the founder of the Han dynasty, or the poems of the military leader and statesman Ts'ao Ts'ao (even if, as gossip has it, Mao's poem was corrected and reshaped by Liu Ya-tzu). But this single example apart, it is not difficult to agree with Arthur Waley's criticism, which used a pictorial comparison and rated Mao's poetry "not as bad as Hitler's painting but not as good as Churchill's". Mao's calligraphy is a fascinating reflection of his personality: it is aggressively unorthodox and mirrors the flamboyance of an ego which will only accept rules of its own invention. In calligraphy, this sort of attitude can create something which is of high value when the calligrapher is in a position to base the liberties he takes upon a confident grasp of the discipline of his craft. Mao entirely lacks formal training, and this gives his calligraphy its unpleasantly bold and bloated air (the bloated impression is exaggerated by enlargement of the small-sized originals when they are reproduced).

But we are not concerned here with the quality of Mao's artistic output. What is particularly noteworthy is the degree to which his conduct and actions are conditioned by his attitude and drive as an artist. This same characteristic applies to several famous statesmen, men whose political designs were the reverse side of a kind of ill-expressed or stifled artistic creativity — or a substitute for it; unable to master the language of literature or the plastic arts, these men have used peoples and empires as their material, as an outward expression of their inward vision.*

---

* This characteristic does not appear with uniform intensity: Julius Caesar's prose, Frederick the Great's music, Napoleon's unfinished novel, Churchill's historical prose and his painting, de Gaulle's essays and memoirs, Ts'ao Ts'ao's poems, Mao's poetry — all of these generously reveal the particular nature of the political genius of these differing individuals; but in their case the artistic urge, while helping to explain their most brilliant political successes (and their most outstanding failures), remained largely subordinate to the rationale of their political

A second characteristic of the "Great Leap Forward" was its rejection of the external world, of modernity, and its urge to return to the familiar bosom of the age-old, unchanged, self-sufficient Chinese countryside, that native soil of which Mao was himself the pure product. It is well known that Mao was little if ever exposed to the influences of the modern world; he was barely acquainted with the intellectual and urban side of China which had begun to open up to contemporary ideas. Works of marxist doctrine carried little weight in the moulding of his thought, compared with the Chinese classics which from childhood had never ceased to kindle his mind. Several biographers have pointed out the influence upon Mao of the classical epic novel, such as *Shui-hu* ("The Water Margin" or "All Men are Brothers") and *San Kuo* ("The Romance of the Three Kingdoms"), but the importance and significance of yet another of his favourite books — *Tzu-chih t'ung chien* ("The Universal Mirror of History as a Reference-Book for Rulers"), written by Ssu-ma Kuang in the eleventh century — has not been sufficiently emphasised. This old-fashioned political handbook for the use of the imperial mandarinate was Mao's constant reading; he even saw nothing unsuitable in having himself shown in a recent official photograph at his desk with this corner-stone of the old bureaucratic order at his elbow, in preference to any other work. An eloquent symbol. Within this bygone, enclosed world, Mao feels most completely at home. It was the scene of the most brilliant part of his career; within it he needs fear no rival, as the subjective intuition of his genius unhesitatingly matches objective reality. But these psychological roots in the country life of the past, the basis of his strength up to 1949, were to become his heaviest handicap after that date. This was brought out clearly in the crisis of the "Hundred Flowers", which calls at this point for some digression.

---

aims. In Hitler (who, it seems fair to say, might never have been tempted into politics had he been able to distinguish himself as a painter and architect), the phenomenon reached paroxysmal proportions; his military campaigns were subjected alternately to lightning flashes of strategic intuition and bouts of frenzy totally out of touch with objective reality. In the cases, on the other hand, of Nero, of Ludwig II of Bavaria, of the last Southern T'ang sovereign Li Yü, and of the emperor Sung Hui-tsung, the artist took over the man — ineffectually in the first two cases, triumphantly in the others. Finally, it would be worth examining the case of artists by vocation and training who are later attracted to the illusory world of politics (Chateaubriand, D'Annunzio, Malraux, Kuo Mo-jo, etc.). There is room for a psychological study of the influence of aesthetics on politics.

With the conquest of power in 1949, Mao found himself in an entirely new situation, confronted with problems of a kind which his earlier experiences could give him no help whatever in solving; what is more, these experiences were soon to hold back the advance of the machine he had set up. Guerrillas fighting barefoot in a countryside with which they were familiar, using patched up equipment, improvising their strategy in the epic vein of Ts'ao Ts'ao and Chu-ke Liang: these were no longer needed. What was needed was the building and organisation of a great modern state capable of facing present-day realities and the external threat. Henceforth, his political judgement would have to tackle endless specialised problems beyond the scope of his experience. His grasp of them was uncertain and he was forced to count on the special qualifications of a category of persons towards whom he had long fostered ambivalent feelings: the academic authorities (ch'üan-wei) and the experts (chuan-chia). The roots of these feelings lay deep in the past. As a young man Mao Tse-tung, driven by a devouring intellectual curiosity, had admired and envied those of his comrades who had the opportunity to study abroad. In Shanghai in 1919, as he was seeing off a group of friends to the ship taking them to France, he confided in one of them — who has since told me what he said — all the discouragement and (justifiable) bitterness he felt, knowing that he was denied a similar opportunity to develop his talents. These feelings were exacerbated by his humiliating experiences as a lowly messenger in the library at Peking University. We need simply refer to the well-known passage in his confession to Edgar Snow twenty years later, which brought to light the unhealed wound in his self-esteem:

"My office was so low that people avoided me. One of my tasks was to register the names of people who came to read newspapers, but to most of them I didn't exist as a human being. Among those who came to read I recognised the names of famous leaders of the renaissance movement, men like Fu Ssu-nien, Lo Chia-lun, and others, in whom I was intensely interested. I tried to begin conversations with them on political and cultural subjects, but they were very busy men. They had no time to listen to an assistant librarian speaking southern dialect."[2]

His frustration drove him to make a myth out of these inaccessible beings and to ascribe to the academic world a power which it in no way even claimed; and at the same time, the resounding successes which he achieved without the benefit of academic training led him in turn to deny that such people had any value.

On taking power, the régime had adopted a welcoming and liberal attitude towards the intellectuals, inviting them to offer their skills in the service of the people. The great majority of intellectuals enthusiastically seized the chance thus given them to serve their country; even the large number of Chinese scientists and academics who had settled abroad were moved by patriotic fervour and returned of their own free will.

However, Mao accepted only with the greatest reluctance the need to call upon the services of a modern intellectual élite for which he felt an instant and almost uncontrollable mistrust and dislike, and which was in a position to call his judgement in question in each particular discipline. To begin with, however, he was lulled into believing that this élite had rallied to him in his personal capacity. The "Hundred Flowers" campaign (late 1956 to early 1957) brought a rude awakening. It would be misleading to think that the "Hundred Flowers" movement was some sort of machiavellian trick played by the régime in order to get its opponents to throw off the mask and expose themselves to repression; the wave of repression in which the movement ended was not the last act of a scenario prepared in advance but rather an emergency measure, hastily improvised to cut short an unforeseen and catastrophic development.

The "Hundred Flowers" movement had been launched on Mao's personal initiative and against the advice of his collaborators who, better aware of what to expect from the state of mind of the cadres and intellectuals, foresaw a dangerous fiasco. Experience proved them right: the country's élite certainly made use of the freedom of expression suddenly granted it, but not in the manner foreseen by Mao. Mao envisaged it as producing positive criticism, which would purify and strengthen the régime and bring it a wave of voluntary and spontaneous adherence, but in fact it became an increasingly rebellious and destructive criticism which called into question the authority of the party and even that of its supreme leader.

The "Hundred Flowers" left permanent scars. For Mao, the experiment finally confirmed the prejudices he had built up towards the intellectuals and led him from then on to consider the modern mind as the natural and unmanageable enemy of his power. For historians studying the rise, decay and final collapse of maoism, the "Hundred Flowers" campaign will remain a crucial date — the turning-point in an evolution and the first seeds of a disintegration. This first, apparently feeble tremor was to be followed by the violent earthquake of the "Great Leap

Forward" and finally by the fatal shock of the "Cultural Revolution". Although at the time it was possible to varnish over the first thin cracks made by the "Hundred Flowers" campaign and so fool the superficial observer, the crack widened until it became the open breach of the "Great Leap Forward" and the final explosion of the "Cultural Revolution". The sudden ending of the "Hundred Flowers" destroyed, once and for all, the liberal illusions thanks to which the first years of the régime had been a period of enthusiasm and intense energy. The régime thus utterly alienated the support of the intellectuals. In the short run the consequences of this might appear to have been slight — the intellectual élite represented only a slender minority within the population as a whole — but this alienation set a direction for maoism which in the long run would be fatal to it. The "Hundred Flowers" brought to an end Mao's constructive and revolutionary phase and opened the period of negative and retrograde activity. The repression that he would from now on mete out to all vital and outward-looking forces of criticism and modernisation is an echo of the blindly reactionary policy of the Dowager Empress Tz'u-hsi as she strove, in the decline of the Manchu dynasty, to exterminate the small élite of progressive intellectuals and disseminators of modern ideas. This parallel between Mao and Tz'u-hsi should not be understood as wholly offensive to the former. Tz'u-hsi was anything but a mediocre personality, in fact she had a brilliant political sense; for her, the tragedy (and the catastrophes she brought upon China) came from the fact that this sense, which was perfectly well adapted to the parameters of her traditional and exclusive world, was lost in the new world which a twist in the path of history had confronted her with. Nor is this comparison an arbitrary one; to some extent it was suggested by the maoists themselves, in the notorious controversy that grew round the film *Secret Episode at the Ch'ing Court* (*Ch'ing kung mi-shih*, see below, p. 65). In the maoists' own judgement on this crisis in Tz'u-hsi's reign, it was the primitive and superstitious Boxer movement, mobilised by the Dowager Empress herself, which was the revolutionary force, while Kuang-hsü and the group of progressive intellectuals crushed by Tz'u-hsi were in the traitors' camp.

A further important consequence of the "Hundred Flowers" experiment was the evidence of a split between Mao and his faithful collaborators and henchmen. For the first time, they found his judgement lacking; for the first time they had been more farsighted than he and, once the damage had been done, it was their efforts that had to be mobilised in order to redress the situation. Mao would never be able to forgive them for having rescued him, and they would never be able to forget this near-disaster. From now on, they were watching their leader with astonishment and dismay.

Their dismay was to have the worst possible confirmation a year later with the launching of the "Great Leap Forward" — a movement which, even more appallingly, crystallised the most negative and destructive forces of Mao's ego: the poetic subjectivity of an aesthete and visionary unaware of the limitations of everyday life, the inspired artist's impatience with unyielding matter, a wilful idealism which seeks to use a kind of mystical energy to control science and technology, a peasant hostility towards modernisation and a systematic reference to all the most archaic and backward aspects of life at the Chinese grass roots. Three themes in Mao's thinking give us a clue to the "philosophy" of the "Great Leap Forward". (1) China's strength lies in her very poverty: China is a "blank page" lying open to Mao's inspiration so that he may paint upon it the unspoken poem of his revolution.* (2) Revolutionary fervour alone can and must effectively overcome material obstacles and so transform matter (the primacy of the "red" over the "expert"). (3) The villager's gift for improvisation and native "make-do and mend" (t'u fang-fa) can and must effectively replace the scientific, technical and industrial means.

In fact, these were the age-old recipes of the guerrilla warfare which was conducted in the early isolation of China's inland provinces, and which in the past had brought Mao his most resounding victories. But he had by now lost sight of the fact that the problems he faced in building a modern China in the 1950s were radically different. And it was here that Mao's thinking revealed its pathetically out-of-date character — in his desperate hanging on to his old fighting formula, the only one that he really knew. Ill-at-ease and out of his depth when confronted with the authority of "specialists", when problems were set out in economic and technological terms that were new and, for him,

---

* "The two most obvious characteristics of the six hundred million Chinese are first their destitution and secondly their ingenuousness. This latter is not a bad thing: on the contrary, it's an advantage. At this extreme point, change must necessarily come; one must act, make the revolution. A blank page is free of ornament: it invites one to inscribe the newest and most beautiful words, to paint the newest and most beautiful picture."[3]

alien, he sought to bring the struggle back at any price to the only terrain familiar to him — the countryside, the scene of the epic years of his youth. He preferred to slow down and hold up his country's development rather than see it escape his control; he not only brought it to a standstill but *deliberately took it backwards*. The idea of China's "destitution" and "blank pages" (*yi k'ung erh pai*), while applicable to some extent to the areas in which communist guerrilla fighters had operated forty years earlier, could clearly not cope with the genuinely complex realities of China as a whole. And the principal obstacle which Mao's thinking encountered stemmed precisely from the fact that the page was not "blank". Rather than maoism being adapted to the reality of China, the latter was forced to adapt itself to maoism. As a result, the only truly cultural part of the "Cultural Revolution" was to consist, as we shall see further on, of an immense effort to paste over, rub out or scratch away from the Chinese "page" the countless rich and living traces that the centuries had left on it, so that on the "blank" page the Chairman could write his poem (and his wife find a stage for her famous piano).

Originally, the idea of making up for the lack of modern equipment by ingenious local improvisation and, *for want of anything better,* resorting to a full range of makeshifts, grew out of an intelligent and realistic policy; in an emergency it produced remarkable results. The revolutionaries were rightly proud of having marched barefoot to victory, and their poverty added an extra dimension to their heroism. All this falls within the positive and creative phrase of maoism, but where maoism begins its senile and retrograde phase is when shortages are presented as advantages and underdevelopment as a positive factor, and when the ingenious makeshift is no longer considered as temporarily better than nothing but as the ideal solution, and is deliberately preferred to the scientific solution of the "experts".

In the "Great Leap Forward" Mao was concerned both to lead China back to this archaic, parochial model, the epic battleground of his youth and, at the same time, to catapult China ahead of all modern nations; this fantastic, contradictory dream brought about the catastrophe. Not only did the movement fail to achieve the exhilarating aims it had set itself, but the entire Chinese economy was plunged into chaos when the construction effort met paralysis and breakdown. Natural catastrophes followed, to complete the disaster. The population, already exhausted by the frenzied and fruitless efforts enforced upon it, began to experience the miseries of famine. The credit and prestige that the party had gained among the peasants suffered irreparable damage, and the régime's authority was directly threatened by the discontent and despair of the masses.

There was consternation in the party's upper levels at this new lurch in policy, which was infinitely more serious than the "Hundred Flowers" and was due, once again, to one of Mao's irresponsible initiatives. This time it was important to take emergency measures to save the régime, and to prevent any repetition of such hazardous ventures.

In December 1958, at the Wuchang conference, Mao was forced to relinquish his position as Head of State in favour of Liu Shao-ch'i. The decision became official in March 1959. The Shanghai conference (seventh plenum of the eighth central committee, April 1959) produced a first critical examination of the "Great Leap Forward", and a first series of amendments was made to the idea of the people's communes. The party apparatus thus began to impress upon Mao the weight of its disapproval, but did not express its displeasure by means of a direct attack. This, however, was to come immediately afterwards. It was led by Marshal P'eng Teh-huai, and culminated in the famous Lushan conference of July-August 1959.

P'eng Teh-huai was a formidable individual. There is a vivid character sketch of P'eng and a fairly complete biographical sketch in Edgar Snow's *Red Star Over China* (pp. 285-305). In 1961 Snow, in *The Other Side of the River*, took the trouble to deny outright that P'eng had organised a plot against Mao two years earlier or that he had been punished: "The Chinese party leadership does not work that way" (p. 642), the implication being that the paying off of old scores in this way could not exist in such an admirable ruling élite, and must therefore necessarily be the product of the perverse imagination of the foreign press. In fact *two years earlier, on 16 August 1959, the central committee had unmistakably denounced P'eng as the leader of an "anti-party plot"*. Unfortunately for Mr Snow, the central committee document which set out his crime ("Decision of the eighth plenary session of the eighth central committee of the Chinese Communist Party concerning the anti-party group led by P'eng Teh-huai") was finally made public, on Peking's initiative (see the *People's Daily*, 16 August 1967). Mr Snow can justly flatter himself on being one of the best-informed foreign observers and one of the most experienced witnesses of Chinese communism, but that he should have blundered so ingenuously and so thoroughly gives food for thought on the quality of Western information on the problem of China.

P'eng Teh-huai was outspoken, warm-hearted and truculent; his heroism and military genius had played a decisive role, first in the Hunan-Kiangsi guerrilla campaign, then in the success of the Long March. Among the masses his prestige was almost legendary and nearly the equal of Mao's, while his popularity in the army was hardly less than that of Chu Teh. He would share his rations with his troops as if they were his family. Having learned all he knew from childhood upwards in the school of life, he was without any academic education and a lifelong stranger to the sophistications and tactical twists and turns of politics. In contrast to so many of his colleagues who, after the Liberation, cut themselves off from the masses in order to enjoy all the privileges of a new bureaucratic class, P'eng maintained his simple and frugal style of living and had remained in direct contact with the people. (During the "Cultural Revolution", this austere style of living which he had always adopted — and which had become a kind of reproach to the new ruling class — was seen as one of his crimes, as yet another aspect of his "hypocrisy". As for the military feats and heroism that had marked his whole career, they were twisted against him as evidence that he was an "opportunist", an "ambitious adventurist" and a "warlord".) So it was he, more than any of the other dignitaries of the régime, who was in a position to hear the complaints of the peasants. He resolved to speak for them, and to make their voice heard in the leader's ear. To do this, not only did he rely on his own position within the régime's apparatus but, above all, he maintained the simple man's belief that it should always be possible for former fighting companions to speak frankly. ("Did we not eat from the same pot?" demanded Chu Teh later on, as he pleaded P'eng's case before the central committee.) He could not understand why, for Mao, there could no longer be companions, only lackeys. (This was to explain the extremely poor quality of the ruling team that emerged from the "Cultural Revolution", which was recruited by Mao from within his private circle — Ch'en Po-ta from the servants' quarters, Chiang Ch'ing and Yeh Ch'ün from the women's quarters, Lin Piao and Huang Yung-sheng from among the generals, and K'ang Sheng and Hsieh Fu-chih from among the policemen.)

In July 1959, during the preparatory sessions for the eighth plenum of the eighth central committee at Lushan, P'eng circulated a memorandum (see appendix, p. 213) which he had sent Mao, in which he bluntly criticised the policy of the "Great Leap Forward"; he accused Mao of having erred towards "subjectivism" and "petty-bourgeois idealism" in his line, and showed how his policy, in its scorn for and ignorance of objective reality, had laid an unbearable burden on the Chinese people.

The growing disquiet and discontent which Mao's autocratic and foolhardy style of government had generated among the top leaders crystallised behind P'eng's manifesto, which had dared to shout aloud with a brutal frankness what most of them believed in their heart of hearts.

During the Lushan conference, Mao found that he was confronted by a formidable opposition. P'eng's standing was high in the army, the party and among the masses. He held high office, standing in fourteenth place in the régime's hierarchy; he was a member of the politbureau, Vice-Chairman of the State Council and Minister of National Defence. He had the open support of other important figures such as Huang K'e-ch'eng (member of the central committee, Vice-Minister of Defence and Chief of the General Staff) and Chang Wen-t'ien (deputy polit-bureau member and Vice-Minister of Foreign Affairs), as well as the tacit support of the majority of central committee members.

At this critical juncture, in order to ward off the most pressing danger, Mao was forced to beg the help of his deputy, Liu Shao-ch'i, who controlled a good number of the levers to the bureau-cratic machine. Liu thus found himself placed in the privileged position of arbiter; he manipulated the majority and had P'eng, Huang and Chang condemned and at once relieved of their party and government posts. But although in the event Mao was spared for the immediate future from the political death which would have sprung from his finding himself in a minority on the central com-mittee, the price he had to pay in order to be rid of his most formidable opponent was nonetheless exorbitant: the transfer of real power to Liu Shao-ch'i.

A digression is called for at this stage, in order to prevent any misunderstanding and to kill outright a kind of Liuist myth which has gained credence in the West. It would be as pointless to try to find any trace of an "ideological" confrontation or of a "philosophic" contradiction between Mao Tse-tung and Liu Shao-ch'i as it would have been to find one between, for example, de Gaulle and Pompidou. Liu's career had been that of a second-in-command, who was somewhat colourless, but devoted and efficient. The case later made against him by the "Cultural Revolution" consists of such clumsy falsifications that they could hardly fool a child. For instance, the accusations consist either of fragmentary documents shorn of their context, or of oral statements quoting unverifiable sources, all attempting to demonstrate that in the past Liu had adopted a treasonable policy in calling for collaboration with the Kuomintang when, in reality, Liu had never done anything but docilely repeat Mao's instructions. In fact this collaboration policy, which had been judged expedient for tactical reasons, was advocated with the greatest force *by Mao himself* in a celebrated article (*Lun hsin chieh-tuan*, "A new stage"), which was later withdrawn from circulation and carefully removed from the definitive edition of the Selected Works of Mao Tse-tung. The article was the text of a speech which Mao had made to the sixth plenary session of the sixth central committee in October 1938. It was initially considered as one of Mao's more important works. Anna Strong presented it then as one of his "six great works". On the eve of the Liberation it was republished in a separate edition by the New Democracy Publishing House (Hong Kong, 1948); after the Liberation it was completely withdrawn from circulation, and all traces of its existence were carefully rubbed out. Only one of its eight chapters, number seven, was reprinted in the definitive edition of the *Selected Works*,[4] and even this was unrecognisable; it had been submitted to a considerable amount of alteration, and its title had been transformed into "The place of the Chinese Communist Party in the national war". The original text, now prohibited, spoke about Chiang Kai-shek in terms of the utmost respect, eulogising him as "the supreme leader of the nation"; he spoke of the "bright future of the Kuomintang" and made exhortations such as the following: "Let us all, with unanimous sincerity, support President Chiang, let us support the national government, let us support the collaboration between the Kuomintang and the Communist Party; let us oppose all enemy undertakings which are harmful to this collaboration of the Communist Party with President Chiang and the national government." He praised "the united leadership of the supreme leader of the nation and the supreme generalissimo, President Chiang" and "the republic based on the three principles of the people".

Liu was also accused of having made a pact with class enemies, industrialists, capitalists and bourgeois intellectuals after the Liberation. Here again, all he did was to apply the political line laid down by Mao* himself. Liu was accused of connivance with Soviet

---

* See for instance Mao's report to the second session of the seventh Central Committee (*Mao Tse-tung hsüan-chi*, vol. iv, pp. 1425-40: ". . . For a long

revisionism — the accusers forgot that it was under Liu's "reign" that the break with the Soviet Union was completed. This notion of Liu's "revisionism" is a fanciful myth, a complete forgery — and a clumsy one at that — used in "Cultural Revolution" propaganda; it can never stand up to the slightest attempt at historical analysis. But since Western commentators of the current Chinese scene are in no way concerned to apply historical analysis, the myth is generally accepted; and it was helped by the sheer volume of sound with which Peking's loudspeakers boldly and endlessly repeated it. Incidentally, it is at this point that those observers most hostile to the Peking régime meet Western maoists in a common gullibility: the latter see Liu's "revisionism" as a sign of dastardly criminality, the former suddenly discover in it an indication of liberal virtues; both thereby, at a stroke, and under the influence of the falsifications of the "Cultural Revolution", forget all they previously knew about Liu's personality and actions. If the "Cultural Revolution" had genuinely been a struggle against revisionism, the group it should logically have brought down was that of Chou En-lai and Li Hsien-nien (who in fact emerged from the whole affair in stronger positions!), and nobody would have thought of tacking the names of Liu Shao-ch'i and Teng Hsiao-p'ing to this concept of liberal pragmatism. Liu's team has all along been associated with the stalinism of the purest, narrowest and most sectarian kind. By what miracle has he now been transformed into a sort of Chinese Dubcek? Any attempt to outline a Liuist "philosophy" with a specific content and in opposition to Mao's Thought must inevitably fail, for the simple reason that a *Liuist philosophy has never existed*. Apart from official communications and various speeches for which Liu Shao-ch'i functioned simply as a transmission belt for the orders of his master, he has written only one theoretical work: "How to be a good communist" (*Lun kung-ch'an-tang-yuan ti hsiu-yang*, Yenan 1939). This slender work is leaden of expression (unlike Mao, Liu is by contrast a man of only mediocre literary culture) and dull of content; were it absol-

---

period after the victory of the revolution, it will be necessary to make a maximum use of all the positive aspects of private capitalist enterprise in the cities and in the countryside, to benefit the development of the national economy. During this period, all the private capitalist elements which are not harmful to the national economy and which are useful to it should be allowed to survive and to develop. . . . We must treat the great majority of democrats outside the party as if they were our own cadres . . . we must give them work and entrust them with responsibility and authority . . .").

utely necessary to credit it with an ideological line, it could best be described as a child's guide to the stalinist virtues of discipline and blind obedience, all perfectly natural in a work coming from Mao's immediate circle. (This should give food for thought to credulous Westerners who imagine that a China led by Liu rather than Mao would take the primrose path of "revisionism". They forget that China was in effect under Liu's leadership from 1959-1965: where then were the primroses?) The child's guide in question was, incidentally, so utterly orthodox that it appeared with Mao's approval, was constantly republished and remained, for over a quarter of a century, a standard work and recommended reading for all members of the party, without anyone ever realising that it was a "poisonous weed"! (The Thought of Liu Shao-ch'i did not appear so "poisonous" at the outset, since Mao himself did it the honour of quoting it; and the quotation was reproduced again in the 1966 version of *Mao chu-hsi yü-lu.*) The theory of blind obedience contained in it was condemned during the "Cultural Revolution", not on principle but because it came from Liu. The "Cultural Revolution" recommended precisely this kind of blind obedience towards Mao: see, for example, the article by Wu Wei-tung in the *Liberation Army Daily* which was reprinted by the New China News Agency on 30 October 1967: one must resolutely obey the Thought of Chairman Mao and resolutely oppose everything that goes against it; Chairman Mao's instructions must be obeyed, *even when they are not understood.* The navy's oath of allegiance to Mao, taken at the beginning of December 1967, is similar: "We shall follow closely step by step, we shall grasp in all its depth, we shall apply phrase by phrase and word by word every instruction from Chairman Mao; those which we understand we shall carry out, those which we do not understand we shall also carry out resolutely, and in the process of carrying them out we shall deepen our understanding; we shall make the Thought of Chairman Mao the substance of our souls, so that it commands each nerve, each movement." And Liu Shao-ch'i was accused of wanting to use his theory of obedience to transform the party members into docile tools!

The troubles and difficulties that the "Cultural Revolution" was to encounter in making out a case against Liu are instructive. The true reasons for purging him could not be mentioned, for they were connected with the "Great Leap Forward" controversy and — on that point — a catalogue of Liu's "crimes" would all too probably make him more popular among the masses. It was only possible to use outlandish and futile pretexts (for example, the film *Secret Episode at the Ch'ing Court,* see p. 65) or to falsify past incidents. This latter task was a particularly delicate one: a case against Liu based on facts from the past would in effect be the equivalent of a case against Mao, since the words and actions of one had always in the past been closely taken for those of the other — Liu having never been anything more than Mao's tame spokesman and henchman. The well-known opinion of another Head of State concerning his chief minister comes to mind:

> "Having long tested his worth and his devotion I have judged him capable and worthy of undertaking this high office. . . . He is inclined by nature to consider the practical side of affairs. While revering brilliance in action, risk in enterprise and daring in authority, he tends to be cautious in his attitudes and reserved in his bearing, and excels in covering all the aspects of any problem and in clearing the way for a solution. Thus it is that this newcomer to public life finds himself suddenly, by my action and without having sought it, invested with an office of boundless scope. . . . Protected from above and supported from below but, in addition, trusting in himself notwithstanding his natural discretion, he gets to grips with the problem."[5]

De Gaulle's judgement of Pompidou is much like the judgement that Mao might have expressed concerning Liu. The working of the relationships between the two pairs — relationships which first drew them together then drove them apart — shows a remarkable parallelism: in neither case did ideology play any part. It was therefore out of the question that the disciple who had usurped his master's place should disown his master's philosophy; that would have been to saw off the branch that supported him. In each pair there is a man of genius who is nevertheless out of his time, an egocentric who can tolerate neither criticism nor contradiction, a creator inspired by a historic culture but ignorant of "management" problems, impatient and cursory in his approach to the technical trivia of administration, organisation, and detailed performance. This man discovers a devoted follower, a Sancho Panza whose zeal is total, who owes to his master all that he is and all that he owns, who is all submissiveness, no dreamer but a doer: so good a doer that he soon makes himself indispensable, and ends by taking over and meticulously controlling the complex machinery of government which his master will now touch only with clumsy irritation. The daily practice of politics at the working level and the practical experience of finding concrete solutions to concrete problems keep his feet on the ground, and he is in close touch with the ever-changing reality of men and circumstances — while his master, freed from these mundane tasks, can withdraw into his visionary world. A crisis occurs. The follower now sees his master, in spite of all his exhortations, tilting disastrously at windmills, and suddenly discovers the extent both of the latter's aberrations and of his own talents.

What was Liu Shao-ch'i going to do, now that he was at the helm? Above all, nothing that might directly affect the maoist continuity on which his own credibility rested and which legitimised his power. (The history of the Taiping insurrection provides an interesting historical parallel to this kind of muffled takeover within a political movement, where there is no change in the general ideological line. Yang Hsiu-ch'ing, an executive who was capable but had no personal vision, ended up by restricting Hung Hsiu-ch'üan — the brilliant, inspired but light-headed leader — to a symbolic and isolated position as a prophet, while he took over all the real power himself. Hung, like Mao with his "Cultural Revolution", later made a successful counter-attack; but his fight to regain power involved such a wide-scale purge of the movement's ruling élite that this haemorrhage precipitated the ultimate ruin of his own régime.) This explains the official condemnation of the P'eng Teh-huai line, as well as the maintenance of Mao as Chairman of the party's central committee. (This is a purely formal position: the real authority lies not with the Chairman but with the Secretary, who at the time was Teng Hsiao-p'ing.)

But Liu had come to power in order to solve an urgent crisis which was threatening the very survival of the régime. He was in a better position than anyone to know that P'eng's description of the catastrophic results of the "Great Leap Forward" was not a "counter-revolutionary calumny" but a realistic diagnosis of the situation. Liu was an apparatchik from top to toe; above all, he wanted to save the régime. He was therefore forced to tack from one side to the other. At all costs, he had to avoid any premature, spectacular demaoisation (which is what P'eng's crude and maladroit initiative had threatened to stir up), for this would have deprived the régime — which had already been dangerously shaken — of its credibility in the eyes of the country, its "cement". But on the other hand, he also had to backtrack

immediately and get the country out of the wild lurch of the
Great Leap Forward. In other words, he had to admit in *fact* that
P'eng was right and neutralise Mao's initiative, but as a matter
of *form* he had to condemn P'eng and safeguard Mao's prestige.
He executed this double manoeuvre with great skill. The political
line of P'eng, Huang and Chang was officially denounced at the
end of the Lushan conference, and P'eng was forced to humiliate
himself publicly by writing Mao a letter confessing to his faults
and humbly begging his pardon (see appendix no. 2). But it is
a remarkable feature of the affair that neither P'eng, Huang nor
Chang were subjected to any punishment. They were discharged
from their effective functions in the party, army and government,
but were allowed to retain their respective titles of member of
the politbureau (P'eng), deputy member of the politbureau
(Chang) and member of the central committee (Huang).* This
degree of clemency seems extraordinary when one compares it
with the fate previously meted out to the rebellion of Kao Kang
and Jao Shu-shih, for example; and when one considers the
seriousness of the facts, one gets a good idea of the extent to
which P'eng's views had found support in the central committee.
P'eng had already been assured of large-scale support before the
Lushan conference. It was on 16 June, in fact, that Wu Han
(under the pseudonym of Liu Mien-chih) had published his
resounding article "Hai Jui reprimands the Emperor", a trans-
parent historical parable in which P'eng could be recognised
beneath the features of Hai Jui, the upright and courageous
Ming civil servant who dared to plead to the Emperor Chia-
ching on behalf of the oppressed peasants. This article appeared
in no less a place than the *People's Daily*, the régime's official
organ. In other words the party's central organs — and above
all the propaganda department, which is one of its more sensitive (not to say sore) points — had already been largely won
over to P'eng's views, and supported his denunciation of Mao's

---

* P'eng retired for a while to his native province of Hunan. By the eve
of the "Cultural Revolution" he had found an official post again,
though a very lowly one: he was third deputy director of the construction committee of the central committee's South-Western bureau. Chang
Wen-t'ien was rehabilitated in 1962 as a special research assistant at
the Institute of Economic Research in the Academy of Sciences. Huang
K'e-ch'eng had re-established himself in a more spectacular way, and on
the outbreak of the "Cultural Revolution" he held the post of deputy
governor of the province of Shensi. From the beginning of 1967
onwards, they were once again stripped of their functions, and all three
were pilloried (see appendix, documents nos 4 and 5).

mistakes. No less remarkable was the fact that the official disgrace of P'eng and his associates did not involve any silencing of their various supporters, who soon made themselves heard once more, and with a growing audacity and eloquence.

P'eng's disgrace thus afforded Mao scant satisfaction for his self-respect. This was emphasised at the same time by what happened on the solid terrain of the political measures that were adopted. The Lushan conference soon produced an official confirmation of P'eng's criticisms. In its communiqué of 26 August it admitted that the statistics previously published on the economic results of the first year of the "Great Leap" had been artificially inflated by between forty and fifty per cent, and in particular that the grain harvest had only been two hundred and fifty million tons (a statistic which was itself probably inflated) as against the three hundred and seventy-five millions previously proclaimed.[6] An even more serious setback for Mao was the fact that the Lushan conference completely removed the mystique concerning the "Great Leap" and deprived the new institutions which it had tried to impose of their original content. The "people's communes" were gradually reduced to mere administrative organs, while their functions in production were transferred to the lower level of the "brigade" and later to the even lower unit of the "production team". From the beginning of 1961, after the decision of the ninth plenary session of the eighth central committee meeting to make official the amendments to the "Great Leap" and the communes, all that remained of the old maoist initiative was simply the name, devoid of any real content.

It should not be thought that by dismantling the whole "Great Leap Forward" movement Liu Shao-ch'i had deviated ideologically and had taken a "revisionist" route. I repeat yet again: the problem was not in the least an ideological one. It was simply a crude choice of life or death for the régime: it was a matter of extreme urgency to take some concrete steps, whatever they were, to rescue the economic situation and reactivate the production of basic foodstuffs, in order to feed a population which had reached the point of despair as a result of their excessive deprivation.

But this about-turn was not in itself sufficient for Liu Shao-ch'i. He still had to consolidate the power which he had acquired, and above all to prevent once and for all any threat that Mao Tse-tung might lapse back into some of his "lyrical improvisations". Mao thus found himself gradually restricted to the role of some kind of ancient totem: everyone genuflected to him, but he was completely powerless in his wooden immobility. Proof of the fact that retirement had been very effectively imposed on him is supplied once again by the "Cultural Revolution". In Teng Hsiao-p'ing's confession of his "crimes", which was extorted from him during the "Cultural Revolution", he admitted that over this whole period he had settled all the party's affairs directly, without ever referring them to Mao.[7] And in a remarkable speech in 1967,[8] Mao recalled this state of isolation and impotence to which he had been reduced, saying that he could not even publish articles defending his own positions in the official Peking press: he finally had to fall back on a Shanghai newspaper, *Wen-hui pao,* to publish the famous article by Yao Wen-yuan (10 November 1965) which lit the fuse of the "Cultural Revolution", though even this demanded the use of many ruses and diversions. And the whole history of the preparation and initial steps of the "Cultural Revolution", which I shall outline later, adequately illustrates the extraordinary difficulties which Mao encountered at the start of his attempt to regain power, and shows precisely how real his enforced withdrawal had been between 1959 and 1965.

In order to make himself more secure, Liu Shao-ch'i strengthened his own team: for example, he got Lu Ting-yi and Lo Jui-ch'ing on to the secretariat of the central committee. At the same time he eventually took over the criticisms which P'eng had made of the "Great Leap", and announced in January 1962 to an enlarged working session of the eighth central committee (the so-called "conference of seven thousand"): "The 'Great Leap' was launched too hastily and lacked balance. After three years of 'Great Leap', some eight to ten years of hard work will be required in order to clean up the mess: at this rate, it is not really worth it. . . . The People's Communes were premature. . . . The backyard furnaces in the countryside produced nothing. . . . There were serious economic and financial difficulties. . . . Too much energy has been wasted; it will be difficult to get back to normal, even in seven or eight years."[9]

From the end of 1959 to the end of 1962, the party authorities consolidated the normalisation process by filling in the cracks opened up by the "Great Leap", and warding off any risk of a return to light-headed maoist improvisation. They did not hesitate to enlist the collaboration of the intellectuals. An ambiguous kind of "thaw" prevailed during these three years: ambiguous because

it was the result of a quite temporary union of interests which in
the long term were still irreconcilable. For the intellectuals, the
free pursuit of truth and the denunciation of tyranny and
mendacity constituted an absolute and permanent mission. For
the ruling group, it was simply a question of mobilising these
voices for a limited and concrete tactical aim: on the one hand,
to discredit the autocratic and subjective political line of Mao
Tse-tung, for good, and on the other hand to set in motion once
more the scientific activity in the universities which had been
paralysed by the "Great Leap", so that the country would again
have the "experts" who were needed for the modern development of China, and whom Mao had so stupidly thought he could
do without. It would therefore be a complete mistake to deduce
that Liu Shao-ch'i nourished a real desire to "liberalise" intellectual life: such a desire would not have fitted in with his strictly
stalinist career, and it corresponded even less to the style of such
dogmatic and sectarian bureaucrats as Lu Ting-yi and Chou
Yang, whom Liu had confirmed in their posts as the dictators of
arts and letters. As soon as these tactical aims had been achieved,
from the end of 1962, Liu Shao-chi's administration did not
hesitate to put the muzzle back on the intellectuals and send them
back to their kennel. But the voices which the intellectuals had
raised in the meantime were not forgotten so quickly.

Let us leave aside the discussions on philosophical and literary
theory and the university work on classical studies, history,
literature, philosophy, fine arts, archaeology etc. (The astonishing
outburst which occurred during this short truce is enough to
make one dream. What an influence contemporary China could
have on world culture, if only its potential for intelligence, knowledge and talent could be freely and fully employed.) Achievements in this sphere do not fall within the scope of this present
enquiry. Let us look instead at work of a directly political and
polemical nature. Two personalities in particular catch the attention, both for their talent and for their boldness: Wu Han and
Teng T'o. It is perhaps no exaggeration to say that to future
historians who approach this period of bureaucratic tyranny, people
such as Wu Han and above all Teng T'o will appear as those who,
throughout these shameful years, really saved the honour and
dignity of the Chinese intellectuals. The price which they eventually had to pay was heavy. They knew this in advance, but they
did not shirk their mission. Teng T'o took as his moral pattern
the scholars of Tung-lin (a group of intellectuals at the close of
the Ming period, who risked the worst kinds of torture by making

political criticisms of a corrupt imperial régime), and foresaw his own destiny in the following lines:

> Do not believe that men who wield the pen only know how to chatter emptily
> When they are under the executioner's axe, they know how to show their red blood!

After Wu Han's short article of 1959, "Hai Jui reprimands the Emperor", in 1960 he composed the libretto for a classical Peking opera, *The Dismissal of Hai Jui*. The historical figure of Hai Jui (1515-1587), who was dismissed from his post by the Emperor because he had taken the side of the oppressed peasantry, served once more as a covering name for P'eng Teh-huai; the libretto in fact appeared as a plea for his rehabilitation. Resorting to historical parables in order to criticise the present is a Chinese tradition which is as old as historiography itself (even the "Chronicle of Springs and Autumns", which is attributed to Confucius, was read by the old commentators as a kind of coded message, with each word concealing scathing judgements on political morality); through centuries of autocracy and imperial censorship, Chinese scholars have had little more than this with which to challenge orthodoxy and make unconventional opinions heard.

This form of parable, which is the traditional weapon of Chinese polemics, was used with a superior dexterity and verve in the political writings of Teng T'o. From the beginning of 1961 until September 1962, Teng T'o published a series of short articles in various Peking newspapers (*Pei-ching jih-pao*, *Pei-ching wan-pao*, *Kuang-ming jih-pao* and the periodical *Ch'ien-hsien*). Under the guise of moral fables and historical anecdotes (sometimes serious, sometimes humorous), literary and artistic commentaries and various other pieces, they present a devastating critique of maoism. These articles deal with a wide range of issues, but certain broad themes can be distinguished.

(a) A plea for the rehabilitation of P'eng Teh-huai, under the guise of sketches of various historical figures who had incurred the displeasure of the sovereign by attempting to alleviate the sufferings of the people.

(b) Attacks against the person and style of Mao: his taste for hollow slogans, his tendency to substitute words for reality, his thirst for personal glory, his vanity, his intolerance of criticism, his lack of realism, his inability to listen to the advice of competent people, his blind obstinacy. It is false that Mao is a "great man". He is a "whining Chu-ke Liang", an amnesiac who forgets his own promises and goes back on his word; he should, as a matter of urgency, "keep quiet and take a rest", or he will find that his psychologically unbalanced nature has turned to "wild insanity".

(c) A criticism of the maoist political line. Mao, with his subjective and arbitrary political line, resembles the emperors of former times surrounded by their little circle of corrupt eunuchs; his policies are worked out without any consideration for suggestions from the base, and he ignores and despises the opinion of the masses. Lacking specialised knowledge and practical experience, Mao pursues unrealisable chimeras; he substitutes trickery for real intelligence, and practises a despotism which is based on violence and coercion, in defiance of the principles of social and political morality.

(d) A criticism of the "Great Leap Forward". This was carried through without any consideration for the natural limits of human strength, and imposed too heavy a burden on the peasants. Mao's dream of a fantastic multiplication of a modest initial capital merely led to the evaporation of this capital; illusion was substituted for reality as the point of departure, and an unrealistic "moral factor" was substituted for objective material conditions, so that the whole enterprise came up against a wall of realities.

(e) On the positive side, Teng T'o reminded the intellectuals of their responsibilities and their mission. Their duty was to right wrongs, as the wandering knights used to do. They had to shout the truth aloud and "meet the tyranny of the wicked with indomitable resistance", even at the risk of their lives; they had to remain attentive to the world around them, and politics had to remain their constant concern. Their studies and their teaching had to be opened to political commitment; in their writings, they had to learn every means possible of making the truth heard, directly or indirectly.

Together with these public attacks, a secret burrowing operation began which was even bolder and more serious, and was aimed at destroying Mao's political existence once and for all. This was the famous "Ch'ang-kuan-lou affair", the details of which were first revealed by the "Cultural Revolution".[10] Under the aegis of P'eng Chen (who was mayor of Peking, secretary of the Peking municipal party committee, member of the politbureau and secretary to the secretariat of the eighth central committee), a small working group met at Ch'ang-kuan-lou, a park in West Peking, to make a secret, detailed and critical re-examination of maoist policy of recent years, and particularly of the "Great Leap Forward". By gathering together the conclusions of enquiries conducted during the campaign, and by analysing the documents of the central organs of the party, they compiled a dossier on Mao's mistakes. P'eng Chen gave Teng T'o the job of organising this dossier.

Mao had already been removed from the levers of power, and now — while still alive — he was about to suffer the fate which Stalin had encountered after his death. But this final step was never actually taken. The dossier was not used at the famous "Conference of the Seven Thousand" of January 1962, for which it had been prepared. At this gathering, Liu Shao-ch'i was content to castigate the failure of the "Great Leap", without transforming his criticism into a public trial of Mao himself. As I have already pointed out, Liu was an apparatchik *par excellence*; he was afraid that such a trial would shake the entire system, and above all that it would endanger his own position. All his political credibility sprang from the sole fact that he was Mao's right arm and successor, and any attack against Mao would necessarily ricochet against himself. The fact that there might have been some divergence between Liu's prudence and the extreme attitude of P'eng is further suggested by the striking difference between the relentless fate meted out to P'eng during the "Cultural Revolution" and the relative circumspection with which Liu was treated.

There was something else hampering the demaoisation process. Although he had been deprived of direct power, Mao's prestige remained considerable, and certain by no means unimportant quarters were faithful to him. During the "conference of the seven thousand", two defence counsel supported Mao against the criticisms coming from the apparatus: Lin Piao and Chou En-lai. Several years later, the "Cultural Revolution" rewarded both of them for refusing to desert Mao in this tight spot. In particular, this act of personal fidelity on Chou's part explains to a large extent the astonishing immunity with which he succeeded in surviving the most dangerous vicissitudes of the "Cultural Revolution".

Far from resigning himself to the retirement which had been imposed on him, Mao immediately began to carve out the long and devious path which would take him victoriously back to power. The direct confrontation at Lushan, in which P'eng and Mao opposed each other, had led to a reciprocal defeat: P'eng was formally denounced and stripped of his functions, Mao lost real power, and Liu — the third party and referee of the conflict — reaped the advantage. However, P'eng was not completely beaten. In the years which followed, he saw the party make a *de facto* ratification of his criticism, while an increasingly eloquent movement of opinion sought his official rehabilitation. But nor had Mao lost everything. To begin with, he had maintained a bridgehead at the summit: Lin Piao. By obtaining the nomination of Lin Piao to the position of Minister of Defence (in place of P'eng Teh-huai), Mao had secured a trump card, a pledge for his future return to power. Of course Mao's adversaries under-estimated at the time the effects which this promotion of Lin Piao was going to have in the long term. Like mediocre chess players confronted by a superior tactician, they were all obsessed by the opportunity of making a big gain immediately — the neutrali-sation of Mao; they paid too little attention to the movement of an apparently insignificant pawn. But it was a move which in the final analysis was to turn the game and ultimately to precipitate their own downfall.

Lin Piao was a sickly and secretive character with a mediocre education, devoid of presence or eloquence; he was extremely nervous, and had a dull and timid look about him. But he had an intense capacity for hard work, concentration and calculation. He was a professional soldier who, within the limits of his trade, had acquired the reputation of being an exceptionally competent strategist. He had a network of men faithful to him, but these were quite strictly limited to his former subordinates in the Fourth Army; besides this, it was difficult for him to rival the prestige of more assertive personalities such as P'eng Teh-huai or Ho Lung. Lin Piao had scarcely succeeded in making an impression even on the most favourably disposed witnesses; in 1961, Edgar Snow described him as "a more compliant and less colourful figure" than P'eng Teh-huai. His influence in the party was practically nil. But beneath his sickly and unobtrusive exterior, he was devoured by ambition; only the "Cultural Revolution" was to reveal the full extent of this. He nursed a long-standing rivalry with P'eng Teh-huai, the favoured elder son who had blocked his promotion for a long time. In 1954 the post of Minister of Defence in Chou En-lai's cabinet, for which Lin already entertained ambitions, was allotted to P'eng. Later in the same year Lin suffered an enigmatic eclipse from public life, which lasted a year and coincided with the purge of Kao Kang. In the 1951-3 period, Kao Kang — probably at the instigation of Beria

— had set up the basis of an "independent fief" in Manchuria; he was purged in February 1954. Lin Piao, who had been closely associated with Kao Kang during the Manchurian campaign of 1947, had also made long stays in the USSR between 1939 and 1942 and again between 1951 and 1953; he enjoyed the favours of Stalin. Immediately after the purge of Kao Kang, *Lin disappeared from the political scene for a year* (from March 1954 to March 1955).[11] Such are the pieces of this ambiguous jigsaw puzzle. In April 1955 Lin rejoined the politbureau, where he figured in twelfth position in the hierarchy, immediately after P'eng. From this moment on, his rise accelerated: in 1956, after the eighth party congress, Lin rose to seventh position in the new politbureau while P'eng fell back to fourteenth position. The eighth central committee had four vice-presidents (Liu Shao-ch'i, Chou En-lai, Chu Teh and Ch'en Yün); in Spring 1958, Lin — who in the previous year had distinguished himself in the rectification campaign against the right — was made fifth vice-president. In 1959 the P'eng Teh-huai affair definitively fused Mao's interests with those of Lin. Seeing the chance to eliminate his old rival, Lin distinguished himself as the main inspiration behind the purge of P'eng; the latter's disgrace was pronounced at an enlarged conference of the central committee's military commission, and the chairman of this conference (held in August 1959) was Lin Piao.[12] As a reward for his efforts, Lin was given his victim's hide: on 17 September he replaced P'eng as Minister of Defence.

Once he was installed in this new position, Lin got down to forging the new instrument which, some years later, would enable Mao to carry out a successful coup d'état against the party: namely an ideologically reorganised army which, during the decisive moments of the "Cultural Revolution", would be able to *replace* the party apparatus, over which Mao had lost all control. He had scarcely been at his post for twelve days when he published an article entitled "Let us march forward with giant steps, waving high the red standard of the general line of the party and the military thought of Mao Tse-tung". Lin Piao had now committed himself: once and for all he had staked his political future on the Mao Tse-tung card, and he glued himself unconditionally to Mao as servant, defender, devotee and prophet. The experiments which Mao had been prevented from pursuing in the party and from executing over the country as a whole were now, through the agency of Lin Piao, going to be tested out at the narrower level of the army. Within the army, as if in an airtight chamber, the "philosophy" of the "Great Leap" and the communes was applied, having been battered, denounced and abandoned in the outside world: revolutionary virtue was substituted for professional expertise, the spiritual factor took priority over the material and technical factors, and there was a return to the archaic principles of the peasant guerrilla. Between 1960 and 1962 Lin was busy developing the people's militias and implanting the ideological basis for "people's war". He launched various movements. First, in May 1960, came the "three-eight" movement (*san-pa tso-feng*), which was inspired by one of Mao's instructions consisting of three principles (a resolute and correct political orientation; a keen and austere style of work; and supple, mobile tactics) and of four terms in eight characters ("unity", "intensity", "seriousness", "liveliness"). Then, in October 1960, came the "four priorities" (*ssu-ke ti-yi*) formulated by Lin. These were: priority to the human factor over the weapons factor; priority to political work over other kinds; in political work, priority to the ideological task over others; and in the ideological task, priority to living thought over books. Then he organised the élite companies (*ssu-hao lien-tui*). The deeper meaning of these various initiatives was not revealed until the advent of the "Cultural Revolution", when the party was disintegrating and the mass organisations were forced to copy these carefully prepared military models. The "élite companies" served as a prototype for the famous "support-the-left detachments" (*chih-tso pu-tui*), the élite detachments which were parachuted to all four corners of the country during the "Cultural Revolution" to crush local revolutionary initiatives, break strikes, impose order in the schools and factories, marshal rebellious youth into disciplinary battalions, protect the local mandarinate, exercise police powers and guarantee the running of industries and railways. (This fell under the heading of the "three supports and two militaries" — *san chih liang chün,* that it is to say, support for the left, support for the workers, support for the peasants; military administration and military education.)

In January 1962, as we have already seen, Lin Piao finally defended in public the maoist line which had been criticised by Liu Shao-ch'i during the "conference of the seven thousand". Throughout this first act of his new political career, the two basic characteristics which he was to display later during his ascendancy in the "Cultural Revolution" appeared. One was a jealous ambition which could not tolerate the presence of any rival; this was to play a big part in the weeding out process during the purges of the "Cultural Revolution", and was largely responsible for the extreme mediocrity of the new ruling team — Lin Piao could only tolerate confederates or insignificant figures around him, and anyone who had some depth presented a threat to him. The other characteristic was his shameless and unstinting flattery of Mao. Lin's sole political capital (he was otherwise incapable of conceiving or formulating any idea of his own) was to pose as the supreme confessor of the maoist Revelation: there is no truth but Mao's truth, and Lin is his sole prophet. (At a certain point during the "Cultural Revolution" Lin was to make a bold and somewhat premature attempt to convey his god to heaven and *keep him there* while the prophet himself took personal care of affairs down below. But Mao Tse-tung called a rapid halt to this attempt to kick him upstairs.)

On 10 November 1965, the Shanghai newspaper *Wen-hui pao* published Yao Wen-yuan's article, "A criticism of the recent historical libretto, *The Dismissal of Hai Jui*". This article sparked off what was eventually to be known as the "Cultural Revolution": it unleashed the formidable chain reaction that Mao used to carry out his coup d'état against the party and regain power. But it did not spring out of nowhere; it was not some fortuitous accident. It was preceded by a slow and laborious undermining process, and there had been several previous attempts to light the touchpaper. These had not been successful, because on each occasion they were scented and defused by those in power. Let us first of all examine the history of these failed attempts of the 1960-65 period.

Between 1960 and 1962 Mao's political career touched its nadir. It is possible that the setback which he suffered at Lushan was aggravated by a physical collapse, the one having provoked the other. (Uncontrollable rumours reported that at Lushan, Mao — suddenly seeing himself put in the position of an accused man — reacted so violently that he suffered a fit. The text of the speech which he improvised on 23 July 1959 is certainly remarkably incoherent.[18]) But after September 1962 (the tenth plenary session of the eighth central committee) he seemed to emerge from his despondency and to renew his energies. In his honorary capacity as Chairman of the party he had no power, but he had a platform; while he was reduced to impotence, he was certainly not reduced to silence. Could he use the prestige of his word alone to turn the situation back in his favour? The history of the period between 1962 and 1965 illustrates the narrow limits of his influence. The men in power let him launch highly incendiary appeals into a vacuum, because they were calmly certain that in the end the means of execution were theirs alone. On each occasion, the application of Mao's various political initiatives was put under supervision and handed over to his adversaries, who neutralised their explosive potential without any trouble.

In September 1962, Mao went back into the arena to take the platform at the tenth plenary session of the eighth central committee. He touched on three themes in his speech; their deeper intentions were to be understood better with the hindsight of the "Cultural Revolution", but at the time their seeds of subversion were quickly eradicated by the apparatus. He dealt first with the problem of youth, whose revolutionary training had to be ensured if China was not one day to change its colours. Secondly, he dealt with the problem of the countryside, where the immobility of the cadres and the peasants' property instincts were threatening the development of socialism. Thirdly, there was the problem of culture, which was monopolised by intellectuals who were defaulting on the socialist ideal and anaesthetising opinion in order to prepare for a capitalist restoration. These three fuses were all to lead to the powder-barrel of the "Cultural Revolution", but Mao had scarcely lit them when the apparatus moved to extinguish them. However, Mao took advantage of the fact that the cultural theme had a relatively minor importance, and succeeded in foxing the vigilance of those in power, so as to relight this last torch suddenly and set off the explosion. (The explosion was christened "cultural" simply because of its initial pretext. It could just as easily have been called the "youth revolution" or the "countryside revolution" if one or the other of these first attempts had made it.)

Of these three different attempts, it was the first which was most quickly rendered harmless. Mao was given no chance to stir up the youth. The maoist initiative was manipulated by a skilled bureaucracy and converted into a dose of chloroform which was administered throughout 1963, with the famous campaigns to emulate model heroes such as Lei Feng and others. As for the educational system, the changes made were purely formal, and teachers continued to encourage the "expert" as against the "red". The second theme, although it too was finally aborted, met greater vicissitudes. There is no doubt that Mao had placed his greatest hopes here. Between 1963 and 1965 he gave birth to the famous "movement for socialist education in the countryside", which was nothing less than a failed first attempt at the "Cultural Revolution". (Subsequently, the "Cultural Revolution" officially recognised this movement's role as a precursor.) The story of the "movement for socialist education in the countryside" is an exemplary illustration of the contradiction between Mao and the apparatus. In this conflict between inspiration and execution, it was always the latter which had the last word, by diverting, sabotaging and neutralising all the attempts launched by the former. When the movement did not succeed in getting off the ground, Mao tried to invigorate it by means of the campaign of the "four clean-ups": in theory, this meant organising associations of poor and lower-middle peasants and using them to purge the local cadres. This maoist idea of rousing the base against the apparatus was against the interests of the party, which sought to keep the base under the strict control of the apparatus. But the "ten articles" which defined this maoist conception of the movement were followed by a second series of "ten articles" dictated by those in power, which practically annulled the effect of the first series by giving priority to the economic imperatives of production and by consolidating the authority of the apparatus. In 1964 the "associations of poor and lower-middle peasants" were put back entirely under the control of the party committees attached to local government. The peasants were now "roused" only under the strict supervision of the authorities.

Faced with this sabotage of his undertaking, Mao counter-attacked in January 1965, when he decreed the "twenty-three articles". This extraordinary document already contained the whole of the "Cultural Revolution" in embryo. In fact, it declared:

> "There is a sharp class struggle, with the enemies of socialism seeking to take advantage of a 'peaceful evolution' to restore capitalism. This class struggle *is reflected in the party, where various levers of command have been corrupted or usurped.*" (article 1)

> "It is a question of rectifying and purging those who, *bearing the authority of the party,* have taken the capitalist road — some of them *are very highly placed, and beneath their mask have changed their real nature.*" (article 2)

The masses had to be boldly roused, given their head, without control being exercised from above (article 5). On the subject of the cadres:

> "Where power is held by cadres who have committed serious faults, *it will be necessary to seize power by sheer force;*

where necessary, if the local militias are not sound, it will be necessary to disarm them and *give their arms to poor and lower-middle peasants."* (article 9)

Here they are: all the elements of the "Cultural Revolution", already brought together in this initial programme. We find, in effect, the central idea that the party itself is corrupted *to the very top*; the party, in the person of some of its highest authorities, is to be the new movement's target. We also find the principle of "seizure of power", by force if necessary; this is to be carried out against the party authorities by the masses, who are themselves outside the party. This principle is clearly stated. All the objectives and methods of the "Cultural Revolution" were thus already defined. One may note in passing that there was nothing to do with "culture" in all this: Mao's original idea had been to launch his coup d'état on the terrain which he was most familiar with — the countryside. If the real "Cultural Revolution" eventually used the cultural pretext as its point of departure and became essentially an urban movement, that is simply because it was a substitute solution for the aborted peasant movement initially envisaged by Mao.

At first sight, it seems surprising that Liu Shao-ch'i and his associates were unable at the time to decipher the writing on the wall which these "twenty-three articles" constituted. But in actual fact they had little reason to feel uneasy. They were far from being a small and fragile clique of usurpers; they were a majority force, and wielded complete control over the organs of party and government. In contrast to their power, Mao no longer embodied anything but an impotent and isolated opposition. How could they have taken seriously the threats which these maoist initiatives contained? In the last analysis, the execution of the initiatives depended on their own authority. And recent experience had shown that the confidence which they had in their own power was not exaggerated: for all their dynamite, the "twenty-three articles" fizzled out, the peasant masses were kept closely in check by the party and did not show the slightest inclination to "rise up"; one had to wait for the revelations made by the "Cultural Revolution" itself to find out — with hindsight — the kind of explosion that had been avoided at the time.

In the end, therefore, it was the last of the three themes mentioned above — the cultural problem — which gave Mao the opportunity to set his coup d'état in motion. But even on this cultural terrain, Mao still encountered a number of obstacles and often got bogged down. During his September 1962 speech, Mao had opened fire on the writers and artists, who were using the pretext of their creative activity to conduct "anti-party" manoeuvres and to create a climate of opinion that would facilitate the "restoration of capitalism". This initial declaration of war was followed in 1963 by campaigns against various intellectuals, artists and writers. These campaigns on the whole lacked bite, and did not take off properly. In 1964 and 1965 the criticisms directed against the marxist philosopher and theoretician Yang Hsien-chen and the "synthesis of contraries", as well as against the novelist and critic Shao Ch'üan-lin and his literary theory of "ambiguous personalities", turned into a quite Byzantine affair; the authorities succeeded in confining the discussion to a purely academic framework, and did not allow it to generate the political developments which Mao hoped for.

Mao, however, was desperately trying to goad the movement on. In June 1964, during his speech to a congress of the All-China Federation of Writers and Artists, he denounced the intellectuals once again as the most dangerous instigators of revisionism in China. Simultaneously Madame Mao (Chiang Ch'ing) emerged for the first time from the shadows to which she had so long been relegated. She tried to bolster her husband's cultural offensive in the specific domain of the theatre. Her reform of the opera would later be hailed in retrospect as one of the starting-points of the "Cultural Revolution". But meanwhile, the attempt to create "revolutionary opera" was sabotaged by the authorities concerned, from the ministerial level down to the actors. The fiasco of the reform of the opera was a snub to Mao, and once again illustrated the state of impotence to which he had been reduced. Madame Mao's speech of July 1964 on the reform of the opera (T'an ching-chü ke-ming) did not even achieve the distinction of being published, and had to wait until 1967 to be finally exhumed to the sound of trumpets by the "Cultural Revolution". (Madame Mao did not forget the insults which she had undergone at the hands of various personalities from the world of culture, cinema and the theatre: during the "Cultural Revolution", not one escaped her vengeance.)

But although Mao saw his various initiatives translated one after another into purely formal movements deprived of their potentially subversive content, where the army was concerned he was preparing behind the scenes (through the agency of Lin Piao) what was to become the real instrument of his coup d'état.

I have already described the role played by Lin Piao between 1960 and 1962, and the way in which the army was gradually prepared for its future political intervention, as a substitute for the party. These preparations were pursued intensively between 1963 and 1965. The campaign to emulate Lei Feng (1963), insipid as it was, at least imposed the new idea that the military could provide a *political* model whose significance went beyond the particular framework of the army and was to become universally applicable. Still more explicit was the fact that from the beginning of 1964 there was a new campaign inviting the whole population to study and imitate the political example of the army. This type of psychological preparation would enable the army to be presented on the outbreak of the "Cultural Revolution" as the source of correct doctrine and the legitimate bearer of political authority in place of the overthrown party. In the same year, in the governmental and administrative sectors, a network of "departments of political work" was gradually installed; it closely followed the system of political commissars in the army, and functioned independently of the normal hierarchy in the party offices.[14] These networks, whose function was purely political, were to play the role of a maoist apparatus parallel to the regular one. This political network was launched with a massive injection of military cadres: from the beginning of 1965, more than two hundred thousand of them found themselves parachuted into civilian life.[15] In the same year, army officers began to occupy posts in propaganda — a key sector which was jealously guarded by the party.[16] In industry and finance, where it would be essential to maintain a modicum of normal activity once the coup d'état had plunged the country into chaos, precautions were taken from 1965 onwards to ensure that the army could take over at some future point: officers were installed in responsible posts normally reserved for civilians, while a number of civilian cadres were sent to the military institutes to be subjected to educational sessions.

At this point, the two parallel movements conducted by Mao — his public interventions in the cultural sphere (which seemed to be headed for failure), and his covert placement of parallel networks (which was the prelude to a military coup d'état) — were about to meet and join together in a pincer movement.

Events speeded up and took a decisive turn in Autumn 1965. In September, during a meeting of the central committee, Mao made another speech denouncing the bourgeois mode of thought. Although the "Cultural Revolution" was subsequently to date its initial impulse from this speech, at the time it seemed destined to the same fate as all the other appeals which the prophet had made from the middle of his desert. The terms of the speech seemed moreover to lack fire: no doubt strong opposition would once more be raised on the central committee against this intemperate overbidding of the "class struggle". In the following month there was an editorial in the *Red Flag*, "Let us adopt the proletarian view of the world in order to build our new world", which, under the pretext of developing the maoist theme of criticising the old world, actually managed to deprive it of its offensive quality, by insisting on the fact that the fight against the traditional view of the world would be long and would therefore have to be conducted in a subtle and patient manner, avoiding excesses.

Was Mao once again about to see his chances of launching the long-prepared offensive vanish? That was how it looked. But on 10 November 1965, the first bomb exploded and set off the chain reaction of the "Cultural Revolution": the Shanghai newspaper *Wen-hui pao* published an article by a still unknown scribe named Yao Wen-yuan. The article was entitled "A criticism of the recent historical libretto, *The Dismissal of Hai Jui*" (*P'ing hsin pien li-shih chü Hai Jui pa-kuan*).

To the uninitiated reader, the article in question scarcely seemed to be more than one of those laborious dissertations crammed with clichés and slogans which the official press produces by the million. Furthermore, the subject was singularly lacking in topicality. The piece by Wu Han which the article took to task was four years old. The major part of the article developed a historical discussion which was deliberately off the point: it was like a critique of La Fontaine's *Fables* based on zoology, or a refutation of *Gulliver's Travels* in the name of geography. The real political implications of the *Hai Jui* piece were only dealt with in an indirect and obscure manner, but the conclusion they led to was quite explicit: "We consider the libretto *The Dismissal of Hai Jui* to be far from a fragrant flower: it is in fact a poisonous weed."

But the article would have struck the initiated reader like a bolt of lightning. Wu Han was the deputy mayor of Peking. He had published the libretto with the general backing of the party organs and the personal backing of P'eng Chen. And here he was, attacked by surprise in public, without any previous discussion within the apparatus, without the normal channels of the official propaganda organs being consulted — and on the sole initiative of an official provincial daily. What could lie behind this inconceivable piece of audacity, bordering on sedition? The first reaction of official circles in Peking was to make direct contact with the Shanghai party committee and ask in threatening tones: "What's behind your decision to publish the article by Yao? Why didn't you warn us? Where's your party spirit?"[17]

Peking was soon to discover what lay behind Shanghai's seditious defiance. Mao Tse-tung had been reduced to impotence in the capital, but he had gradually succeeded in converting Shanghai into a loyal political fortress. More serious still, less than three weeks later (on 29 November) the official army organ *Chieh-fang chün pao* gave its own backing to the attacks on Wu Han. And Lin Piao (who had just published his pamphlet "Long live the victory of the people's war", which defended and illustrated maoist principles and refuted the technical ideas of war espoused by Ho Lung and Lo Jui-ch'ing) continued to urge maoisation on the army: in December he promulgated his "five instructions" on the "pre-eminence of politics" (*t'u-ch'u cheng-chih*).

Peking was beginning to realise that this time the opposition organised by Mao had some real forces at its command, and decided to mark time for a while. But those in power were not unduly disquieted; they remained confident that, as in the past, the surest way of disarming Mao would be to avoid open confrontation. It would be sufficient to give Mao formal satisfaction by organising a purge of cultural circles; this purge would be carefully directed and controlled by the leading party organs, and they could easily arrange for the whole business to remain an inoffensive comedy.

The word "comedy" is no exaggeration. In January 1966, the central committee set up a small group of five members to supervise this cultural purge (which was already being called the "Cultural Revolution" in the party's internal memos). The individual placed at the head of this executive commission was none other than P'eng Chen: in other words, the task of drawing up the prosecution dossier was handed over to the chief defendant. (It was P'eng Chen whom the maoists were aiming at, through Wu Han and subsequently Teng T'o.)

And it was at precisely this crossroads that Mao, that incomparable tactician, was waiting for his enemies. The latter were certain they had full control of the situation, and were blinded by an excessive confidence in their own power; they were to fall headlong into the trap which had been patiently set for them. Prudence should have suggested to P'eng that he disown his protégés and hand them over to be purged, in order to save his own position. With the entire party apparatus behind him, he did the opposite: he counter-attacked. On 7 February 1966 he presented a "draft report"[18] on the work of the Group of Five to the central committee. This draft had an insolent formality about it. It began by recalling the proposals once made by Mao himself in 1957 during the "Hundred Flowers" campaign, concerning the need for "a great blossoming" and for the "expression of all different kinds of opinion, even non-marxist ones". It proposed that the rectification movement should only be carried out slowly and carefully: "problems of a cultural order are complex and cannot be dealt with in the twinkling of an eye". The guiding principle should be "the search for truth on the basis of facts, and the equality of all before the truth". In passing, he launched a ferocious swipe in Mao's direction: "We must not behave like those intellectual tyrants who always act in an arbitrary manner and resort to force in order to gain the adherence of others; we must encourage the maintenance of truth, and always be ready to correct our faults." The central idea in the draft was that the problem of Wu Han's writings belonged to the sphere of historical studies; the discussion should therefore be led away from the political domain and brought back to the academic domain, where it could be analysed at leisure (this may have been disingenuous, but P'eng Chen was giving Yao Wen-yuan a taste of his own medicine). If at the end of this discussion opinions continued to differ, one would have to reserve judgement and postpone the conclusion till later. Everything seemed to indicate that the men in power would once again switch the points and shunt the maoists into the engine-shed. Were they not in a majority on the central committee? And in fact the draft was approved by the central committee several days later (12 February).

But P'eng inadvisably abused his advantage. He authorised the Peking press to defend Wu Han and to counter-attack against Yao Wen-yuan. The moment he did this, he exposed himself: when the wind turned, no one wanted or dared to come to his rescue.

Three months later the same central committee that had ratified the draft (the "February outline") rescinded it, and accompanied this decision with a circular (the famous "16 May Memorandum"[19]) which opened the floodgates of the great purge. P'eng was to be the first victim.

What had happened between the ratification of the draft (12 February) and its denunciation (16 May)? The real "Cultural Revolution" had taken off, openly and irreversibly. It is the army which holds the key to the story of how Mao managed, in the space of these three months, to overturn the balance of forces and make his breakthrough. The details of this military coup d'état are still unclear, but the broad lines are known. For several years Lin had been preparing the army for direct intervention in the political scene, as we have seen above. He still had one obstacle to overcome, and it was a considerable one. His grip over the army was not total: it was countered at the top by someone who held considerable power. This was Lo Jui-ch'ing, the chief of the general staff, who was supported in turn by Ho Lung; the latter had since 1961 maintained a controlling grip on all the activities of the central committee's military commission. This obstacle was finally eliminated at the beginning of 1966. Lo was arrested on an obscure pretext (conspiracy against the state) in February or March; he was submitted to sessions of self-criticism, and on 18 March tried to commit suicide by jumping out of a window — but he only succeeded in breaking his legs. Lo was thus the very first victim of the "Cultural Revolution": he was purged on the quiet, and the affair was not made public until much later. It was revealed at mass meetings in Peking in December 1966 (the 21st and 24th). We can see from this how much "spontaneous initiative" came from the "maoist masses": the bird presented to them was already slaughtered and trussed.

This secret operation left the way open for Lin Piao. With the assistance of Yang Ch'eng-wu (first deputy leader of the general staff), who got troop movements held in the Northern military region of China, and of Fu Ch'ung-pi (second in command of the military region of Peking), Lin Piao was assured of the military control of Peking. Yang Ch'eng-wu and Fu Ch'ung-pi were rewarded for this decisive action, which put Mao back in the saddle: the former was put at the head of the general staff and the second was promoted to commander of the Peking military region. But their moment of glory was not to last. In 1968 they were both ruthlessly eliminated: the means was an obscure accusation that they were plotting a coup d'état! The "Cultural Revolution" was an incredible *grande valse*, glittering with promotions and purges: not only does one search in vain for an expression of the "spontaneous will of the masses" (they have always been presented with *faits accomplis*, and play the role of a choir or of a hired audience — they have no decision-making power over events, and are not even considered worth the trouble of informing properly once the event is over), one cannot even decipher any ideological coherence. The skittles were used to knock each other over.

Once Lin Piao had deployed his troops behind the scenes, the "Cultural Revolution" could begin. The job of announcing officially that it had been launched went fittingly to the army: it was in fact the *Chieh-fang chün pao* ("People's Liberation Army Daily") which published the two articles marking the beginning of the movement: "Let us wave on high the great red standard of the thought of Mao Tse-tung, let us participate actively in the great socialist Cultural Revolution" (editorial, 18 April), and "Let us never forget the class struggle" (editorial, 4 May). In this context, the central committee's repudiation of the P'eng Chen draft which it had approved three months earlier is easily explained. After he had rallied Lin Piao's troops, Mao obtained the services of the police and the secret apparatus of the security police. P'eng Chen found himself alone, and no one now dared to compromise himself by coming to his aid. He fell in June, and this skittle also knocked over Lu Ting-yi, the head of propaganda. The great slaughter had begun. Nothing could plug the breach which Mao had opened, and it grew with dizzying speed until it engulfed everything.

What were the men in power to do now that they were faced with this situation — Liu Shao-ch'i, Teng Hsiao-p'ing, and their whole apparatus? They realised that they could no longer stop the vast upheaval which had now set in, but they continued to believe that they were in a position to control the way it was going, and to limit its range. With the aim of controlling events from the summit, they delegated "working groups" to go into action on the ground; the job of these groups was, of course, to suppress the "revolution". In this way they would avoid condemning themselves out of their own mouths as P'eng Chen had done with the appearance of his draft. They were under the illusion that once a clearing had been cut (with the sacrifice of P'eng Chen, Lu Ting-yi and Chou Yang), the flames would not spread. The illusion was quite understandable. An extension of the purge to the summit of the apparatus was *unthinkable*, since it would have involved the destruction of the party and the scuttling of the régime. But this was precisely the flaw in their logic: Mao did the unthinkable, and cornered his rivals precisely by destroying the party and scuttling the régime. The man who, during the "Great Leap Forward", had already demonstrated that he was prepared to sacrifice the interests of China for the interests of the régime, was to demonstrate during the "Cultural Revolution" that he was prepared to sacrifice the interests of the régime for those of his own personal power.

The military coup d'état gave the maoists control of Peking; but the apparatus still controlled its vast network in the provinces. This too was dealt with by one of Mao's master strokes. He succeeded in luring T'ao Chu out of his powerful South China citadel by offering him the post of head of propaganda in Peking and a dizzying rise to fourth position in the new hierarchy. T'ao made it to Peking in July 1966. He was thus cut off from his base: this was a part of Mao's game, and T'ao fell a few months later. Liu and Teng thought that by unloading P'eng Chen and Lu Ting-yi they had saved their position; T'ao Chu deluded himself into thinking that he simply needed to betray Liu and Teng in order to obtain a magnificent promotion; Yang Ch'eng-wu and Fu Ch'ung-pi thought they deserved their new power because they had made the initial contribution, by force of arms; Wang Li, Ch'i Pen-yü and the Red Guards, trusting the word of Mao Tse-tung, put themselves in the front line of his "revolution". All of them, one after the other — colleagues and rivals, betrayers and betrayed, victims and executioners, friends and enemies — eventually found themselves cast into limbo; they had not realised that in this lottery, in which all the dice were rigged, there was only one winner, and he had been appointed in advance — Lin Piao. Where is the "culture", and where is the "revolution"? In fact, the whole affair was simply a settling of accounts in the corners of palace corridors. And drunk with its very first victory, the maoist faction allowed the mask to slip for an instant, and confessed that the whole mechanism of the "Cultural Revolution" had only been an ingenious ploy to get rid of the individuals who held power. After P'eng Chen and his acolytes had fallen, the *Red Flag* (9 July 1966) wrote:

> "The full exposure of their revisionist nature required a certain interval of time and the development of a certain favourable climate. Even a poisonous snake does not come out of its hole unless there are certain favourable climatic conditions. The moment these poisonous snakes came out of their hole, they were captured by Chairman Mao."

Now that Mao had the forces of the Peking garrison available to control the seat of power, he felt in a position to convene a plenary session of the eighth central committee (the eleventh session, 1-12 August 1966) — the first to be convened since 1962. Even in Peking, the coup d'état had already sealed the fate of the members of the apparatus: in this sense, the "Cultural

Revolution" was over before it had even started. The gigantic
task which Mao was to be faced with over the next three years
was to seize power in the provinces, and to reabsorb the innumerable and powerful local pockets of resistance. The discipline and
cohesive strength of the party were too great to allow the base
of this monolithic organism to rise against the top. And while the
party as a whole did not remain actively faithful to Liu Shao-
ch'i, at least it remained hostile and deliberately passive towards
the injunction to "rise"; the rigidity of its network, which covered
the whole country, prevented it from responding to Peking's
appeal. It therefore became urgently necessary to improvise a
new force simultaneously and all over the country, which would
reproduce the Peking coup on a local scale. The army had enabled
Mao to take power in Peking, but it could not be entrusted with
the same task in the provinces: the troops on whom Lin Piao
could count unconditionally were not numerous enough to enable
a simultaneous action to be carried out all over the country.
There were still powerful groups within the army whose allegiance
was to chiefs such as Ho Lung and Lo Jui-ch'ing. These groups
were largely impervious to Lin Piao's influence; in several military
regions they held territorial bases which could have been turned
into a fortified camp, deaf to the orders of Peking. At that
moment it would have been dangerous to entrust the seizure of
power in the provinces to the local garrisons; in several military
regions, this would have involved an inordinate growth in power
for certain commanders of whom Mao and Lin were not exactly
sure, and would have given the apparatus an advantage by creating autonomous fortresses. For a time, the army had to be
restricted to the position of a neutral observer. The battering-
ram which Mao used to dismantle the party apparatus was therefore made up of the "revolutionary masses", with the youth in
the front line. The way in which Mao mobilised and used the
Red Guards is very similar to the way in which the Dowager
Empress Tz'u-hsi manipulated the Boxers. He turned against his
enemies the mass of popular discontent which had been brought
about by *his own* régime and which, with greater understanding,
should have been turned against himself. Just like the Boxers, the
Red Guards were inspired by a genuine, powerful revolutionary
dynamism and patriotism, but they were likewise lacking political
experience and informed, educated cadres. Their naive and
primitive mysticism was at the disposal of an old and experienced
politician who, once he had reached his objective, did not scruple
to rid himself of these innocent helpers. The bureaucratic despot-

ism which Mao himself had established had for a long time been the cause of dissatisfaction and frustration among the youth, and they were on the point of exploding. All Mao needed to do was denounce his personal rivals as the sole origin of a system of which he himself was in fact the author and then open the floodgates of popular anger against them, and he had got rid of them. But when this wave had accomplished its task and turned back on itself, it would see that it had not in fact accomplished anything at all: it had drowned the puppets, but the puppetmaster remained the same and was sitting high and dry on the bank, already closing the lock gates. The Red Guards realised in the end that they had been tricked, but it was too late: at that moment, when their role was finished, Mao was able to abandon them to military repression and replace them with a collection of mandarins who were identical to the original ones.

But in 1966 the illusions of the young people were still intact; they enthusiastically grasped the unheard-of freedom offered by the famous sixteen-point charter of the "Cultural Revolution" (promulgated on 8 August by the eleventh plenary session of the eighth central committee). According to the terms of this document, the masses were handed the right to denounce and overthrow the party authorities that were oppressing them. From mid-August to mid-September, China exploded and fell prey to its young people. Throughout the provinces, the Red Guards put the local authorities on trial; but the authorities defended themselves by organising their own Red Guards. The confusion was total.

The chaos at one point benefited the local authorities which sought to emancipate themselves from Peking. Faced with this situation, Peking attempted to regroup its forces and to regain control over the Red Guards: a unified command was imposed on the latter in order to co-ordinate their activities; they were given military "instructors", which made the movement dependent on the army. In mid-September Chou En-lai issued a warning to the Red Guards: their job was to get rid of certain designated individuals, not to call the system in question. Peking strove from this point on to direct the Red Guards by remote control, but its success-rate was uneven.

From 1967 onwards, new elements began to appear. Peking exercised uncertain control over the provinces, and found itself boxed in between contradictory imperatives. Either it could press on with the movement for local seizures of power at the risk of plunging the country into anarchy and civil war, or it could re-establish order by reinstating those local authorities which the

coup d'état had tried to eliminate; either it could keep the army
to the margins of the conflict at the risk of getting bogged down
in the chaos, or it could let the army intervene and see an
uncontrollable growth in the power of regional commanders who
were hostile to the maoists. In the diary of the period between
1967 and 1969 which occupies the next section of this book, we
shall follow these developments at the level of the day-to-day
conflict.

II
A Diary of the "Cultural Revolution"

"In China, the majority of individuals endowed with a powerful ambition have from antiquity onwards dreamed of becoming emperor. . . . This kind of ambitious person has always existed in all periods of history. When I began to advocate revolution, six or seven out of ten of those who rallied around were harbouring this type of imperial dream at the outset. But our aim in spreading the revolutionary ideal was not only to overthrow the Manchu dynasty, it was in fact to set up the republic. We therefore gradually succeeded in ridding the majority of these individuals of their imperial ambitions. Nevertheless, there remained among them one or two who, as much as thirteen years after the founding of the republic, had not yet abandoned their old ambition of becoming emperor, and it was for this very reason that even in the ranks of the revolutionary party people were continually cutting each other's throats. . . . If everyone retains this imperial mentality, a situation arises where comrades fight each other, and the whole population of the country is divided against itself. When these unceasing fratricidal struggles spread throughout the country, the population is overwhelmed by endless calamities. . . . Thus in the history of China through the generations, the imperial throne has always been fought over, and all the periods of anarchy which the country has then gone through have had their origin in this struggle for the throne. In China there has for the last few thousand years been a continual struggle around the single issue of who is to become emperor."

Sun Yat-sen, *San min chu-yi, Min-ch'üan chu-yi*, I

1967

February — March

The Shanghai experiment in January was supposed to provide a pattern of action for the "Cultural Revolution" throughout the rest of the country. In fact the disappointments and the latest rebounds of the Shanghai experiment have turned out to be a prototype of the problems which the "Cultural Revolution" is meeting everywhere. Let us briefly go over the facts.

In November 1966 the maoist activists in Shanghai formed themselves into a body called the "Headquarters of the Shanghai revolutionary-rebel workers". A powerful league called the "Headquarters of the workers' red defence units for the defence of Mao Tse-tung thought" was immediately formed in opposition to the first group. This league had at least 780,000 supporters and was in fact set up by the party committee of Shanghai municipality. Its aim was to protect the latter from the activities of the "rebel" maoists.

On 3 January the "rebel" maoists succeeded in taking possession of the offices of the daily newspaper *Wen-hui pao* and took by storm those of *Chieh-fang jih-pao* ("Liberation", another Shanghai daily) on 5 January. This was officially hailed by Peking as a great revolutionary victory, and the whole country was urged to imitate the example of this "January revolution". These shouts of victory were premature. Peking had misjudged the local situation as well as the balance of forces confronting each other. The "red defence units" counter-attacked, cutting off water, gas and electricity, organising strikes, bringing the port to a standstill and creating a "vicious current of economism" by distributing strike pay and dividing social security reserve funds among the workers. Bloody street battles broke out between the "red defence units" and the maoists. Events became confused.

Mao Tse-tung had counted on the army regaining control of Peking and therefore of the centre of power. However, he could not contemplate using the army in the same way on a large scale throughout the country. There were still too few generals giving unconditional loyalty to Lin Piao. To instruct the army to take power everywhere would have meant dangerously strengthening the authority of the regional military leaders, whose loyalty to Mao was more than doubtful and who maintained strong ties with the local Liuist party apparatus. But Mao was faced with chaos in Shanghai; soon he no longer had any choice, and was forced to call in the army.

On 25 January the *Chieh-fang chün pao* ("People's Liberation Army Daily") called on the army, in the name of Mao Tse-tung, to "support the left". It carefully specified that the "left" should be supported *even when it was in the minority,* which speaks volumes for the real position of the Shanghai masses.

On 5 February, when — and only when — they had obtained the support of the army, the maoists in Shanghai succeeded in gaining control of the municipal party committee and announced the setting up of the Shanghai Commune. On the same day, Radio Shanghai praised this as the direct descendant of the Paris Commune and the new contribution of Mao Tse-tung to international communism. But two days later, on 7 February, the term "commune" was disclaimed by Peking. It was to be replaced on 24 February by a new organ, the "Revolutionary Committee" of Shanghai, based on the "triple union" (*san chieh-he*) of the army, the rehabilitated cadres and the "revolutionary rebels". (Meanwhile three other "Revolutionary Committees" had already been formed in Heilungkiang on 31 January, in Shantung on 3 February and in Kweichow on 13 February. After Shanghai, a fifth Revolutionary Committee was to be set up in Shansi, on 18 March.)

All the elements in the execution of the "Cultural Revolution" are now in place. The slogan "seizure of power" sets the maoist activists against the local party authorities. The latter defend themselves by organising their own activists and by trying to stage a simulated "seizure of power" with these activists (this is called "brandishing the red flag to fight the red flag"). The struggle between the two sides remains unresolved, and is degenerating into violence and chaos. Peking itself has had some difficulty in recognising its own supporters, since the opposition groups frequently crystallise around individuals, rivalries and problems which are strictly local. (Incidentally, notice the remarkable amount of time which has elapsed between the setting up of these five Revolutionary Committees and the official announcement in the Peking press. The official communiqué has only been issued several days later at the earliest, and in certain cases several weeks and even a month after the victory. This reflects the state of confusion into which the country has been plunged and the difficulty the central government is experiencing in ascertaining the exact identity of the victors in each case — whether they are true or bogus followers of Mao.) The army is refereeing the struggle. In each case, its intervention — when it finally consents to intervene — is decisive. The army is already well placed in the leadership of two of the first Revolutionary Committees. The deputy leader of the Revolutionary Committee of Heilungkiang is Wang Chia-tao, a commander of the provincial military region of Heilungkiang, and the deputy leader of the Revolutionary Committee of Shantung is Yang Teh-chih, who is commander of the military region of Tsinan. This intervention by the army more often than not is tending to tip the balance of forces in favour of the established order (that is, the traditional party apparatus) and to the disadvantage of the "left", which it is supposed to support. Kwangtung is an interesting illustration of this. On 22 January a "federate rebel committee" seized power in Canton. Immediately an "action committee" rose up against it and accused it of being manipulated by the former provincial authorities and of having staged a "seizure of power". The "action committee" went over to the attack and laid siege to the "rebel committee". The army flew to the help of the latter and checked the "action committee". The latter does not consider itself defeated, and it has managed several times to take the army's administrative buildings and barracks by force of arms, urging the troops to rebel against their officers. These struggles have gone on for two months, and the outcome is still uncertain.

But the central government cannot allow these disturbances to continue indefinitely; they are threatening to paralyse the country's economy. Therefore the slogan of mobilisation of all forces for spring ploughing has rapidly been replacing the slogans of rebellion. Priority has now been given to the needs of agricultural production over the requirements of the "Cultural Revolution". On 7 March a decree prohibited "seizures of power" within the production brigades of the people's communes during the period of spring ploughing. According to the decree "it must be remembered that the majority of agricultural cadres are good or good enough". As for those who have made mistakes, there must be an effort to rehabilitate them rather than to crush them.

On 8 March the *People's Daily* published an important article denouncing the dangers of the "anarchist current". It is becoming clear that if the "Cultural Revolution" is to succeed promptly, it has to accept the unconditional support of the army. (Already when the "Revolutionary Committee" of Shanghai was being set up, the newspaper *Wen-hui pao* acknowledged unreservedly that the collaboration of the army had been a decisive factor in the victory.) The problem is that the "Cultural Revolution" alienated the sympathy of a large proportion of the army from the beginning. While the old wounds from the purge of P'eng Teh-huai have not yet healed, the recent elimination of individuals as powerful as Lo Jui-ch'ing and as influential and as popular as Ho Lung has led to serious unrest among the General Staff. The excesses of the Red Guards who invade the barracks and loot the armouries has aroused the wrath of the local military authorities. Under these conditions the army threatens to become a double-edged sword for Mao Tse-tung. It is undoubtedly capable of re-establishing order, but the risk is that it may not be a maoist order. . . .

Things have gone so far that Peking no longer has any choice. In order to placate the army, the maoists have made a vague turn to the right and have attempted to bring their supporters into line. In a short speech made on 14 February, Wang Li was obliged to convey the new message to the rebels. They are to adopt a "correct attitude" towards the army. They are forbidden henceforth to try to instigate any rebellious activity within it. The army is to be considered *a priori* as a body free from blemish whose offending elements constitute only a tiny minority. The violence which the Red Guards have indulged in has been publicly condemned on several occasions. In Peking, the establishment of a general assembly of Red Guard students (the inaugural meeting was chaired by Chou En-lai) is a sign of the desire to discipline the movement. Last but not least, the order given on 7 March to all "itinerant" Red Guards to get back to their respective home towns before the 22nd does seem to point to the end of their independent activity. Measures have been taken to prohibit the anarchic proliferation of "rebel" organisations (and severe punishment has been promised for people who write wall posters which disclose secret party or state information — which is an important indicator of the value of the information which we have previously obtained by this means).

But the most effective way of neutralising the influence of the rebels is still the new formula for the seizure of power: the "triple union". Since the setting up of the Revolutionary Committee of Shanghai, there has been a remarkable insistence upon the diffusion of this new slogan, which has been the topic of several articles in the official press. The seizure of power by the "triple union" is opposed to the unilateral seizure of power (i.e. that which is carried out by the rebel masses alone and attempts to overthrow all the authorities indiscriminately), and has been given Mao's blessing as the only orthodox formula. In the "triple union" the previously structured and organised rebel groupings no longer act on their own initiative, but operate in conjunction with the old rehabilitated and reinstated cadres on the one hand and the local military authorities on the other. The attempts at unilateral seizures of power have caused chaos. By vaguely threatening all the cadres, they weld them into a unanimous and efficient body of resistance; the administration has tended to be suddenly deprived of all its competent personnel, and the seizures have been carried out in confusion, with the rebels themselves splitting into rival factions. On the other hand the "triple union" formula offers a guarantee of order, but is in fact a disguised step backwards. Theoretically it is still a "revolutionary seizure of power", but in practice the rebel masses have lost their dynamising role to former local bureaucrats and in particular the army, which has been called upon to direct and consolidate the alliance. Even before the Revolutionary Committees were set up, the army in fact already found itself in power. It has naturally stepped in to fill the gap created by the disappearance of the party, since it is the only organised and disciplined force capable of standing in for the enormous bureaucratic apparatus. The army is now taking on the most varied tasks: it is taking over local administrations, staffing factories (to prevent sabotage, waste and looting and above all to compel the workers to stay at their workplace), supervising transport, propaganda and the schools. All that remains is to get the country to accept this rigid framework. Chou En-lai has been getting down to this recently: in his speeches at two large rallies which have been held in Peking, one consisting of peasants' delegates and the other of workers' delegates, he stated: "The army is there to help you. . . ."

The leading role that has recently fallen to Chou En-lai is a good illustration of this tactical withdrawal which the "Cultural Revolution" has made. At the Peking reception for the "revolutionary rebel" delegates from Kweichow, in the presence of Mao and Lin Piao, it was Chou En-lai who took the floor, to lay down the new policy of prudence and tolerance deemed appropriate towards former cadres. On 22 February it was Chou again who presided over the general assembly of Red Guard delegates in Peking. There was an even more remarkable event at the end of February, when it was he and not the Minister of Defence who gave the army orders to march on Honan province to quell the disturbances there. (This also indicates the limits on Lin Piao's influence over the army; it was deemed more effective to use Chou as the intermediary, yet Chou has no formal authority over the army.) Some wall newspapers have even gone so far as to award him the title officially reserved solely for Lin Piao — that of "close comrade-in-arms of Chairman Mao".

However, Chou's position is not absolutely secure. He is always being attacked indirectly, through his close supporters. Li Fu-ch'un, Li Hsien-nien, Yü Ch'iu-li, T'an Chen-lin and Ku Mu have been subjected to incessant and vicious attacks. But Chou has launched a vigorous counter-attack, publicly defending those concerned. The source of his strength is primarily that his skills are irreplaceable, all the more so now that the purge has created a dramatic void at the top. (Out of thirteen members of the secretariat of the central committee, nine have been purged by the "Cultural Revolution". Of the four remaining in office, three have recently been the subject of repeated attacks, and of the three newly installed members, one has already been removed and the position of another is threatened. . . .) Secondly, Chou has always shown unfailing personal loyalty to Mao (in 1962 he was the only one to come to Mao's defence besides Lin Piao). Moreover, out of all those in the ruling group, only he cannot be accused of personal ambition. He has always voluntarily confined himself to a purely administrative role, and in the past he has never tried to seize the available opportunities to manoeuvre himself into first place under Mao.

But for the moment he is walking a tightrope. The need for order and production (which he has done his utmost to re-establish) directly contradicts the requirements of the "seizure of power" advocated by the Cultural Revolution Group of Ch'en Po-ta and Chiang Ch'ing. In several ministries where Chou's protection is particularly effective, the activity of the rebels has been thwarted and the seizure of power carried out by those people who held it in the first place! The conflict between the pragmatic and the extremist tendencies is illustrated by a series of totally contradictory articles which have appeared in the *People's Daily* and the *Red Flag*. Chou En-lai harangues the workers in terms such as the following: "At all costs you must do eight hours of efficient work per day. You may only engage in revolutionary activity outside your eight hours. During working hours you are forbidden to leave your place of work." To which the Cultural Revolution Group, scarcely veiling the accusation, retorts: "Under the pretext of production they are attempting to put down the revolution. . . . There are some people who pretend to be preoccupied with the problems of production but who are using this opportunity to prevent the rebels from securing the power held by the revisionist faction. Always and under all circumstances the revolution is the motive force of production. The revolution is of supreme importance."

The Cultural Revolution Group draws all its strength — which is not negligible — from its direct and close association with Mao. Its activity corresponds to Mao's deep and spontaneous aspirations, while Lin Piao and Chou En-lai represent respectively the law of the gun and the pressure of hard facts (the reality with which the maoist ideal is periodically compelled to come to terms). This insoluble contradiction between design and execution has given rise to uncertain and piecemeal interventions; violent advances and prudent withdrawals are made, sometimes simultaneously. Driven by a team of horses pulling in different directions, the "Cultural Revolution" is getting bogged down in confusion.

Of the innumerable recent purges, that of Chu Teh has aroused particular interest. The charges brought against him have been published in detail in a document published by *Hsin Pei-ta*, the organ of the Red Guards at the University of Peking. The main counts on the indictment relate to events which took place more than thirty years ago! In fact this old man of eighty-one has practically retired from active life. The accusations against him (he is described as a warlord, ambitious, opportunistic, and a usurper of a military glory which is Mao's alone) revolve chiefly around his biography, which he had written by Liu Po-yü in 1939. But these recent slanders make it difficult to forget that for a long time he was Mao's senior and then his right hand man, and that during its heroic period Chinese communism was in fact a two-headed body, with Mao as its political and Chu as its military head. In actual fact, Chu's only real mistake, which Mao could not forgive him and which could not be referred to, was in 1959, when on the strength of his reputation Chu ventured to speak his mind and came to the defence of P'eng Teh-huai.

As I stated above, circumstances forced the central authorities to appeal to the army to regain control of the situation. But military intervention has since turned out to be a double-edged sword for the maoists, because it has brought about a consolidation of the power of the commanders of the military regions, several of whom are hostile towards the "Cultural Revolution". The problem is particularly acute in regions like Sinkiang and Tibet, where in the past the norm of the division of political and military power has not been observed, and where the commander of the military region carries out many of the duties of the first secretary of the party committee. From such a position of strength it is easy for the local satrap to take advantage of the "Cultural Revolution" and make his territory an "independent fief". Wang En-mao is ruling Sinkiang in this manner. In Peking the Red Guards denounce him as the butcher of the "Cultural Revolution", and have issued a call for "the liberation of Sinkiang from the tyranny of Wang En-mao". But in his kingdom, Wang — who controls the army, the administration and propaganda — has had the local press praise him as an "exemplary supporter of Chairman Mao". In Tibet, Chang Kuo-hua is playing a similar role. His troops control the administration, the press and the radio, and up until now the Red Guards have been given no freedom of action. In Inner Mongolia, the army has used force to disband three groups of rebel maoists. In certain provinces like Szechuan and Honan, the military command is loyal to Ho Lung, is closely linked with the local party apparatus and has sided wholeheartedly with it. This has led to violent clashes between the local garrisons and "revolutionary rebel" groups.

April

Ch'i Pen-yü's article ("Patriotism or Treason", *People's Daily*, 1 April) has aroused much interest, and marks the beginning of a spectacular personal attack against Liu Shao-ch'i. But this offensive is really more of a restriction on the development of the "Cultural Revolution" than an escalation of the struggle. By implicating all the local cadres, the efforts to "seize power" have driven the cadres to adopt a unanimous position of resistance and sabotage which is proving to be formidably effective. The *People's Daily* itself recently emphasised that if the majority of attempts to "seize power" have so far failed, it is precisely because the rebels have indiscriminately attacked too large a number of cadres and have stirred up the opposition of the majority. The

"Cultural Revolution" is equally incapable either of backtracking or of rapidly reducing this enormous resistance from the local party apparatus, and therefore has now centred its attacks on Liu Shao-ch'i alone, trying to use this manoeuvre to try to create a diversion. On the pretext of taking the struggle as far as possible, an opportunity has been found to uncouple the "Cultural Revolution" from its base. The Shanghai press (*Wen-hui pao* and *Chieh-fang jih-pao*) has made some illuminating remarks on the real significance of the campaign now being waged against Liu. "All the revolutionary mass organisations which are at the moment engaged in 'civil war' activities (in inverted commas in the original text) *are to stop these local struggles immediately* and are henceforth to direct all their energy to denounce the crimes of China's Khrushchev", and "The greatest possible number of people must be rallied to strike the tiny minority at the top". In other words, the maoists — rather than get caught up in an unpredictable struggle against a substantial and many-sided opposition — have replaced these adversaries with an isolated scapegoat who has already been rendered powerless.

The pretext that has been chosen for this campaign against Liu is amazingly feeble. He has been taken to task for having once approved a showing of the film *Ch'ing kung mi-shih* ("Secret episode at the Ch'ing court"), which he was supposed to have judged a "patriotic work" when in reality it was a "vindication of treason". This old film (made in Hong Kong, 1948) is perfectly ordinary and has lain buried in oblivion for many years. Why exhume it now, as the main exhibit at Liu's trial? Liu's whole career makes it difficult to imagine him being a hardened cinephile, and it is even doubtful that he has ever seen or paid any attention to the film in question. Is this, then, the most heinous and exemplary of crimes? This kind of affair is going to deprive the "Cultural Revolution" of all credibility (assuming that the people involved have ever bothered about its credibility). The only motive which may explain the choice of such a baroque pretext once again depends on petty personal factors. Mao's wife has to be given an opportunity to shine on the political scene at all costs. Before the "Cultural Revolution" the only official post she had held was that of member of the cinematographic industry steering committee of the, Department of Culture, and it was in this capacity that she once opposed the screening of the film in question and had been in the minority among her colleagues on the committee. Consequently, the only way of portraying Liu Shao-ch'i now as an opponent of the revolutionary line defended by Mao's wife is to fabricate a criminal past for him *in the field of cinema.*

But with Chiang Ch'ing's name up in lights, there has been a new and sudden increase in the activity of the extremist faction. Once again the Red Guards have the wind in their sails, and once again the authorities are underwriting their activities. An article in the *People's Daily* has just recalled their merits as revolutionaries. At the same time, the army is now being called to order. Its interventions so far have all too often led it to support "right-wing" organisations, forcibly disband rebel groups and persecute the Red Guards. To prevent a recurrence of such events, a decree of 1 April explicitly states that the army has no authority to decide which mass organisations are revolutionary and which are counter-revolutionary. On 2 April an article in the *People's Daily* reminded the army that it should "treat the Red Guards properly". On the 6th, an editorial in the *Liberation Army Daily* called upon it to "remain moderate". Also on the 6th the military commission of the central committee enacted a ten-point decree forbidding the army, among other things, to use its weapons against mass organisations, to make arrests or use physical violence. The decree also orders the army not to take any specific initiatives before consulting the opinion of the "Cultural Revolution" committee, and it stipulates that it should trust the mass organisations, and should only use methods of intellectual persuasion in its dealings with them, and that this should be done patiently.

As I have already indicated, the army is far from achieving the political homogeneity which Lin Piao dreams of. It is divided into different fiefs, which are organised along the invisible but restrictive lines of personal loyalties consolidated during past campaigns; it is crisscrossed by contradictory tendencies and is subject to unrest, which has revealed itself in several recent purges. Hsü Hsiang-ch'ien, who has recently been promoted to the leadership of the army's Cultural Revolution Group, has been ousted from this post to make way for Hsiao Hua. (Hsiao Hua, Lin Piao's right-hand man, has become famous as a result of his open struggle against Chiang Ch'ing in January. He rebuffed her when she tried to interfere in the supervision of "Cultural Revolution" activities in the army. In retaliation, Hsiao's residence was sacked in a Red Guard raid.) Yeh Chien-ying has disappeared. As for Ch'en Yi, even though he has formally become a civilian cadre, he has kept his close personal links with the military world, where his prestige remains considerable. And the virulent attacks which the rebels continue to pile on him have created sharp dissatisfaction in the army.

But even though Peking is theoretically trying to devise a new turn to the "left" by restraining the army, there is a large gap between the official instructions of the central authorities and actual experience in the provinces. The case of Wang En-mao, the warlord of Sinkiang, is a good example. Continually denounced by the rebels between October 1966 and February 1967 as responsible for massacres of maoists in Sinkiang, he has just been made head of Sinkiang's "Cultural Revolution" committee! (When a brigand cannot be defeated, he is made a baron.) He went covered with official flowers to Peking, where he had discussions with Chou En-lai. Incidentally, this confirms the rumour that Chou (the only person in the maoist camp who remains an acceptable intermediary to the dissidents among the military) is busy negotiating a compromise with the opposition leaders in the army. He has already had similar dealings with Chang Shu-chih, who is a supporter of Ho Lung and commander of the provincial military region of Honan.

May

The provinces continue to be the scene of uninterrupted violence. Extensive and bloody clashes have taken place in Szechuan, at Chungking and especially at Chengtu. The seriousness of the situation in Szechuan has led to upheavals in the local administration. Li Ching-ch'uan, the first secretary of the party bureau of the South-West region (he is also a member of the politbureau of the central committee) has been held responsible for the events which soaked Chengtu in blood for over a month, and is accused of seeking to transform Szechuan into an "independent kingdom". He has been removed from office and replaced by Chang Kuo-hua. The latter is likewise an equivocal figure. He is a soldier who used to reign over Tibet, and succeeded in counteracting the influence of the "Cultural Revolution" in his province. There are two possible motives for his transfer to Szechuan. By promoting him, Peking has succeeded in diverting him far from his entrenched position in Tibet; and his nomination is a compromise solution for Szechuan, where in the existing turmoil someone who supports the "Cultural Revolution" would be unacceptable. At the same time the commander of the military region of Chengtu, Huang Hsin-t'ing, has been deposed and replaced by Liang

Hsing-ch'u (previously the deputy political commissar of the military region of Canton).

Serious clashes have also taken place in the north-east. Twenty thousand workers at the car factory at Changchun went on strike and sacked two schools which were being used as Red Guard centres. In Heilungkiang during a pitched battle, a large group of maoists were crushed by a coalition of workers and soldiers. Bloody clashes have broken out once more in Honan (Chengchow and Kaifeng). In the same province, police at Hsinyang crushed a demonstration of Red Guards who were celebrating the establishment of the new Peking Revolutionary Committee — which took place on 20 March!

There have been disturbances in Inner Mongolia, and Ulanfu has been demoted.

Even the few provinces which have already been "conquered" are not free of disturbances. Out of the five provincial Revolutionary Committees which have already been set up, three (Shantung, Kweichow and Heilungkiang) were not represented at the 1 May celebrations in Peking. Fights have even broken out at Changping, a stone's throw from the capital.

It is obviously difficult to determine the exact scale of these various clashes. The wall newspapers often mention hundreds and thousands of dead and wounded, and tens of thousands of combatants. A large amount of rhetoric has certainly gone into the writing of these accounts, but this bloody fighting is nonetheless quite real; it is a source of grave concern to the Peking authorities and is recognised as such by the official press. On 22 May the *People's Daily* published an important editorial under the headline, "Put an immediate stop to the armed struggle". It denounces the "vicious current of violence which throws the general line of the Cultural Revolution into confusion, destroys production, the national economy and revolutionary order and threatens the life and assets of the population."

The most serious and most violent clashes are generally those in which the coalition of workers, peasants and soldiers confronts "rebel" maoist groups. Another type of conflict is that which has broken out between rival maoist factions struggling for the power to monopolise various kinds of equipment (vehicles, means of propaganda, printing equipment etc.).

The "triple union" formula, which is supposed to facilitate the "seizures of power" and thus to hasten the normalisation of administrative and economic activity through the rehabilitation of former cadres, has so far been a failure. The rebels torpedo any attempt to reintegrate the cadres, while the latter — having learnt from previous experience — take refuge in discreet inaction. As an example of the former cadres' reluctance to respond to the "triple union", the Revolutionary Committee of Peking Municipality, which was set up at the end of March, has managed to recruit only one member of the former apparatus, Wu Teh, to its leadership. Furthermore, the ferocious attacks which continue to be made against Ch'en Yi augur quite badly for the policy of tolerating former cadres, even though from time to time he continues to resurface amid the turmoil. He was present at the reception given by the Tanzanian ambassador on 26 April and even gave a short speech. He was also on the rostrum on 1 May. A whole succession of people who have been the subject of recent attacks also took part in the 1 May celebrations: Chu Teh, Tung Pi-wu, Ch'en Yün, T'an Chen-lin, Li Hsüeh-feng, Li Hsien-nien, Liu Ning-yi, Chang Kuo-hua etc. This forms part of the seduction policy which the maoists are now using on the cadres who have been investigated, in order to try to obtain their support and persuade them to resume their activities. This conciliatory venture is a question of urgent need. The isolation of the maoists at the top has assumed dramatic proportions. This is illustrated well by the list of absentees from the 1 May ritual. More than 60% of the members of the central committee and more than 80% of the deputy members of the central committee did not take part in the festivities. Several departments of the central committee were not represented. An Tzu-wen, the director of the Department of Organisation, and his three deputy directors were absent. Hsü Ping, the director of the Department of the United Front, and his six deputy directors, the leaders of the Department of Propaganda, the members of the Supervisory Commission of the central committee, the leading members of the judiciary and five deputy ministers of the Security Department were also not in evidence. The vacant seats were no less numerous among the armed forces, especially among the ranks of the General Staff of the navy, airforce and artillery.

The general refusal of cadres to enter into the "triple union" is increasing the importance of the role played by the army. At the level of each province and each town, the attitude of the army is becoming the decisive factor in the outcome of the struggle. Peace or disorder, victory to the rebels or to the opposition: everything is entirely dependent on the action or inaction of the army, and on the way in which it sides with this or that faction. But while the army remains the ultimate arbiter of power every-

where, it is generally too slow to make up its mind, and when it
does come to a decision, it usually does so in such a way as to
damage the "Cultural Revolution". Once again the central
authorities are handling the army with the utmost caution. The
Red Flag (no. 6) has reminded everyone that the army is the
"pillar of the revolution", and that "at no time nor in any circumstances should the spearhead of the struggle be turned against it".
(Chou En-lai stressed this point in his speech at the inauguration
of the Revolutionary Committee of Peking Municipality.) Still
on the same topic, the *People's Daily* of 12 May added that the
actual outcome of the "Cultural Revolution" is entirely dependent
on the support of the army.

But the army has its own demands, and it apparently does not
feel inclined to blindly accept orders dictated by the Cultural
Revolution Group of Ch'en Po-ta and Chiang Ch'ing. Furthermore, Chiang Ch'ing has been deprived of the position which
she won for herself in the army as "adviser" to the military committee of the "Cultural Revolution", while her adversary, Hsiao
Hua, has been made head of this committee. The indignation of
the army has been roused by the purging of several of its most
prestigious and popular commanders, and it is exasperated by the
rebel maoist excesses which have been directed against them on
several occasions. Peking's job now is to paper hastily over the
cracks by infusing the ranks with a general mystique of personal
loyalty to Chairman Mao, which he can use as a kind of cement.
This propaganda campaign is turning into a kind of folk-lore.
By order of the military committee, a special medal bearing the
head of Mao and the inscription "Serve the people" was given
out on 13 May to every soldier in the land, sea and air forces,
in the course of liturgical ceremonies which the New China News
Agency described with religious fervour.

In the doctrinal and historical sphere, the event of the month
was the publication on 17 May of a very important document
of the "Cultural Revolution", which was officially made known
to the country one year after it had been secretly circulated
inside the party. Very special publicity was given to this text, and
its publication was accompanied and followed by numerous
doctrinal commentaries.

The document in question, which is simply called *Memorandum*
(it was in fact a memorandum of the central committee addressed
to all levels of the party, dated 16 May 1966), sheds extra light
on the first stage of the "Cultural Revolution" and shows that
from May 1966 the "seizure of power" had already been decided

upon, and the fate of Liu Shao-ch'i and his associates had already been irrevocably determined. The first aim of the *Memorandum* was to inform all levels of the party that the "draft" of the Group of Five, which had been ratified by the central committee on 12 February 1966, was henceforth abrogated; that the Group of Five was itself disbanded, as were all the other bodies which were dependent on it, and that it had been replaced by a new, smaller-scale committee (that is, the existing Cultural Revolution Group led by Chiang Ch'ing and Ch'en Po-ta). The *Memorandum* denounced the draft as being the work of P'eng Chen alone — thus clearing the other members of the group, among whom was the equivocal K'ang Sheng (who had either been put beside P'eng Chen deliberately to act as "stool pigeon" or who had changed tack of his own accord when the wind changed and had bought his reprieve by betraying P'eng). The *Memorandum* made a detailed analysis of the criminal designs revealed by the draft: namely, the desire to evade the political repercussions of the criticism of the *Hai Jui* libretto by diverting the discussion to the purely academic level and attempting to lead the "Cultural Revolu- tion" away from its true aims: "These individuals who follow the capitalist road and who have infiltrated the *central committee and all the organs which are dependent on it in each province, each town and each autonomous region . . .* ; among these people there are some that we already know, others have not yet been exposed, *some of them enjoy our confidence and we have moulded them to be our successors — individuals who are like Khrushchev and who live alongside us!*" (On the question of the draft of the Group of the Five and of the *Memorandum*, see Section One above, p. 48.)

June and the First Fortnight of July

The "Cultural Revolution" seems to have been swallowed up. For almost four months now the "seizures of power" movement has been at a standstill in the provinces, the great majority of which still have no Revolutionary Committees. The "seizure of power" policy is hardly even mentioned any more at the moment, and the slogans which crop up again and again refer to a less exciting policy: "make the revolution with thrift", and "fight against waste". The *People's Daily* has gone so far as to devote its front page to cheaper recipes for making the glue for wall posters. (Formerly the revolutionary poster-writers used glue made of flour, thus wasting large quantities of this precious foodstuff.) The *People's Daily* has also vigorously denounced (through "readers' letters") the misuse of loudspeakers: the simultaneous uproar of opposing factions who make use of them everywhere and without intermission, preventing workers both from working and from relaxing, and therefore harming production. The Red Guards are to stop borrowing trucks and cars for their revolutionary ventures, because by doing so they are monopolising plant required for production and are wasting fuel.

There are increasing orders to fight against anarchy and violence. The term "civil war" (used in inverted commas) appears frequently. It is often applied to quarrels in which one maoist faction opposes another. The "Cultural Revolution" has in actual fact produced an extraordinary proliferation of rebel factions, whose only common feature is their unconditional loyalty to Mao — the rest of the time they spend tearing one another to pieces to gain control locally. These internal divisions have ended up by paralysing the progress of the "Cultural Revolution". In principle, the army is instructed to adjudicate all conflicts: the rival factions come and denounce each other to the local military authority, which adopts drastic measures only as a last resort.

These endemic outbreaks of violence have led to a steady increase in the powers accruing to the army, since it alone has proved to be ultimately capable of keeping some order. In several provinces already won over to the "Cultural Revolution" a real military régime is beginning to take shape. (It is remarkable that in Peking, for example, even the directives of the ordinary police, such as those which refer to city traffic etc., are now issued by the military authorities.)

By its very nature and its practice of discipline the army, even a "People's Liberation Army", spontaneously leans towards the traditional side in the defence of order and respect for authority. And its interventions more often than not result in restraints on the activities of the extremists and the Red Guards. The setting up of schools under the control of the army has already resulted in the dissolution of a large number of "rebel" groups.

Mao's problem is that on the one hand he has been forced to call in the army to contain the chaos, but on the other hand this recourse to the military is usually rebounding against his own supporters. Szechuan is again a good example of this. It is a particularly recalcitrant province, as politically it is an old and solid bastion of Liu Shao-ch'i and Teng Hsiao-p'ing, and militarily it has been staffed for a long time by Ho Lung's men. Szechuan has thus been convulsed by violent struggles. Disturbances have just broken out once again in Chungking, where the army has crushed factions of maoist activists. Significantly, this repression is specifically the work of two soldiers (Lan Yi-nung and Pai Pin) who were sent to this province by Peking in May to lay the foundations of the future Revolutionary Committee there.

The reopening of some universities has been announced. The initiative came from the Aeronautical College of Peking (the Red Guards there have been one of the most advanced groups of the "Cultural Revolution"). But the time-table fixed by the college is almost entirely monopolised by study of the thoughts of Mao, sessions of criticism and discussion, military training and initiation into industrial and agricultural tasks; practically no time is devoted to specific teaching activities. To judge from this, the principal aim of the reopening of the universities seems to be simply to contain the students between four walls and to hinder the "revolutionary" activity which they were pursuing outside.

The few Revolutionary Committees which have successfully been set up are already subject to a rectification campaign. This is aimed at restoring their purity and revolutionary ardour, and at dragging them out of the rut of mandarinism in which they seem to have been bogged down since their inception. Of the new sets of rules adopted by various Revolutionary Committees, one of the most typical is that which has appeared in Heilung-kiang (see the *People's Daily*, 29 June):

> "Study of the thoughts of Mao: the members of the committee will devote one hour every day to this before work, as well as the entire morning on Wednesdays and Saturdays. During the hours of study of the thoughts of Mao, there will be no discussions, the offices will remain closed, no visitors will be received and the telephone will not be answered.
>
> The leading cadres must get closer to the masses, personally receive deputations from the masses, reply to letters, accept criticism modestly and humbly and criticise themselves. The committee will periodically undergo rectification campaigns.
>
> One third of the administrative cadres of the Revolutionary Committee and in particular of the leading cadres will be sent in permanent rotation into the factories or into the fields to take part collectively in the work of production. One third will devote themselves to enquiries among the

masses, and one third will remain in the offices to carry on the administrative work.

It is forbidden to praise members of the committee by name. Members will not give official receptions, will not allow themselves to be photographed or filmed, will not have their photograph or news about themselves published in the newspapers, will not have themselves applauded on their arrival at meetings, will not have themselves called by their official title but will quite simply be called 'comrade'.

In the buildings of the committee there will be no domestic personnel. Cleaning and domestic duties will be performed by the cadres themselves on a rota basis.

Adopt a frugal and austere attitude. There is to be no waste or privilege. Members of the committee will not have the right to provide themselves with a personal secretary, whether in the name of the committee or in their own names. It is forbidden for members of the committee to hold banquets, to give presents or to accept them."

The recent explosion of the Chinese hydrogen bomb has been heralded as a victory for the "Cultural Revolution" — which is quite paradoxical, since the nuclear research sector has been quite specifically isolated from the influence of the "Cultural Revolution" (see article 12 of the *Sixteen Points*). This paradox is, moreover, that of the régime as a whole: the "revisionists", the "specialists", the "economists" and the "experts" have equipped the country with the political, administrative, scientific, technical and economic foundation to enable the doctrinaires to periodically allow themselves the ruinous luxury of denouncing and dismantling this infrastructure, while giving themselves credit for its latest fruits. The contradiction which Mao has not managed to solve is that China can only achieve material success at the expense of deviating from ideological purity. This contradiction can only be resolved by the lame and terribly costly formula of perpetual alternation: swings of the pendulum between the shame-faced fat cows of reality and the noble lean cows of ideology — the latter feeding exclusively on the reserves accumulated by the former. Given this ideological ball and chain which is regularly hung around China's neck, it is not surprising that her economic development has progressed only slowly and sporadically. The miracle is that, although paralysed by such a régime, China has nevertheless succeeded in making unquestionable progress. Chou En-lai continually takes fastidious care to tell his foreign visitors (of whom the author of this book has been one) that no one should labour under any illusions about China's material progress, that China is still in many respects an underdeveloped country, that it has a very long way to go etc. In fact although the debts which the communist régime inherited at the seizure of power of 1949 were heavy (and even this liability should not be exaggerated: in railway communications and industry, the new régime has largely survived on the achievements of the Nationalist Republic before the war), the fact that today after twenty years there is still only little to show is a matter for shame. The potential of the Chinese people for intelligence, inventiveness, endurance, ingenuity and activity is such that it can adapt itself even to inept governments, providing that they are content with being simply parasitic (like the British colonial government in Hong Kong or the Kuomintang government in Taiwan), and to discriminatory legislation (as in the majority of countries of South-East Asia): and it still manages to perform miracles. By comparison, the results which the People's Republic of China can lay claim to are deeply upsetting to informed observers rather than a cause for admiration, for they know only too well that China would achieve infinitely more and better things if only its government had not undertaken systematically to inhibit and waste its human resources.

In the ideological sphere the spread and teaching of the classical passages of maoist doctrine continues on an intensive scale. Very special importance is being given to the 1957 text *On the correct Handling of Contradictions among the People*. The inspiration for this article came from the threefold impact of the denunciation of Stalin's crimes by Khrushchev, the Hungarian uprising and the failure of the "Hundred Flowers" movement. It develops the essential point of maoist doctrine, which consists in the theory of the permanence of class struggles within socialist society itself. It marked the starting point of what was to become the "anti-revisionist" struggle.

At the same time the personality cult of the "great Helmsman, great Leader, great Commander-in-chief, great Teacher, supremely beloved Chairman Mao" has become more than just a tribute paid to his thoughts; it has reached heights of mysticism and hysteria. Various hymns to his glory (reproduced *in extenso* on whole pages of the *People's Daily* together with the musical score, so that the tens of thousands of readers of this austere official gazette can learn to sing them at home) sing his praises in the form of sun-worship litanies: the radiance of his person is compared to the activity of the sun, spreading universal life etc.

The commemoration of the forty-sixth anniversary of the founding of the Chinese Communist Party provided a new opportunity to intensify the maoisation of the party: the party only exists through Mao, it is "his personal creation" (so much for historical facts!), "all the victories which the party has won were victories for the thought of Mao Tse-tung". Mao is the only salvation: "to deviate from the thought of Mao Tse-tung is tantamount to the fundamental rejection of marxism-leninism and is equivalent to prohibiting the possibility of erecting a true marxist-leninist party" (the *People's Daily*, 30 June, and the *Red Flag*, no. 11). On the same occasion the unique and privileged position of Lin Piao was sanctified: "for several decades he has implemented and defended the revolutionary proletarian line of Mao Tse-tung in the most loyal, the most resolute and the most profound way, and he brandishes the great red flag of the thought of Mao Tse-tung. . . . Comrade Lin Piao is the closest comrade in arms of Chairman Mao, his best pupil and the most brilliant example for the whole party and the whole country of the living study and living application of the thought of Mao Tse-tung". In fact the consecration of Lin Piao became normal and necessary once the personal authority of Mao was substituted for the timeless collective authority of the party. The repository of absolute truth is no longer the party but Mao. This is a transfer of authority from a permanent and abstract body to an individual who, however "immortal" his thought, is nevertheless himself mortal, and this constitutes a considerable threat to the continuity of the régime: hence the need now to designate a Crown Prince who is also endowed with this unique quality of infallibility. However, the elevation of Lin Piao is a precarious way of remedying the enormous breach which Mao has opened by substituting his personal authority for that of the party. It does not meet with unanimous approval even within the maoist group. While it is still comparatively easy to deify Mao, with his historical stature, a similar undertaking on Lin Piao's behalf is a much more arbitrary affair, and whatever the propaganda efforts it is going to be difficult to persuade public opinion that the chosen one is equal to his calling.

The Second Half of July: the Wuhan Mutiny

The seriousness of the Wuhan mutiny would seem to have no precedent in the whole history of the régime.

Wuhan, a complex consisting of the three towns of Wuchang,

Hankow and Hanyang — a total of 2,500,000 inhabitants, is situated in the centre of China, in the Hupeh province on the Yang-tze river, and occupies a position of vital importance from the economic and strategic points of view. Political power was previously held there by Wang Jen-chung. (Wang was initially the mayor of Wuhan, and first party secretary of Hupeh province. He was then promoted to first party secretary for the Central Southern region, replacing T'ao Chu when the latter was made head of the Department of Propaganda after Lu Ting-yi was purged. After this meteoric ascent, T'ao Chu was himself purged at the end of 1966.) Wang seemed to enjoy Mao's favour — it was in his company that the Chairman went for his famous swim in the Yang-tze river. But at the end of 1966 he was violently attacked and finally purged. As everywhere else, the tornado of the "Cultural Revolution" had left the army as the sole organised authority in Wuhan. It was under the orders of General Ch'en Tsai-tao, who since 1955 had held command over the very important military region of Wuhan (including the provincial military regions of Hupeh and Honan). Ch'en Tsai-tao had at no time in the past belonged to Lin Piao's group of loyal supporters, and was on the contrary closely linked with the powerful regional commanders Wang En-mao (commander of the military region of Sinkiang), Ch'in Chi-wei (commander of the military region of Kunming) and Huang Hsin-t'ing (commander of the military region of Chengtu). These men were all former subordinates of P'eng Teh-huai, Ho Lung, Hsü Hsiang-ch'ien and Liu Po-ch'eng; by way of solidarity with their leaders, they had put up an active resistance to the maoist current.

From the beginning of 1967, Wuhan was the scene of continual struggles. The three towns had no less than fifty-four groups of "revolutionary rebels" which, vying in the struggle for power, fought with each other continually in bloody clashes. Ch'en Tsai-tao chose to give military assistance to a powerful organisation called "the Million Heroes", which consisted chiefly of factory workers (two thousand workshops and mining establishments went on strike from 29 April to 30 June to increase its ranks), railway workers and peasants — all sworn enemies of the maoist Red Guards. Supported by the army, this workers' militia undertook to crush the maoist activists. The crisis reached its first climax at the end of June, culminating in the closure of the railway bridge over the Yang-tze river and in a street battle which resulted in two hundred and fifty dead and one thousand five hundred wounded. In July, in response to appeals from the maoists who saw themselves on the point of being wiped out, Peking sent to Wuhan two of its highest-ranking emissaries, Hsieh Fu-chih and Wang Li, to try to impose a truce.

Hsieh Fu-chih, vice-president of the Council of Ministers, Minister for Security and leader of the Revolutionary Committee of Peking Municipality, has become one of the leading personalities of the "Cultural Revolution". He has an ambiguous past. For a long time he was Teng Hsiao-p'ing's right-hand man, but his rallying to the "Cultural Revolution" at its inception in fact made the initial development of the movement possible. By placing the security forces at the disposal of the maoists, he played a decisive role in the military coup d'état in Peking which turned the balance of forces in Mao's favour.

Wang Li, who does not have as varied a career as Hsieh behind him, is an upstart. He is a product of and a chief spokesman for the "Cultural Revolution"; his association with Chiang Ch'ing and his major role in the Cultural Revolution Group has catapulted him into the highest spheres of the hierarchy. After the purge of T'ao Chu he was put in charge of the Department of Propaganda, and in this capacity is considered one of the brains behind the maoist movement.

That Peking should send two such eminent ambassadors to settle Wuhan's problems already conveys an idea of the seriousness of the situation.

Hsieh and Wang arrived in Wuhan on 14 July.

What happened in the days which followed did not become known immediately. The first indication that something serious had occurred in Wuhan was disclosed abruptly in Peking during the evening of 21 July, with a sudden demonstration (including army detachments) which marched to shouts of "overthrow Ch'en Tsai-tao! Liberate Hupeh! Release Wang Li immediately!"

Details of the affair were described a little while later in the wall newspapers and in Red Guard publications. On the 17th — three days after the arrival of the emissaries of the "Cultural Revolution" — the local maoists, wishing to take advantage of the support which had at last arrived from Peking, organised a demonstration to celebrate the arrival of Hsieh and Wang. They ran right into a counter-demonstration by the "Million Heroes". Ch'en Tsai-tao was exasperated by the interference of the Cultural Revolution Group, and was conscious of the strength of the support of his colleagues from the adjacent military regions. He unleashed his troops. On the 20th a military detachment (unit 8201), backed up by the proletarian militias of the "Million

Heroes", laid siege to the airport, the railway station, the wharves
on the Yang-tze river and the main thoroughfares of the city.
The place where Hsieh and Wang were staying was taken by
storm. Wang was carried off, dragged in front of the crowd,
savagely beaten and then locked up.

If at this point the authorities of Peking had yielded to the
temptation to make a direct military intervention to free Wang
Li, they would have carried the internal divisions in the army to
breaking point. This would have almost certainly led to civil war.
Instead, they skilfully adopted a flexible and conciliatory
manoeuvre. On the same day, the 20th, Chou En-lai went to
Wuhan to negotiate the release of Wang Li.

On the 22nd five hundred thousand demonstrators marched
in Peking to shouts of "Down with Wang Jen-chung and Ch'en
Tsai-tao!"

During the afternoon of the 22nd Hsieh Fu-chih and Wang Li
returned by plane from Wuhan to Peking, where they received a
hero's welcome at the airport in the presence of all the régime's
highest dignitaries. Radio Peking announced their "glorious
return" in a special programme which was broadcast three times.
On the 23rd, the *People's Daily* celebrated their return with
particular emphasis, but without mentioning details of the episode.
The official communiqués limited themselves to stating that Wang
Li and Hsieh Fu-chih had "returned in glory from Wuhan where
they had gone to sort out questions relating to the Cultural
Revolution" and that "their glorious return to Peking was an
event which should fill all the revolutionary masses of the country
with enthusiasm."

On the 24th the gunboats of the Eastern fleet of the Chinese
navy sailed up the Yang-tze as far as Wuhan, while paratroop
units regained control of strategic points of the city and disarmed
unit 8201 as well as the "Million Heroes". On the same day
Ch'en Tsai-tao and his chief subordinates were taken to Peking.

Contrary to some commentators, it does not seem that the
troop movements determined the outcome of the crisis. It had
already been solved through diplomatic channels, with Chou
En-lai's intervention on the 20th. It should be noted that the
release and return of Wang Li and Hsieh Fu-chih to Peking was
effected on 22nd, that is to say, previous to the despatching of
the central government troops. The sending of these troops, the
disarming of the rebels, the departure of Ch'en Tsai-tao for
Peking and his replacement at the head of the military region of
Wuhan by Tseng Szu-yü — all this did not come about through

the use of force, but was simply the result of previous negotiations. Thus the disarming of the mutineers took place without a struggle, and Ch'en Tsai-tao was simply relieved of his command without being punished.*

Vast demonstrations, still celebrating the return of the two emissaries, have subsequently been organised in several large Chinese cities; the most important of them took place in Peking, where on the 25th a million people marched past T'ien An Men (the Gate of Heavenly Peace) in the presence of all the leaders of the régime. The demonstrators' slogans ("We will defend Chairman Mao with our blood and our lives!") scarcely resemble shouts of victory, but rather the rallying-call of a minority threatened by a powerful enemy.

The Wuhan incident marks a decisive turning-point in the development of the "Cultural Revolution". The army, which in the past has often already been partial to the forces of resistance, has gone one step further and adopted an attitude of open defiance. As a consequence, this has led the extremist wing of the "Cultural Revolution" (Ch'en Po-ta, Chiang Ch'ing, Wang Li, Chang Ch'un-ch'iao, Yao Wen-yuan, Ch'i Pen-yü, etc.) to harden its distrust and hostility towards the army. It has substituted the old phrase denouncing "the handful of revisionists who hold power in the party" with the expression "the handful of revisionists who hold power in the party *and those who hold it in the army*". This refers to the immunity which puts the army above all suspicion and has kept it sheltered from the unrest of the "Cultural Revolution".

But it is difficult to see how Mao can bring himself to approve of this declaration of war which his all too fervent followers are making on the army. If he does, he will run the risk of alienating himself from the sole organised force which, since the undermining of the party, has been the régime's last bulwark against anarchy. The army for its part, although it has shown itself to be one-sided in its repression of rebel maoists in the provinces and largely deaf to the orders of Lin Piao (whose artificial promotion to the position of Crown Prince is still unacceptable to the former old guard of P'eng Teh-huai, Ho Lung, Liu Po-ch'eng, Hsü Hsiang-ch'ien etc.), has mostly remained loyal to

---

* The price Peking paid for the submission of the provincial army would gradually be disclosed by the subsequent development of the "Cultural Revolution". The central authorities would sacrifice their extreme left and abandon it for good to military repression, in return for which the provincial garrisons would nominally recognise Peking's authority.

Mao. Even if in some cases this loyalty is more formal than real, it is nevertheless preventing the opposing factions from crystallising around a common element of dissatisfaction. Although the opposition is immense, it is still hopelessly fragmented and impotent, precisely because it cannot bring itself to denounce Mao directly. By stopping on the brink of sacrilege, it has been reduced to trickery, local insurrection and sabotage, and lacks any organic nucleus. The case of Liu Shao-ch'i is a good example. He refuses to counter-attack when accusations are made against him, and he confines himself to a single line of defence, pleading error in good faith and declaring his unalterable past, present and future loyalty to Mao.

August

A year after the beginning of the "Cultural Revolution", the country does nothing but fall deeper into the chaos and violence from which hardly any province is now spared. (The situation is particularly serious in Hupeh — the after-effects of the mutiny in Wuhan have not yet been eliminated — and also in Hunan, Kiangsi, Szechuan, Kwangsi, in Nanking, Shanghai and especially in Canton. Disturbances have also been reported in Honan, Shensi, Chekiang, Fukien, Shantung, Inner Mongolia, Yunnan and in Kweichow. Several towns in the north-east are the scene of uninterrupted violence — Shenyang, Fushun, Changchun, Harbin — and the central authorities have sent Kuan Feng there on a peace mission. In Heilungkiang, in principle a model maoist province, the commander of the military region, Wang Chia-tao, and his political commissar, P'an Fu-sheng, have been treated violently by the Red Guards.)

The disturbances vary in character. There are confrontations between rival groups of "revolutionary rebels", who accuse each other of betraying the line laid down by Chairman Mao; there are clashes between Red Guards coming from outside and workers and peasants organised by the local authorities to drive them off; and there are outlaw groups which are taking advantage of the disorder to indulge in looting and other excesses.

The maoists' major weakness is that they are hardly ever able to rely on anyone but the Red Guards, who are young and inexperienced, while the opposition (generally speaking) has the people's militias and some support from peasants and workers at its disposal.

The major weakness of the opposition is its lack of a unified command and of a common rallying slogan: its generalised disorder can never take the form of an organised front, and the situation is not turning into one of civil war.

Peking is divided more than ever between the contradictory demands of the extremists and the army. Have they really decided to restrain the extremists? There are some indications of this. On the 23rd, Hsieh Fu-chih broadcast an appeal on the radio, calling upon the Red Guards to reject violence and not to undertake any more marches through the provinces. Chou En-lai is vainly trying to get the warring factions in Canton to lay down their arms. On the other hand, in several areas the maoist authorities have decided to arm certain élite groups of Red Guards (like those of the Aeronautical College in Peking, as well as some groups from Kiangsi and Hunan).

But it is obvious that in the last analysis the army will still be the ultimate arbiter of the "Cultural Revolution". The army is therefore one of the main concerns of the maoist authorities, and they are giving it carrot-and-stick treatment. The carrot was the anniversary celebration of the founding of the People's Liberation Army on 1 August. This celebration commemorates the Nanchang insurrection of 1 August 1927. The leading instigators of this insurrection in the political sphere were Chou En-lai, Li Li-san, who was violently attacked in February and according to a news item dated 5 August has just hung himself, Chang Kuo-t'ao, who defected in 1938 and after the Liberation settled in Hong Kong, recently emigrating to Canada, and T'an P'ing-shan, who subsequently left the party. In the military sphere they were Ho Lung, who has been purged by the "Cultural Revolution", Yeh T'ing (deceased) and Chu Teh, who has been taken to task violently by the "Cultural Revolution". The "Cultural Revolution" is trying to minimise the historical significance of the Nanchang insurrection, first because Mao did not take part in it and secondly because all the heroes of this event, with the sole exception of Chou En-lai, have now fallen into disfavour. This celebration has just been observed with a lavishness which is all the more striking as there have recently been suggestions of abolishing it (last year it was practically dispensed with, and was limited to a discreet reception at the headquarters of the General Staff). On this occasion many army personnel who had recently been attacked, such as Chu Teh, were reinstated to the platform. (It is obviously out of the question that Chu Teh can ever play an active role again. His presence at the 1 August celebrations should be interpreted as a symbolic gesture of appeasement and conciliation towards the top military hierarchy, which has been weakened by attacks made on it.) The stick, on the other hand, is that the military commission of the central committtee has instituted a purge of unprecedented scope among the political commissars in the army, affecting a third of their total strength. In seven of the thirteen large military regions, the first political commissar has been replaced, as well as in nine of the twenty-seven military sub-regions.

All things considered, how far can Mao count on the support of the army? There are some disturbing signs: of the ten field-marshals, only two have followed him (Lin Piao and Nieh Jung-chen); the others have either been purged or subjected to violent attacks which can hardly endear the "Cultural Revolution" to them. Scarcely more than half the commanders of the military regions were present at the 1 August celebrations. The General Staff of the airforce was almost entirely absent, and the navy was hardly represented. Moreover three of the thirteen large military regions have already had to be given new commanders (Inner Mongolia, Chengtu and Wuhan). The commander of the military region of Sinkiang, Wang En-mao, has a highly ambiguous attitude. The military regions of Nanking and Kunming are commanded by well-known opponents of Mao (Hsü Shih-yu and Ch'in Chi-wei) who still hold office, without any attempt having been made to challenge their authority. And within the maoist camp itself there is constant friction between Lin Piao's subordinates and Chiang Ch'ing's Cultural Revolution Group. In this respect the attacks on Hsiao Hua, which have been resumed this month, are a dangerous portent.

The chief causes of discontent in the army result from the fact that, as I indicated above, the "Cultural Revolution" has attacked several of its most popular and respected leaders: the cadres of the military regions have a long and close association with the provincial party apparatus, and the excesses of the Red Guards, which are often directed against local garrisons, have provoked the exasperation of the latter and an impatient desire to reimpose order by force.

The composition of the Revolutionary Committee which has just been set up in Chinghai (12 August) points quite clearly to the only course which is capable of pulling the "Cultural Revolution" out of its present impasse: although in theory it is the product of one of the "triple unions", this Committee is in fact no more than an extension of military authority. The situation of military control in the provinces has not been modified at all — it has simply been disguised with a "revolutionary" label. The new Revolutionary Committee is in fact chaired by the commander of the military region (Liu Hsien-ch'üan), while the deputy chairman of the Revolutionary Committee is second-in-command of this same military region (Chang Chiang-lin). However on 13 August, in an article welcoming the setting up of this committee, the *People's Daily* did not fail to emphasise that it was the army which had made this victory of the "revolution" possible.

The disclosure of old documents of the régime has shed more light on how the "Cultural Revolution" came about. On 16 August the *People's Daily* published an abridged version of the "Decision of the eighth plenary session of the eighth central committee of the Chinese Communist Party regarding the anti-party group which had P'eng Teh-huai as its leader", a decision taken on 16 August 1959 at the Lushan Conference. This text and the commentaries on it (*Red Flag*, no. 13) provide a number of important revelations. It becomes obvious now that the Lushan Conference was a major crisis which led to Mao's eclipse, and allowed the ascent of this "power-holding faction" which the "Cultural Revolution" is now endeavouring to bring down. In other words, the "Cultural Revolution" can be defined essentially as an attempt by Mao to regain what he lost after the Lushan Conference. It is an attempt to counter threats to his own political survival — the threats which were posed by the new forces born at this conference.

September and October

The Wuhan mutiny, which at the end of July brought the country to within a stone's throw of civil war, has been a terrible blow to the maoist forces. They are now drawing the conclusions, and are beginning to change course completely. If this new orientation lasts, it will soon succeed in emptying the "Cultural Revolution" of all its content: such is the exorbitant price Peking is having to pay for the support of the army.

Not only have the instigators of the mutiny gone unpunished (Ch'en Tsai-tao, the main instigator, has simply been let off, though he has had to undergo a "session of study of the thought of Mao Tse-tung" in Peking): on the contrary, in order to appease the mutineers, *it is their victim Wang Li who now finds himself in disfavour*! Wang Li is accused of having issued a slogan denouncing the "revisionist faction which holds power *in the army*". This slogan has now been repudiated: the maoist forces depend on the goodwill of the army, and everything possible is being done to gain its collaboration. The army has been raised on to a pedestal above the squabbling, and is sheltered from criticism. The myth of a pure and infallible army is being created. The downfall of Wang Li is highly significant. Wang Li was one of the ideological pillars and main spokesmen of the "Cultural Revolution" (since the elimination of T'ao Chu he has been in charge of the key Department of Propaganda), and his removal indicates that the "Cultural Revolution" has in fact just renounced its extreme aims and no longer exists, except as a label stuck on a precarious coalition of interests.

The elimination of Wang Li is not an isolated incident: it corresponds to a new political course. The heads of the leading thinkers of the "Cultural Revolution" are beginning to roll, one after the other. Lin Chieh, who like Wang Li was a journalist on the *Red Flag*, has also fallen. He is accused of being an accomplice of Wang Li, of leading the "counter-revolutionary" group known as "the group of 16 May" from behind the scenes, of spreading slogans praising the purge of leading heads of the army, and of having collected material for a "black book" dossier against Chou En-lai. After him Mu Hsin, the editor of *Kuang-ming jih-pao*, was arrested on a charge of "collusion with the counter-revolutionary clique of Lin Chieh". Yao Teng-shan, the famous "red diplomat", has also fallen into disfavour. On his return from Indonesia in April he received a triumphal welcome in Peking. Feeling the wind of revolution in his sails, he led the "Cultural Revolution" in an attack on the bureaucratic stronghold of the Ministry of Foreign Affairs. Leading the attacks on Ch'en Yi, he went so far as to accuse Chou En-lai (not without reason) of protecting the mandarins in this ministry. What is more, it was said to be at his instigation that the Red Guards set fire to the premises of the British Chargé d'Affaires in Peking. But now Yao is being dragged into a public trial and can hear himself being called a "political pickpocket"! Such are the rewards which the "Cultural Revolution" offers to those who are naive enough to believe in it and take it literally, for this is precisely the "crime" of Wang Li and his comrades. The various points of the charge make a quite coherent picture. The "group of 16 May", with which Wang Li and Lin Chieh have been associated, is a faction of extremists who advocated leading the "Cultural Revolution" to its conclusion, refused to deal with the old bureaucracy, and talked of extending the "Cultural Revolution" to the army. Initially these extremists were supported and directed at the top by the Cultural Revolution Group, but when their intransigence began to stand in the way of the compromises which the maoists in power wished to negotiate with the bureaucrats and generals, they were denounced ruthlessly and outlawed.

But while in Peking it is still relatively easy to eliminate the main leaders of the activist movement of the "Cultural Revolution", it is at local level that the problems have been thorniest, and the chief concern of the maoist authorities is no longer so much to struggle against "revisionists" as to bring its own followers to heel, whose sincerity and zeal is becoming far too dangerous. This anxiety is reflected in the official press, which has devoted numerous articles to the denunciation of this extreme left, which is always described as being "of the extreme left in appearance, but in reality right-wing". Orthodoxy being "left" by definition, opposition necessarily has to be described as "right". And when for opportunist reasons the authorities veer to the right and are challenged by the left, the right is normally christened "left" and the left "right". The same terminological waltz is used for concepts like "capitalist" and "proletarian"; it does not correspond at all to socio-economic realities but simply consists of moral judgements. Likewise "revolutionary" and "counter-revolutionary" do not refer to a political content but simply indicate those in power and the opposition. Thus one is "capitalist" because one is a criminal and "revolutionary" because one is on the winning side, and not vice-versa — which brings to mind Lu Hsün's sardonic aphorism, "The individual who is condemned is guilty because he is condemned and not condemned because he is guilty." The range of the accusations which have officially been lodged against the activists demonstrates their position quite clearly. They refuse to share Peking's view that the "state of the Cultural Revolution is excellent" and that the "Cultural Revolution has won a decisive victory". On the contrary, they consider (and one can understand their point of view) that the "Cultural Revolution" has not yet achieved its objectives and is in danger of being stifled. They complain about the fact that authority is in the hands of bureaucrats while authentic "revolutionary rebels" are being persecuted. They either refuse to contribute to the "great alliance" or sabotage it with divisive manoeuvres. Their failing is their egocentricity: they attribute revolutionary qualities to themselves alone, and refuse to see them in other groupings. They divert the masses and refuse to carry out the instructions of the central authorities. In the struggle they have resorted to physical violence and attempted to wreak personal revenge. They slander all those who loyally obey orders from the central authorities, calling them rightists. At the same time, in order to swell their own ranks, they do not hesitate to recruit conservative groups and bad elements. They systematically mistrust all former cadres, and accuse those among them who get into the saddle again of being mere opportunists. They have published threatening tracts against local authorities, which speak of "shelling their general headquarters". They have adopted an incorrect attitude towards the army, and advocate carrying the purge into its ranks.

The indictment is clear. Once again, these activists are accused of taking the "Cultural Revolution" seriously, of wanting to wage it in earnest, of rejecting the parody which Peking is now attempting to put in place of it.

In fact Peking's only wish now is to put a quick end to the whole adventure. At the national celebrations of 1 October, which this year were on an appreciably more modest scale than the previous year and resembled more a ceremony of personal homage to Mao Tse-tung than a national festival, the army was given the place of honour and the Red Guards were relegated to the background. In his speech, Lin Piao extolled "the victory of the Cultural Revolution" as if it were an event in the past.

But in order to get the defeated and frustrated rebels to give up the struggle and docilely help reinstate the bureaucratic machinery against which they revolted, is it going to be enough simply to tell them, "now that you've won you can have a rest"?

The "Revolutionary Committee" formula, a mere semblance of the "seizure of power" based on the trinity of the army, the rehabilitated cadres and the representatives of the "revolutionary rebels", was drawn up in order to put the rebel element into the minority and neutralise it. This element is too weak to ever hope to take control of the new organ, but it is at least strong enough to hinder its establishment. Even the meagre success of the first seven Revolutionary Committees (Heilungkiang on 31 January, Shantung on 3 February, Kweichow on 13 February, Shanghai on 24 February, Shansi on 18 March, Peking on 20 April and Chinghai on 12 August) seemed impossible to extend rapidly throughout the country. The rebels were powerless to face military repression directly, but had two weapons with which they could sabotage the setting up of "triple unions". They used blackmail against the cadres, to prevent them from taking part in Revolutionary Committees. This blackmail proved very effective. The cadres were indeed invited by Peking to take up active struggle again and to resume service. But they were scarred and terrorised by their recent experiences and, given the choice between the distant encouragement from the capital and nearby threats from local rebels, they preferred to restrict themselves to prudent speculation. Had not Peking already abandoned them to the fury of the rebels once before? Secondly, the rebels resorted to violence to prevent the more docile groups influenced by the army and by the former party machinery from joining the Revolutionary Committees. This created a climate of civil war.

In order to evade the obstacles which the rebels have thus created, the maoist authorities are now trying to impose the new policy of the "great alliance" (ta lien-he), which is seen as a preliminary condition for the "triple union". The "great alliance" is a cloak which has been thrown over the conflict between rebel factions and bogus rebel factions in such a way as to set up a provisional ceasefire. Instead of the problems being solved, they are being spirited away (just as the victory of the "Cultural Revolution" has been announced, now that it is no longer deemed politic to continue it). The authority of Mao himself has been invoked for the announcement that "within the proletariat there are basically no conflicts of interest and there is consequently no reason to see mutually exclusive rival factions develop". Because of this strategy of "great alliances", the "revolutionary rebels" are no longer directly represented on the Revolutionary Committees; they are represented only indirectly, through a preliminary "great alliance" where their activist virulence is diluted by contact with pseudo-rebels. This is theoretically supposed to facilitate the rehabilitation of former cadres, which Peking is now trying to speed up by all the means at its disposal. (See the *Liberation Army Daily*, 20 October; *Wen-hui pao*, 20 October; the *People's Daily*, 21 October. According to these, offending cadres must be shown understanding. All they have to do to be able to resume their former positions is to become aware of their past errors, and to be determined to follow the thought of Mao Tse-tung from now on.)

But as I have indicated above, the rebel factions are refusing to walk compliantly into this trap of the "great alliance", and their obstinate refusal continues to paralyse the whole normalisation process.

To complicate matters, the struggle is still going on at the top between the three rival groups whose uneasy coalition makes up the maoist faction. With the elimination of Wang Li and Lin Chieh, the Cultural Revolution Group (Ch'en Po-ta, Chiang Ch'ing) has been suddenly tricked by the army into losing some of its best men. But it has responded by having Hsiao Hua, Lin Piao's right-hand man, eliminated. (Hsiao Hua dared to prohibit Chiang Ch'ing from interfering in the affairs of the army.) Lin Piao has himself been affected by the elimination of his lieutenant, but to deaden the blow somewhat, Lin's wife Yeh Ch'ün has been given an official position by way of compensation. She has been appointed a member of the Cultural Revolution Group and is beginning to appear, well-placed, on official platforms. This rise to power on the part of wives is a worrying sign for the health of the régime. On the one hand, it indicates the crisis in confidence which is rife at the top: for want of reliable advisors, the leaders have resorted to relying on their bedfellows, somewhat like the emperors in times of decline who, seeing treason everywhere, could only trust their eunuchs. On the other hand the leadership has now set the example for promotions to be made no longer on the basis of objective ability but of private favour.

In the covert struggle which continues around Mao, the blows being exchanged are still merely oblique. In the Chiang Ch'ing-Lin Piao - Chou En-lai triangle, a temporary community of interests has united the latter two against the former. This alliance would have succeeded in toppling Chiang Ch'ing a long time ago, were it not for the fact that she holds a unique but decisive trump card: the personal support of Mao. Meanwhile, even if direct clashes are still being avoided, these three leaders are fighting one another through their subordinates. While Chiang Ch'ing has lost Wang Li and his associates, Lin Piao has lost Hsiao Hua; and Chou En-lai, after several desperate rescue attempts, seems incapable of saving Ch'en Yi.

November and December

The right turn described above is becoming more marked. Following the downfall of Wang Li, Lin Chieh and Mu Hsin, the radical element within the "Cultural Revolution" has been completely decimated: and now Kuan Feng has been eliminated, by association with Wang Li and the clandestine activity of the "group of 16 May". (Kuan Feng was deputy editor of the *Red Flag*, Wang Li was editor and Lin Chieh a member of the editorial committee. With these purges the *Red Flag*, which gathered together the whole ideological vanguard of the

"Cultural Revolution" and acted as spokesman and doctrinal guide to the movement, has now been practically reduced to silence.)

These purges do not accord with Mao's personal wishes. All the champions of *his* "revolution" have disappeared one after the other, but he is obliged to sacrifice them in order to appease the army.

The Cultural Revolution Group has thus been reduced to a minimum and the Red Guards have been forced to suspend their activities, while the army holds the levers of power everywhere. Propaganda is being used to brush up the army's image; a great educational and moral campaign is being conducted, on the theme "the army loves the people, the people support the army". The point is to impose the myth of a Red Army which is pure and infallible, protecting the population which idealises it like a father. In order to erase the memory of the army's ruthless repression of activist youth — and to divert attention from repression which is still in progress in some areas — the press is continually giving edifying accounts of the heroic sacrifice of soldiers, drowning to save foolhardy Red Guards who get into difficulties while swimming in a river, etc., etc. Military personnel, who were for a long time the butt of the Red Guards, have proudly reappeared on the scene. The best example is that of Huang Yung-sheng in Kwangtung. Huang, the commander of the Canton military region (covering the two provincial military regions of Kwangtung and Kwangsi) was violently attacked by activists who accused him (not without reason) of being an instrument of T'ao Chu and of having had groups of Red Guards maltreated by the army. At the height of the crisis, that is in August, Huang was recalled to Peking and for three months nothing more was heard of him. He finally resurfaced on 14 November: a communiqué from the New China News Agency mentioned his presence in Mao's retinue (along with a series of other survivors — Ch'en Yi, Hsü Hsiang-ch'ien, Yeh Chien-ying, Li Hsueh-feng) on the occasion of an audience granted by Mao in Peking to a group of diplomats and technicians who had returned home from Indonesia and Burma. And now, according to the latest intelligence, he has been not only cleared but put back in the saddle. He has got back to Canton as leader of a group which is to prepare the setting up of the Revolutionary Committee of Kwangtung, which in fact gives him full powers over the province. In this preparatory group he is seconded by an experienced bureaucrat from the previous party apparatus (Ch'en Yü, secretary of the Bureau for

the Central and Southern regions) and by two political commissars
of the Canton military region (K'ung Shih-ch'üan and Ch'en
Teh). The rebels, who can see their former adversary returning
with his authority strengthened, have no representation on the
leadership of this preparatory group. Similar preparatory groups
have also been set up in Hunan, Kiangsi, Honan, Szechuan and
Kansu. They all offer the same combination of the two traditional forces, the army and the cadres, and deny the rebels any
representation. And the two new Revolutionary Committees
which have just been set up (in Inner Mongolia on 1 November,
and in the municipality of Tientsin on 6 December) clearly illus-
trate the position which the "Cultural Revolution" has finally
adopted. The "seizure of power", of which the establishment of
the Revolutionary Committee was supposed to be the outcome,
is nothing more than a conventional formula. In Inner Mongolia.
the Revolutionary Committee is led by a soldier, T'eng Hai-
ch'ing formerly second-in-command of the military region of
Peking and now acting commander of the military region of
Inner Mongolia. He is assisted by three deputy leaders: a soldier
(Wu T'ao, political commissar of the military region of Inner
Mongolia), a former party cadre (Kuo Chin-ming, party secretary
of Inner Mongolia), and a revolutionary delegate (Huo Tao-yü).
In Tientsin, they have not even bothered to grant token representation to the "revolutionary rebels" at the head of the Committee. It is led by someone from the previous party apparatus
(Hsieh Hsueh-kung, secretary to the secretariat of the North
China Bureau and first secretary of the Tientsin Municipal Committee), backed up by three adjutants who are none other than
the commander of the Tientsin garrison (Cheng San-sheng), the
head of the Police Headquarters of Tientsin (Chiang Feng), and
the political commissar of the Tientsin garrison (Hsiao Ssu-ming).
It is a strange "seizure of power" that consists of putting back
into power people who already hold it; a strange "revolution"
which denies any power to revolutionaries, and instead con-
solidates the authority of the representatives of the traditional
order, namely the bureaucracy, the army and the police. We can
measure the path taken by one year of "Cultural Revolution"
thus: an attempt at unilateral "seizures of power", followed by
the watered-down formula of the "triple union"; then the "triple
union", further diluted by the stratagem of the "great alliance".
In Tientsin even these last pretences have now been dropped.
Neither in the long official victory communiqué (*People's Daily*,
7 December) nor in the inaugural speeches delivered by the

leaders of the Committee was there any mention of a "triple
union". The reason for this is very simple. For there to be a
"triple union", there have to be three elements. But in the Tientsin
Committee, no room — not even theoretical room — is left for
the "revolution" between the bureaucracy and the army.

In Peking, Chiang Ch'ing has been absent from a number of
official gatherings. According to the Red Guard newspapers,
Chou En-lai stated in a recent speech that Chiang Ch'ing was
exhausted by her labours and would do well now to take some
rest. And at the same time the unsinkable Ch'en Yi, whom
people had lost hope of seeing ever again after all the attacks
against him, has resurfaced. (He has already made five public
appearances in recent weeks and on 6 December he even
delivered an official address at a reception given by the Finnish
ambassador.) Just as on peasant barometers, where the appearance of an old crone with an umbrella heralds bad weather and
that of a yokel in shirt sleeves the return of the sun, so the Peking
Punch and Judy show, with its display of successive changes in the
fortunes of Mao's wife and the old bureaucrats, reflects
quite clearly the variations in the political climate of the country.
The unexpected reappearance of Ch'en Yi (when someone has
been dragged through the mud like he has, you would not think
he could ever be clean again) in effect coincides with a renewal
of impetus in the campaign to "release the cadres". From
Peking's point of view, the application of this policy is supposed
to enable all the bureaucrats from the apparatus to be reallocated
their former positions, the only exceptions being a small minority
of people at the top who are in direct and close communication
with the former leaders.

But by betraying all the declared objectives of the "Cultural
Revolution", the maoist authorities have only further kindled the
anger of the "extreme left" who, in the provinces, are fighting
on desperately. Vigorous clashes continue to occur more or less
everywhere (the chief regions affected recently have been Liaoning,
Hunan, Szechuan, Kwangtung, Kweichow and Yunnan). What is
more, official sources have just confirmed the existence of inner
divisions which are tearing the maoist group apart. On 22 December the *People's Daily* published the "new directives of Chairman
Mao": "Each of the *two factions* should not dwell too much on
the shortcomings and mistakes of the other. Each should leave it
to the other to discuss its own shortcomings and mistakes; each
should carry out its own self-criticism in such a way as to obtain
a broad unity within which only minimal differences continue

to exist". This is the very first time that the existence of *two* factions has been officially noted. They can be easily identified: one is obviously a military and bureaucratic coalition (Lin Piao and Chou En-lai), and the other consists of survivors of the Cultural Revolution Group who refuse to submit to defeat.

Lin Piao's rise to power is becoming increasingly ostentatious. Yang Ch'eng-wu, who is chief of the general staff and ranks second in the army after Lin (remember that it was Yang's decisive intervention which gave the maoists military control of Peking Municipality and thus enabled the "Cultural Revolution" to be launched) had a long article published in the *People's Daily* on 3 November, which claimed to be an indictment of Lo Jui-ch'ing but in fact was a ratification of the privileged position which Lin Piao now occupies; in it, the Mao-Lin relationship was portrayed in a subtle way which ran the risk of only half pleasing Mao. According to the article, true supreme authority can only rest with Mao himself; but it deifies him to such an extent that he is in fact promoted to the clouds, leaving only Lin Piao, his sole high priest and qualified interpreter on earth, to decide the exact meaning and mode of application of his thoughts.

A little later, on 18 November, a meeting of army delegates who had taken part in a study session on the thought of Mao Tse-tung in Peking paid a special tribute to Crown Prince Lin. This was only a prelude. The new propaganda campaign to exalt Lin and his role has now reached a hysterical climax. At the end of November Lin Piao made a gift of a calligraphic inscription, written in his own hand,* to a navy delegation at a study session on the thought of Mao in Peking. It read: "To sail the high seas one relies on the helmsman, to make revolution one relies on the thought of Mao Tse-tung". This event, in itself insignificant, gave rise to festivities on an extraordinary scale. On 1 December, the *People's Daily* and the *Liberation Army Daily* devoted the whole of their front pages to this event. In the next few days, various celebrations took place in the navy to hail the event, and troops swore an oath of loyalty to Lin Piao. These ceremonies were described in lyrical terms by the press. The English version of the communiqué of the New China News Agency (published in *Peking Review*, 1967, no. 50) was heavily adulterated to make it palatable for foreign consumption. To give

---

* Lin Piao obviously wields the sword better than the brush: he is a lousy calligrapher, and makes himself ridiculous with his servile and clumsy way of imitating Mao's style.

an idea of the orgy of superlatives which was lavished on Lin
Piao's calligraphic inscription, it is necessary to adhere to the
original Chinese version:

"The inscription of Vice-chairman Lin is not only an honour
for the navy but is also an honour for the whole of the
armed forces and for the whole nation. It not only represents
the greatest concern, the greatest encouragement, the greatest
stimulus and the greatest teaching for the navy but it also
represents the greatest concern, the greatest encouragement,
the greatest stimulus and the greatest teaching for all the
armed forces and for the whole nation. . . . Vice-chairman
Lin is the comrade in arms of our great leader Chairman
Mao. He is Chairman Mao's best pupil, his best successor
[*chieh-pan jen*, literally 'he who takes over']. He is the
deputy chief of staff of the entire nation. He has appreciated
the value of the thought of Mao Tse-tung in the most complete, the most rigorous and the most scientific way. In the
most loyal, the most resolute and the most fearless of ways
he has always upheld Chairman Mao's position as supreme
leader. He has defended the thought of Mao Tse-tung as
well as the revolutionary line of Chairman Mao. With the
greatest penetration and dynamism, he has led and organised
the great movement for spreading the thought of Mao Tse-
tung throughout the whole party, the entire armed forces
and the entire nation. . . . Vice-chairman Lin has brandished
the great red standard of the thought of Mao Tse-tung the
highest, highest, highest. He understands the thoughts of Mao
Tse-tung in the deepest, deepest, deepest way and he applies
them in the best, best, best way. Vice-chairman Lin gives the
entire party the highest example of the thoroughness, the
spread and the defence of the thought of Mao Tse-tung
and he will for ever be our brilliant example in this study."

Confronted with this unreadable style, the western reader may
brand the translation as being too literal and delude himself into
thinking that in the original Chinese these turns of phrase are
generally acceptable. This is not the case. The original text is no
less strange for the Chinese reader. These bizarre repetitions of
identical superlatives are only ever found *in Lin Piao's own prose*,
which leads one to assume under the circumstances that he instructed his own stooges on how to write this piece to his own glory.

As we can see, his audacity really goes a long way. Not content
with having himself proclaimed successor to the soverign during
the latter's actual lifetime, the prophet is beginning to inhale the

incense which in principle should be reserved for his god alone. This insolent exhibition has obviously been set up to act as a warning to the Chiang Ch'ing - Ch'en Po-ta clan on the one hand, and to Chou En-lai on the other.

One interesting detail is that K'ang Sheng has recently been denounced in the official publications of provincial rebels. The "Cultural Revolution" put him in Mao's immediate circle, and one would have thought that he would be sheltered from any attacks. K'ang Sheng is a mysterious and equivocal person. During his lengthy stay in the Soviet Union in the thirties, he worked very closely with Wang Ming. On the eve of the "Cultural Revolution" it was he who was seconded to P'eng Chen in the famous "Group of Five". It is possible that he saved his head and secured his promotion by betraying P'eng. In 1962, when Liu Shao-ch'i exercised power, it was K'ang who took the initiative to republish Liu's work on "The Spiritual Formation of the Communist", which is today denounced as a "poisonous weed". No doubt he owes his high capacity for survival to the fact that for a long time he has had supreme control over the Intelligence section of the secret police. The eminence of his actual position (while Ch'en Yi was being abused by the Red Guards, K'ang was virtually acting as Foreign Minister) is characteristic of the "Cultural Revolution". Generally speaking, it is not particular about the choice of its chief executives, and prefers to recruit them either from opportunist elements of dubious honesty (such as T'ao Chu, Kuo Mo-jo etc.) or from mediocre and insignificant individuals (such as Ch'en Po-ta, Yao Wen-yuan, Ch'i Pen-yü etc.). These actors are doubly useful: they can be harnessed to unsavoury tasks which would discourage those of a more steadfast character, and they can be dispensed with at any time should the wind change. K'ang Sheng's position, however, is much more secure; his political offices make him at once dangerous and indispensable to the leading élite, and there is every indication that the recent attacks, embarrassing as they may be, cannot seriously threaten his position.

The maoist authorities now wish to normalise the situation, and to fuse the "Cultural Revolution" with bureaucratic legality as quickly as possible. An important indication of this development has already appeared, in a passage from a speech which Hsieh Fu-chih delivered on 14 October to a gathering of student activists in Peking. He announced that the ninth party congress will be convened next year. (Theoretically it is the congress which is the supreme source of power in the party. It votes on and amends the party constitution, and elects the central committee. According to the 1956 constitution the congress must be convened every four years. In actual fact it was not convened in 1960, nor in 1964.) The news given out by Hsieh is of considerable importance. One can easily imagine how impatient Mao is to put an end to the coup d'état situation which still prevails, and that he wishes to legitimise the "Cultural Revolution". His power will only be firmly established when he manages to reconstitute the membership of the central committee, to install his own men in all the departments which require them and to have the purges of the Liuist group officially ratified. But it is doubtful whether he is in a position to initiate this congress quickly. Even in normal times, the preparation of a plenary meeting of the party requires a considerable amount of work, which theoretically falls on the Secretarial Bureau, one of the organs hardest hit by the "Cultural Revolution".

The news announced by Hsieh was confirmed on 26 November by *Wen-hui pao* (note in passing the leading role which this Shanghai daily has played since the beginning of the "Cultural Revolution". It shares the job of setting the pace with the *Liberation Army Daily*, while the *People's Daily*, the official paper, is often content just to copy their editorials). The convening of the ninth party congress is being prepared for 1968. This congress, the *Wen-hui pao* added, will be like a second birth for the party, and will make it truly a party of Mao Tse-tung.

Mao Tse-tung is hampered in the political sphere by the compromises which he has had to make with the army, and by his need to put a quick end to the violence and anarchy in which the entire country is threatening to become engulfed; but at least he has found a field in which he can give freer rein to his old obsession: the reform of education. This time there are at last no more "intellectual authorities" to put a spoke in his wheel. The army has left him to do as he pleases with the universities — to demolish them if he likes — for it is obviously indifferent to the fate of higher education.

On 3 November, the *People's Daily* published a first plan for the reform of education, based upon three pilot schemes: the University of T'ung-chi in Shanghai (civil engineering and architecture), the Forestry Institute of Peking and the University of Peking. The most radical attempt is at T'ung-chi, which has rejected its status as a university in order to turn itself into a commune (the "7 May Commune"). The traditional teaching system has been abolished; the duration of study has been shortened from four to three years. There is no more study in the formal sense of the word, only discussion and practical work carried out in committee. The traditional teacher-student duality has been replaced by a more complex arrangement calling for the participation of soldiers, workers and peasants. Examinations have either been abolished or take place with books open. The selection of students is being carried out on a purely political basis, and the same goes for the awarding of diplomas. This educational reform is an event of considerable importance, which threatens to have a dramatic influence on the country's long-term future. In the past, Mao's visionary inventions (such as the impromptu blast-furnaces etc.) were carried out in a specific, quantitative area and were immediately measurable. They called straight away for remedies; their failure was so obvious that there was no room for discussion, and a change of direction took place immediately. At worst these experiments only resulted in a waste of time, labour, raw materials and energy. But the immediate effects of the educational reform will remain invisible and will only be felt in the long term, when the present generation of scientists, engineers, technicians and teachers find themselves without qualified successors. Once again we can see Mao's impetuous, trenchant style. He has always been prepared to put the future of the whole country at risk on an impulse. He has at last got the chance to settle his old differences with the university, which he has always regarded with the hostile complacency of a self-taught man and the mixed feelings of jealousy and aversion for academic orthodoxy which are typical of a handyman of genius. In the final estimate of the "Cultural Revolution", measures of this nature will weigh more heavily on the fate of China than many initiatives of a purely political nature. The dramatic element is that the destiny of a nation of eight hundred million inhabitants can depend to such an extent on the idiosyncrasies of one old man.

In the doctrinal sphere, several recent articles in the official press are worth mentioning.

On 30 October, the *Liberation Army Daily* published an article denouncing Liu Shao-ch'i's theory on the unconditional obedience to be observed by party members. Does this mean that the maoist line will encourage individual initiative and freedom of judgement? Nothing of the kind. The same article reminded its readers that obedience to the thoughts of Mao must be unreserved, that the struggle against all those who oppose the thoughts of Mao should be absolute, and that Mao's directives should be followed *even when they are not understood*. At the beginning of December, the navy took a solemn oath to "follow step by step, to apply sentence by sentence and word by word each of Chairman Mao's directives, *even if at first we do not understand them* . . . so that the thoughts of Mao may form the substance of our soul and control all our movements." What, then, is the difference between Liu's and Mao's conceptions of obedience? On this point the article gets tangled up in jesuitical phraseology: the characteristic of maoist obedience is to simul- taneously combine "democracy" and "dictatorship", while Liu's conception contains only the second of these two terms. But on the other hand, it must be remembered that real "democracy" would be unable to exist without the framework of unconditional obedience to the directives of Mao. In actual fact, the very obvious fact which emerges from all this is that there has never been the slightest ideological difference between Mao's and Liu's theories. The kind of obedience which is demanded today by Mao is in no way different from that which Liu advocated in his talk in 1939: the best proof of this is the fact that the text of his talk initially received the approval of Mao and was used for more than twenty-five years as a basic manual for the political education of party members without anyone saying anything against it. The only problem was ultimately a *personal* one. To *whom* should this obedience be addressed, and to whose advan- tage should it be? So long as Liu was Mao's loyal right-hand man, the obedience which he advocated could only benefit his master. The day Liu undertook to fly on his own wings, and the party became his instrument and ceased to be Mao's, this blind discipline of the cadres would operate to Liu's advantage, which would then force Mao to coin his famous slogan, "It is right to rebel!" When we get to the bottom of this controversy — and we do not have to dig very deep to do so — what becomes immediately obvious is that Liu's real crime was not that he set up a dictatorial system, but that he turned to *his own* benefit the dictatorial powers that were Mao's alone.

On 9 November the *People's Daily* published an article denouncing the counter-revolutionary attitudes of Lu Ting-yi (the former head of the Department of Propaganda, purged by the "Cultural Revolution"). The attack concentrated on a par- ticular event — the publication of a work dealing with Wei Cheng, on the personal initiative of Lu Ting-yi, in 1962. The event is not very significant in itself, but it provides interesting material for reflection on the nature and extreme limits of the opposition to Mao within the party.

Wei Cheng, a minister of the emperor T'ang T'ai-tsung, had boldly criticised the policies of the sovereign on several occasions. The sovereign had had both the magnanimity not to take offence at this and the intelligence to draw inspiration from the criticism in order to put right several mistakes which he had made. Like Hai Jui, as seen by Wu Han, the *Wei Cheng* of Lu Ting-yi was a plea for P'eng Teh-huai, and a way of suggesting to Mao that he might adopt a less intolerant attitude towards those who in good faith were in disagreement with his policies. Note that like Wu Han, Lu Ting-yi likens Mao to an emperor. That is to say: even if a certain aspect of his policy may be open to criticism, the fundamental principle of his authority cannot be called in question. In other words, one cannot really speak of *opponents* but only of *subjects*, who can only hope that the sovereign, once informed of his mistakes, may one day take their suggestions into consideration. (This same attitude can now be found in Liu Shao-ch'i, whose sole line of defence since his disgrace has been that of protesting his unshakeable loyalty to Mao.) When one thinks of the power which Lu Ting-yi had as head of propaganda, sheltered by Liu's authority — at a time when Mao was stripped of real power and held a purely honorary position . . . ! This kind of case enables us to measure all the better how pathetically impotent the Chinese leaders are to criticise Mao's power. Even when they are in opposition to Mao, they are still incapable of freeing themselves from the feeling of feudal allegiance which binds them to him. And the régime by its very nature appears incapable of reforming itself on its own initiative. Even when the opposition to Mao is in the majority, it remains simply a juxtaposition of innumerable individual and local dissatisfactions which cannot identify or denounce the common source of its ailment. It therefore seems out of the question that a revolutionary shoot will ever bloom again from the régime itself. The future development of the Chinese revolution will necessarily be the achievement of a new generation from outside the present apparatus.

Finally, there has been a series of long doctrinal articles denouncing errors formerly committed by Liu Shao-ch'i and Teng Hsiao-p'ing in sphere of agricultural policy. These articles are interesting, as they indirectly disclose more information on the motives and origins of the "Cultural Revolution".

The first of these articles was published jointly on 22 November by the *People's Daily*, the *Liberation Army Daily* and the *Red Flag*. The argument ran as follows.

In 1949, Mao wanted to strike while the iron was hot and direct the countryside immediately into socialist collectivisation through co-operatives. Liu Shao-ch'i opposed this with all his might. In 1950, Liu made himself the advocate of the exploiting class, and authorised the rich peasants to hire agricultural labourers. "To forbid exploitation would be dogmatism; temporarily, a certain system of exploitation can be beneficial. If the peasantry is left to follow its natural inclinations, and if a greater number of rich peasants are created, no harm will have been done." Collectivisation was one of the basic principles extolled by Mao from 1943 onwards. Liu Shao-ch'i had continually opposed this principle. In 1951, because of his hatred for the poor peasants, he had attacked the co-operative movement. In 1953 Mao launched a successful counter-attack, and in 1955 the co-operative movement spread throughout the country. But in May of the same year, Liu Shao-ch'i and Teng Hsiao-p'ing took advantage of the fact that Mao was absent from Peking and made another attempt to curb and sabotage the movement. Today Liu still refuses to recognise that he was guilty of this sabotage. But the best proof of his guilt is his 1951 statement: "The mechanisation of agriculture should precede its collectivisation." Liu advocated such a principle because he in fact was plotting to restore capitalism. This principle was, moreover, a philosophical heresy. Mao had taught that the determining factor was not industrialisation but revolutionary human resources. During the second half of 1955, Liu's opportunist line was crushed and Mao's line triumphed; the co-operative movement spread over the whole country. In 1958, the "Great Leap Forward" marked a further stage in the collectivisation of agriculture. But Liu, the class enemy, detested this victory and still dreamed of restoring capitalism. The "Great Leap Forward" met with temporary difficulties because of Liu's sabotage and three consecutive years of natural catastrophes. Liu took advantage of this to resume the offensive on the political, economic, cultural and ideological fronts. At his instigation, a free market was restored, as was the right of the peasants to cultivate private plots. The communes were run down. Liu maintained that the re-establishment of the private market was a necessity and that there was no need to be frightened of capitalism spreading to a certain degree. And Teng went one better: "Black or white, the colour of the cat is not important; a good cat is one that catches mice." But in 1962, at the height of Liu's offensive, Mao launched a counter-attack against this opportunist, rightist line. He reminded the country that the class struggle was still a current phenomenon, and assigned it a new task: the "movement of socialist education". It was thus under Mao's personal supervision that first of all the "ten points" were worked out. These were later to be followed by the "twenty-three points". The real nature of the contradiction thus came to light. It was a conflict between two lines, the socialist one and the capitalist one. Teng Hsiao-p'ing was the first to react. Four months later he launched ten additional "points", which completely contradicted the original "ten points". Then Wang Kuang-mei's famous "work teams" experiment took place. This experiment implemented a right-wing policy under a leftist guise. It classified the poor peasants as counter-revolutionaries and deprived them of their power. As for Liu Shao-ch'i, he tried his utmost to hide the fact that the essence of the struggle lay in the opposition between socialism and capitalism. He reduced the movement to a simple confrontation between the "four purities" and the "four impurities", and turned the struggle against the poor peasants and against the good or relatively good cadres — all this to prevent the revisionists in the party from being exposed. He feared the mobilisation of the masses and resorted to the policy of obedience, in the style of the Kuomintang. He crushed mass movements, oppressed revolutionary cadres and froze the movement to protect himself as well as his supporters. But the promulgation of the "twenty-three points", which were personally drawn up by Mao, was to ring the death-knell of these capitalist schemes.

On the sequence of events in the struggle for power and the identification of its chief episodes and turning-points, this document is very illuminating. (I have described all these vicissitudes above — see Section One.) In the ideological sphere, on the other hand, as an indictment it is extremely weak. It is based merely on incomplete quotations which are always taken out of context and are more often than not chosen from sources that are difficult to verify — private conversations and personal correspondence. The opposition between the "Liuist line" and the "Maoist line" is simply artificial; it has been obtained by the deliberately anachronistic use of sources. Thus a remark of Liu's from 1950 is juxtaposed with one of Mao's from 1953 to 1955. This is a classic procedure: since the line of the party has to fluctuate according to the requirements of the time, it is alway easy to get rid of a loyal servant *on the very basis of his past services*. Accusations had already been made in this way against Liu Shaoch'i on account of his compromise policy towards the Kuomin-

tang at the beginning of the war: a policy which in fact was not
his own (did Liu Shao-ch'i ever have his own policy?) but that of
the party and of Mao himself.

Similarly, immediately after the Liberation the policy of tolerating capitalists and private agricultural enterprise, far from being
Liu's personal initiative, was the official party line and was
defined as such in the clearest terms by Mao himself (see p. 25n).
The existence of a "revisionist line" is simply a myth invented
to discredit the adversary. If there has ever been a "revisionist"
tendency in China, it consists of Chou En-lai and his team of
technocrats. If the "Cultural Revolution" were really what it
claims to be, it should direct its attacks in the first instance
against this group. (And in actual fact the young activists, being
logical, wanted to direct the struggle this way. As we have just
seen, this only brought about their own condemnation.) One
really must have a great deal of contempt for the intelligence of
the public to dare present Liu Shao-ch'i as a "revisionist". It
was during the reign of this pedigree stalinist that China completed its break with Soviet revisionism. The real dividing line
is thus not the one that sets "revolutionaries" apart from "revisionists", but rather the one that separates usurping ministers
from loyal courtiers. The crux of the crisis is contained in Liu's
famous remark: "To oppose Mao Tse-tung is only to oppose an
individual." And the political patchwork quilt of the maoist clan
is woven from one single thread: the common loyalty which the
people who make up this group have displayed towards Mao.
Liu and his supporters were not trying to turn the régime to the
right at all, nor to renounce any of its objectives. (The step backwards after the "Great Leap" was not a turn to the right but an
attempt to stop before reaching the precipice. *Liu had no choice*;
the very survival of the régime was at stake.) And how did Liu's
China show signs of bourgeois slackening between 1959 and 1965?
Liu and his followers never questioned any of the régime's
principles (from this stemmed both the ineffectiveness of their
criticism of maoism and the hollowness and obvious falseness of
the charges later drawn up against them). The basis of their
actions and the constant theme of their writings — whether in
Wu Han's *Hai Jui* or in Lu Ting-yi's *Wei Cheng* — were limited
purely to a criticism of the *personal style* of Mao's government
and the arbitrary, subjective, arrogant, impulsive and foolhardy
nature of his initiatives. Liu Shao-ch'i and Teng Hsiao-p'ing
simply wanted to neutralise Mao (P'eng Chen and Lo Jui-ch'ing
wanted to go further and institute a public denunciation of his

mistakes, and this was why the "Cultural Revolution" reserved its most cruel fate for them). The problem was not an ideological but a personal one. *It was not a question of changing the destination of the ship, but simply of changing the helmsman.* The maoist tactic now is, on the contrary, to maintain a systematic confusion between Mao as a person and his thought. This enables anyone who opposes him to be discredited, and it transforms his adversaries into "counter-revolutionaries".

Other articles concentrate more specifically on the "Great Leap Forward", which the maoist authorities are now trying to rehabilitate. The constant reference which is made today to the events of 1958-62 clearly shows that they were a decisive turning-point in the destiny of the régime. Mao has never accepted the failure of the "Great Leap". As one of the texts reproduced below demonstrates, he would have preferred to see China perish from famine rather than readjust his vision or recognise his mistakes. He cannot forgive Liu Shao-ch'i and Teng Hsiao-p'ing for having saved the régime against his will. A long article in the *People's Daily* of 3 December, entitled "Only socialism is capable of saving China", is directed specifically against Teng Hsiao-p'ing. The argument runs as follows.

In 1962, taking advantage of the difficulties caused by the Liu-Teng faction's sabotage as well as by three consecutive years of natural disasters, all the monsters and demons dreamed of changing things, and Liu and Teng launched a new offensive against Mao Tse-tung's proletarian headquarters. Liu launched the slogan *san tzu yi pao,* advocating individual enterprise. (The slogan means "three freedoms and one contract". The "three freedoms" refer to land ownership, free market outlets and the development of small enterprises directly responsible for their own profit and loss. The "contract" refers to the determination of production quotas for family enterprises.) Teng echoed him in an even more crafty manner. "For the time being," he said, "the most important problem is to increase food production. In so far as individual enterprises can further this production they are a good thing. It is not important whether the cat is black or white as long as it catches mice." Thus, according to Teng, it matters little whether there is socialism or capitalism: the main thing is to produce food. Teng went further: "On the question of knowing which form of production is the best (collective or individual), the following attitude must be adopted. The best form of production is that which, within the framework of local conditions, is most likely to restore and develop production." Thus

Teng used the pretext of this need to increase production in order to encourage individual enterprise. Which, in actual fact, is the best form of production? The people's communes are — Mao stated this in 1958. But to listen to Teng, one would think the communes are less beneficial to production than private enterprise! In reality, Teng was aiming a poisoned arrow at our great leader Chairman Mao. He was hoping to stir up the peasants to rebel against the people's communes, which are an initiative of great world significance. Teng equipped himself with fine excuses to advocate private production: "It is a question of satisfying the aspirations of the peasants". He was thus giving himself the airs of a man who felt for the misfortunes of the populace, and who was pleading on behalf of the downtrodden. "An enormous number of peasants", he said, "demand that the land be redistributed to them. The peasants have lost confidence in the collective economy". But he was overlooking the class problem. He was speaking of peasants in general, but in fact was pleading solely for the rich peasants. And on the other hand, by encouraging individual enterprise he was neglecting an essential issue: the bond between agriculture and industry. In reality the crux of the matter, as Chairman Mao had indicated, was the problem of educating the peasantry. Teng covered himself with yet another excuse. It was, he said, an exceptional situation. "To build individual enterprise as a basic political line would be a mistake, but it could be used temporarily to cope with an urgent situation." And further, "We can only progress if we temporarily accept the need to take one step backwards first". Thus according to Teng, the only way to overcome the difficulties was to surrender for a time to individual enterprise. When production had been restored, collectivisation could be resumed. What logic! When socialism comes up against difficulties, help should be sought from capitalism! Finally, in order to attack the socialist dictatorship of the proletariat, he spent his time creating an atmosphere of pessimism: "The illnesses which agricultural production is suffering from are complex and serious. It will take at least three, five or even seven years before it can be restored to health. . . ."

On 17 December, an article called "Long live the Three Red Flags" dealt once again with the same themes. In 1958 Chairman Mao launched the movement of the "Three Red Flags" (i.e. the "general line of socialist construction", the "Great Leap Forward" and the "people's communes"), and this movement developed magnificently, speeding up industrial and agricultural production and the production of basic equipment, and propelling forward the socialist revolution and socialist construction. But after 1959, three consecutive years of natural disasters and the sabotage of the Soviet revisionists brought about temporary economic difficulties. The Chinese Khrushchev took advantage of this to paint a gloomy picture. "Our economy is on the brink of collapse." How should the situation in fact have been viewed at this point? Our great leader, Chairman Mao, pointed out: "The situation is magnificent: there are a good many problems, but the future is very bright." Subsequent developments have confirmed the correctness of these words. It was the "Three Red Flags" that made it possible to overcome the natural disasters quickly and to take a great leap forward into the construction of an autonomous, complete and modern economy. But by distorting the facts, the Chinese Khrushchev has claimed that the disasters came not from nature but from man. Completely rejecting the "Three Red Flags", he spends his time sabotaging the outstanding prestige of Chairman Mao and the central committee. The Chinese Khrushchev, who fears and hates socialism, has slandered the general line, calling it "blind", and slandering the people's communes, calling them "premature". His attacks against the "Three Red Flags" had basically only one motive: the destruction of socialism and the restoration of capitalism. He favours a rebirth of capitalism and private enterprise, etc. He has proposed a reconsideration of the verdicts on the right-wing opportunists. "As for those who adopted the same positions as P'eng Teh-huai," he has said, "in so far as they were not in collusion with foreign countries, their case can be re-examined." In addition, he has advocated that an opposition group be authorised to exist. These facts demonstrate sufficiently well that the Chinese Khrushchev is the general representative of capitalism within our party. If he were to have his way, the peasants and workers would fall back into slavery, China would change colour and revert to semi-colonialism and quasi-feudalism, and a capitalist dictatorship would replace the dictatorship of the proletariat. In 1962, at the tenth plenary session of the eighth central committee, Chairman Mao led a counter-attack and launched the battle-cry: "The class struggle must never be forgotten!" And then came the great proletarian offensive against capitalism. . . .

1968

January

The political programme for the coming year was laid down on 1 January in a joint editorial in the *People's Daily*, the *Liberation Army Daily* and the *Red Flag*. Five tasks have been put before the nation:

1. To develop the movement for "the study and living application of the thought of Mao Tse-tung". In actual fact, this "thought" has been put to use in the context of the "new general directives of Chairman Mao" by the Lin Piao - Chou En-lai coalition, as a means of reimposing order and checking revolutionary initiative: "Any word or deed which is in opposition to the thought of Mao Tse-tung should be resolutely rejected and fought against, whether it comes from the right *or from the extreme left.*"

2. To purify, consolidate and reorganise the party. In reality, the purges are aimed not only at the Liuist faction but equally at the left extremists. This theme of reconstructing the party was also taken up again specifically and expanded in an editorial in the *People's Daily* on 19 January. It should be seen in context with the preparations for the ninth party congress which are taking place at the moment. A speech by Hsieh Fu-chih has provided various pieces of semi-official information on this forthcoming congress. The delegates will be greater in number than at preceding congresses, in order to prevent the assembly from being reduced to a gathering of old men, and to allow it to "absorb new blood". *The delegates will not necessarily have to be elected, but can be appointed from above.* The purpose of the congress will be to revise the party constitution in terms of the central problem of the struggle against revisionism. A Red Guard publication dated 15 January has also spoken of the preparations for the ninth congress. Peking has already sent instructions on this subject to the various Revolutionary Committees as well as

to the commanders of the military regions: where the central authorities have a clear knowledge of the situation, they will choose the delegates. Where they do not have all the information at their disposal, the delegates will be chosen jointly by the central authorities and the local Revolutionary Committee. In plain language, Peking is going to try as hard as possible to pack the assembly with loyal elements. This will not be uniformly workable. In several provinces where the local military authorities are now firmly entrenched, Peking will be forced to make concessions over the choice of delegates. But in order to be absolutely sure of a majority in the assembly, the maoist authorities are allocating to themselves, in advance, the power to swamp the opposition with "new blood" which they can nominate at will, as there is no longer any theoretical limit on the total number of delegates.

3. To continue and to intensify "revolutionary criticism"; to further denounce the crimes of the "Chinese Khrushchev" and his "capitalist clique"; to consolidate the "great revolutionary alliance" and the "triple union"; to rally the majority of the former cadres; to oppose sterile factional disputes; to eliminate sectarianism and the clan mentality. These directives are set in the general perspective of the struggle against "factionalism", which remains the most important problem. The central authorities are trying to reinstate the old bureaucratic apparatus everywhere, but they are coming up against fierce resistance from the revolutionaries. They are therefore trying to divert the latter's activism from the real field of battle and to direct it into the academic and innocuous role of denouncing Liu Shao-ch'i, hoping that if the activities are fully occupied in flogging this dead hourse they will no longer have time to attack the mandarins, who are very much alive and under whose control the authorities wish to place them.

4. To consolidate the unity between the army and the people; "the army is the fundamental pillar of the Cultural Revolution".

5. To develop industrial and agricultural production, strengthen labour discipline and conduct the "revolution" with austerity, fighting the pernicious current of "economism".

The maoist authorities want to bring the "Cultural Revolution" to a rapid end, by hastening the establishment of Revolutionary Committees in those provinces which do not yet have them. They thus hope to be able during the course of this year to declare the "complete victory" of the movement. (Chou En-lai has disclosed to two Japanese MPs visiting Peking that this celebration is supposed to coincide with the national celebrations of 1 October.)

The gradual elimination of the extremists and the consolidation of the military-bureaucratic alliance between Lin Piao and Chou En-lai has reduced the "Cultural Revolution" to a simple reshuffle of party and administrative personnel. The acceleration of the movement no longer presents major problems. This month three new Revolutionary Committees have been set up: in Kiangsi (5 January), Kansu (24 January) and Honan (27 January). The leadership of these committees follows a more or less uniform pattern. The chairmanship has been assigned to the Political Commissar of the military region in question. The posts of vice-chairman have been entrusted to the Commander of the military region and to former local bureaucrats. The symbolic presence of one or two delegates from "mass organisations" is optional. The details of the membership of these committees are as follows:

Kiangsi. Chairman: Ch'eng Shih-ch'ing, Political Commissar of the provincial military region of Kiangsi. Vice-chairmen: Yang Tung-liang, Commander of the provincial military region of Kiangsi; Huang Hsien, former Deputy Secretary of the Secretariat of the provincial party committee and Deputy Governor of the province. Yü Hou-teh and Wang Li-lang have been listed as the delegates from the mass organisations.

Kansu. Chairman: Hsieh Heng-shan, Political Commissar of the military region of Lanchow (note that Hsieh is a former supporter of P'eng Teh-huai and Ho Lung!). Vice-chairmen: Chang Chung, Deputy Commander of the provincial military region of Kansu; Hu Chi-tsung, former Secretary to the Secretariat of the provincial party committee and Deputy Governor of the province. Ch'iu Yü-min and Hsiao Tse-min have been listed as the delegates from the mass organisations.

Honan. Chairman: Liu Chien-hsün, Political Commissar of the military region of Wuhan, formerly First Secretary of the provincial (Honan) party committee. Vice-chairmen: Wang Hsin, second Political Commissar of the provincial military region of Honan; Chi Teng-k'ui, former Assistant Secretary to the Secretariat of the provincial party committee; Keng Ch'i-ch'ang, first Secretary of the party committee of the district of Hsinhsiang; Yang Li-yung, Political Commissar of the K'aifeng garrison. There is no revolutionary delegate among the leaders of this "Revolutionary" Committee.

February

As one might have foreseen, the Revolutionary Committees are being set up with increasing rapidity — now that the "seizure of power" has given way to the simple ratification of an existing situation, and the supervisory authority of the regional military commands over the former bureaucracy is being legitimised by the "revolutionary" label.

This month therefore has seen the setting up of three new committees: in Hopeh (3 February). Hupeh (5 February) and Kwangtung (21 February) At the risk of being too meticulous, let us once again examine how the leadership of these three committees is composed. The identity of their leaders is in fact very illuminating.

The Hopeh Revolutionary Committee is chaired by Li Hsüeh-feng, a remarkable specimen of the old bureaucratic apparatus whose "revisionist" connections are notorious. As the former First Secretary of the Party Bureau in the North China region, his long and close association with Liu Shao-ch'i and P'eng Chen makes him, in the eyes of the Red Guards, a typical representative of the "faction in power" which must be overthrown. He was subjected to such intensive attacks by revolutionary rebels that at the end of 1966 he had to give up his duties as First Secretary of the Peking municipal party committee. The first deputy leader of the committee is himself also a fine old bureaucrat named Liu Tzu-hou. He was formerly First Secretary of the provincial (Hopeh) party committee and governor of the province. He too was violently attacked by the Red Guards, who accused him — not without justification — of sabotaging the "Cultural Revolution". The deputy leaders include three soldiers: Ma Hui, Commander of the provincial military region of Hopeh; Tseng Mei, the Deputy Political Commissar of the provincial military region of Hopeh (previously Commander of the Peking garrison); and Chang Ying-hui, an officer from an army unit stationed at Shih-chia-chuang. Two deputy leaders have been described as delegates from the mass organisations, but the first of them, Liu Tien-ch'en, is in fact a senior civil servant (Vice-chairman of the Federation of Industry and Commerce in Peking). Only the other one, Keng Ch'ang-so, a "national hero of agriculture", can possibly correspond to the theoretical definition of a "representative of the revolutionary masses".

The Hupeh Revolutionary Committee has at the end of the list of its leaders a much larger number of new men who could pass for "representatives of the masses" (Chu Hung-hsia, Jao Hsing-li, Yang Tao-yuan and Chang Li-kuo), but it is firmly controlled at the top by the army and the mandarins. The leader of the Committee is in fact Tseng Szu-yu, commander of Wuhan military region (he replaced Ch'en Tsai-tao, and was previously Deputy Commander of Shenyang military region). Tseng is one of Lin Piao's men. He is assisted by two soldiers (Liu Feng, previously Deputy Commander of the airforce stationed at Wuhan and then promoted to Political Commissar of Wuhan military region, and Liang Jen-k'ui, a senior officer of Hupeh provincial military region), and by two bureaucrats. One of these is Chang T'i-hsüeh, Deputy Secretary of the provincial party committee and governor of the province; Chang was the right-hand man of Wang Jen-chung, who was public enemy number one in the eyes of the revolutionaries of the region and the accomplice of T'ao Chu. The other bureaucrat is Jen Ai-sheng, Director of the Department of Agriculture of the provincial party committee. The Kwangtung Revolutionary Committee is also firmly controlled by the army and its "revisionist" puppets. It is chaired by Huang Yung-sheng, Commander of the military region of Canton, of whom I have already spoken above and who became famous as a result of his repression of Red Guards. The Kwangtung rebel faction "Red Flag" called him "T'ao Chu's sidekick", "the hangman who massacres revolutionaries", the "T'an Chen-lin of Canton". On 5 January, a Cantonese publication called K'an chin chao was still taking him to pieces in the following terms: "The hangman Huang Yung-sheng, having taken it easy in Peking for a few months, has returned to Canton. No sooner has he put aside his butcher's knife than he begins to play the little saint." It continued by speaking ironically about the "buffoons" (very pleasant for Lin Piao and Chou En-lai) who now wish to pass him off as a member of Chairman Mao's head-quarters. The publication referred in passing to the ugly affair involving rape which Huang was supposed to have been involved in long ago, and which T'ao Chu had been so kind as to hush up. This accusation may very well be mere slander, but it is none the less significant of the rebels' state of mind over the provincial leader whom Peking has now imposed on them. The article concludes with a call to vigilance on the part of all revolutionaries, urging them to enlighten everyone about the real identity of Huang, who once in power will not miss the opportunity to make the heads of revolutionaries roll by the thousand.

The Deputy Leaders of the Kwangtung Revolutionary Committee consist of an impressive list of military personnel: K'ung Shih-ch'üan, Political Commissar of the Canton military region, Ch'iu Kuo-kuang, Deputy Commander of the Canton military region, Yen Chung-ch'uan, Chief of Staff of the Canton military region and Huang Jung-hai, Commander of the Kwangtung provincial military region. The latter, another *bête noire* of the revolutionaries, is joint leader of the Revolutionary Committee of Canton Municipality (at the head of this Committee he is assisted by such people as Chiao Lin-yi, a tool of T'ao Chu, whom the Red Guards recently hauled before a public tribunal and accused of being a "triple anti" — anti-Mao, anti-masses and anti-party). The Kwangtung Revolutionary Committee also comprises two more bureaucrats of the old school: Ch'en Yü (previously Third Secretary of the party bureau of the Central and Southern region, Secretary to the secretariat of the provincial party committee and governor of the province) and Wang Shou-tao (Secretary to the secretariat of the South Central Bureau). At the end of the list are two new men: Huang Yü-ying, a teacher, and Liu Chi-fa, a worker who is described as the delegate from the "Red Flag" rebel faction.

These semblances of Revolutionary Committees which the rebels now see being imposed from above, and in whose leadership they have hardly any share, are all the more offensive because they are springing up scarcely more than a year after the flamboyant proclamations which heralded the "Cultural Revolution". The *People's Daily* of 22 January 1967 defined this as being chiefly "a struggle for the seizure of power". In the same period, the *Red Flag* (1967, no. 3) developed this idea of a "seizure of power" even further. According to the official mouthpiece of the movement (which is now reduced to silence, its editorial team having been decimated by the recent purges), "seizure of power" could not simply consist in harnessing the legacy of the old power: one should not be satisfied with gradual reforms, nor should one attempt to conjure away the contradictions by surrendering to conciliatory manoeuvres. In a word, the *Red Flag* was boldly preaching a radical destruction of the existing order. This preliminary dismantling of the old apparatus was in fact scarcely achieved anywhere, except by the Revolutionary Committee of Shanghai. The principle of the "triple union" soon arrived to signal a first step backwards, since it officially made room for former rehabilitated cadres and for the army alongside the revolutionary elements. However, in theory the revolutionary element was supposed to make up "the nucleus and the motor of the 'triple unions' " (New China News Agency, 9 February 1967) and we have since seen how this principle was just not put into operation.

The "revolutionary rebels" are finding it difficult to realise that Peking has betrayed and abandoned them for good, and they continue to struggle desperately. In Canton, for example, they have tried up until the last minute to hinder the setting up of this caricature of a Revolutionary Committee which seals their defeat. They succeeded in delaying it by several weeks. Finally, on the actual day of its inauguration — the 21st — the official ceremony was marked by a clash in the Yueh-hsiu shan stadium between the rival "Red Flag", "Spring Thunder" and "East Wind" factions. There followed such a state of confusion that the official communiqué from Peking announcing the setting up of the committee, had to be deferred until the 23rd, as the central authorities had not managed immediately to obtain a clear picture of the situation. (This embarrassing delay also compelled the *Ta-kung pao* in Hong Kong, which had left the front page of its edition of the 22nd intact for a report on the expected victory, to fill it at the last minute with a padding of revolutionary ditties along with their musical scores.)

The active and militant indignation of the betrayed young people who oppose the setting up of pseudo-revolutionary committees, or who are sabotaging and undermining the authority of those which have already been set up, has been officially christened "factionalism". The evil of "factionalism" is also being continually analysed and denounced in a very revealing way in the official press. The *Wen-hui pao* on the 15th enlightened us on the mistakes of factionalism: "The supporters of factionalism are frequently *individuals who have previously distinguished themselves in the revolutionary vanguard in the struggle against revisionism*. Full of these credits, they let themselves become drunk with the feeling of their own importance and became arrogant towards the masses, whom they divide into irreconcilable groups, sabotaging production and thus weakening the cause of the proletariat." The heroes of yesterday have thus become today's culprits. Now that the "Cultural Revolution" has at last shown its true colours, its original naive shock troops have turned into spoilsports and vicious disturbers of the peace. This is confirmed by the fact that the walls of Peking have recently been covered with posters *denouncing the crimes of Ch'i Pen-yü*, who was, we may recall, one of the first and most ardent heralds of the "Cultural Revolution", his articles exciting nationwide interest — "On the Reactionary Character of *Hai Jui Reprimands the Emperor* and of *The Dismissal of Hai Jui*" (*People's Daily*, 4 February 1966), "Critique of the Reactionary Capitalist Position of *Ch'ien-hsien* and *Peking Daily* (*Red Flag*, 11 May 1966), "Patriotism or Treason?" (*People's Daily*, 1 April 1966). He is accused of having supported the extreme left faction behind the scenes and *of having been opposed to Chou En-lai.* All this is quite in keeping with the successive purges of Wang Li, Kuan Feng, Mu Hsin, Lin Chieh, Yao Teng-shan etc. The entire activist élite of the "Cultural Revolution" is being swallowed up.

As usual, if the adversary is to be neutralised, he must be systematically slandered. In contempt of all probability they are now presenting the extreme left activists, who were in the vanguard of the "Cultural Revolution" and dealt the fiercest blows at the Liuist faction, as agents in the service of Liu Shao-ch'i (and as for Liu Shao-ch'i, he will no doubt soon be presented as an agent of Chiang Kai-shek and the Americans). Thus the article put out by the New China News Agency on 12 February states:

"This division of the revolutionary masses into two large factions which occurred during the Cultural Revolution is the fruit of a plot by those who follow the capitalist road. At the beginning of the Cultural Revolution, as the revolutionary groups were rising against the faction which follows the capitalist road, the latter used its influence to push one section of the working masses to oppose this group of revolutionary rebels in such a way as to protect itself. . . . Those who follow the capitalist road had further recourse to other stratagems and plots. They slipped several of their men into the very ranks of the revolutionary proletarian groups and by all the means at their disposal these men incited the latter to factionalism."

The same article analyses the causes of factionalism:

"In the course of the Cultural Revolution the Chinese people enjoyed democratic rights to an extent without precedent in the history of the world. Under these conditions it was completely understandable that on some questions differences of opinion should have occurred. Thus for example with regard to the cadres: some deemed that so-and-so was fundamentally good, while others judged him to be bad and were of the opinion that he should be overthrown. Owing to these factionalist intrigues, these differences of thought and opinion led to the development within numerous mass revolutionary organisms of situations of acute opposition as well as uninterrupted 'civil war'." [inverted commas in the original]

It eventually sets out the remedy:

"Since the national celebrations last year the mass movement of struggle against factionalism has spread over the whole country. The revolutionary masses with the warm assistance of detachments of the People's Liberation Army supporting the left have organised large-scale study sessions on the thought of Mao Tse-tung, where members of the revolutionary mass organisations who have differences of opinion have assembled and all together conscientiously studied the latest directives of Chairman Mao with regard to the Cultural Revolution".

The article then recalls the content of these famous directives. "1. Within the working class there are fundamentally no conflicts of interest. Under the régime of the dictatorship of the proletariat, there is even less reason for the divisions which develop within the working class to take on the character of irreducible opposition between two large organised factions.

2. The revolutionary Red Guards and the revolutionary students should bring about the 'great revolutionary alliance'; seeing that the two confronting factions are revolutionary mass organisations, it should be possible on the basis of revolutionary principles to achieve the 'great revolutionary alliance'.

3. The two factions should avoid reproaching each other with their shortcomings and faults. Each should leave it to the other to criticise of its own accord its own shortcomings and mistakes. Let each one carry out its own self-criticism in such a way as to create a fundamental unity which goes beyond differences on small points."

The article ends with a new appeal for a struggle against factionalism, and with a call for the establishment of the "great revolutionary alliance", which "alone can create the conditions allowing the establishment of Revolutionary Committees, can mobilise the masses in the struggle against the 'Chinese Khrushchev' and at the same time allow economic production to be firmly maintained".

The corollary to this struggle against left-wing activism is obviously the reactivation of the party apparatus. Preparations for the ninth congress are continuing. Radio Shanghai has announced that in May, Shanghai will convene its local assembly of party delegates (the convening of local assemblies normally precedes the convening of the national congress). This desire to get the party back in marching order includes, by extension, a certain desire to counterbalance the unlimited power which the army has secured. Since the "Cultural Revolution" swept away the basic principle of the division of political and military power, as well as the subordination of the latter to the former, the

commanders of the large military regions have suddenly been
invested with limitless authority, and are often finding themselves
in a position to negotiate on an equal basis with Peking. Peking
is thus once more haunted by the old spectre of provincial
military autocracies, under which the Chinese Republic suffered
so much in the first years of its history, and which the People's
Republic seemed to have finally exorcised. Now that the evil
has been done, will the party in reconstructing itself be able to
take back from the army the prerogatives which it has so
imprudently conceded?

Parallel with the party's reconstruction there are signs of a
desire to normalise government activity. Ch'en Yi, a human
barometer, seems to have been fully reinstated to his former
duties. A communiqué from the New China News Agency dated
12 February, concerning the audience which Ch'en granted to the
new Dutch Chargé d'Affaires in Peking, referred again to his
dual title of Vice-chairman of the Council and Minister for
Foreign Affairs.

The First Fortnight in March

The anniversary of the directive issued by Mao on 7 March 1967 has
just been commemorated throughout China. The directive concerned
the training of the nation (and in particular of youth) by the army:

"By means of a series of groups and sessions, the army
should undertake the military training of universities, middle
schools and higher classes in primary schools, and should
take part in supervising the resumption of classes, rectify-
ing the organisation and establishing the triple union. First
of all experiments must be carried out and conclusions
drawn from them, and then these experiments should be
gradually extended. The students must be convinced, and
the teachings of Marx, according to whom it is only by
freeing all humanity that the proletariat itself can finally be
freed, must be applied. Cadres and teachers who have made
mistakes must not be left out of this military education.
Except for the old and the sick, everyone must be allowed
to take part in the sessions in the interest of their reform.
It will be enough for everyone to work conscientiously, and
the problems will be easily resolved."

In the present state of things — the resumption of classes is still
a sluggish process, while anarchistic tendencies and the intransigence of the extremists are hindering the rehabilitation of cadres
— these instructions are still a pressing issue.

On 3 March the New China News Agency published the conclusions of a "living study and application session on the thought of Mao Tse-tung" held by activist delegates from the airforce. After an obligatory stanza to the glory of Mao, there was a long passage dedicated to Lin Piao:

"In this decisive struggle for the destiny of all humanity, our much loved Deputy Leader Lin Piao has unlimited loyalty towards the great Chairman Mao. He follows Chairman Mao closely and right to the end. He brandishes high the great red standard of the thought of Mao Tse-tung, he unflinchingly defends the great leader Mao Tse-tung as well as the great thought of Mao Tse-tung and the proletarian revolutionary line of the Chairman, struggling directly against the opportunists of the left and the right. With the most resolute revolutionary energy Vice-chairman Lin has won the victory over the handful of capitalists within the party and over the sabotage of class enemies. In the entire army, in the entire party and throughout the whole country, he has unyieldingly promoted and developed with all his strength the movement of the living study and application of the thought of Mao Tse-tung, he has opened the fundamental road which allows the masses to grasp directly the thought of Mao Tse-tung, and he has thus made a mighty contribution to the Chinese revolution and to world revolution."

This is another attempt to create a certain image of Lin Piao, imposing him as a privileged intermediary between the common herd and a Mao who is already half enveloped in clouds.

Ch'i Pen-yü's disgrace has now been confirmed. His career was meteoric. He emerged abruptly from obscurity on 1 April 1967. He had the job of firing the first shot against Liu Shao-ch'i, with the famous article "Patriotism or Treason?" On 1 May he was already in a prominent position in Mao's retinue when it inspected the militants of the "Cultural Revolution" in Peking. On his last public appearance, on 31 December 1967, he was in eighth position in the hierarchy. The accusations now lodged against him, although very obscure, are interesting. He is accused of having *opposed Chou En-lai* by organising attacks against his close associates: Ch'en Yi, Li Fu-ch'un, Li Hsien-nien and Yü Ch'iu-li. In addition, he is supposed to have ordered his supporters to gather compromising information for the purposes of compiling a "black book" *against Lin Piao*. He is supposed to have been in collusion with the Wang Li - Kuan Feng clique etc., and to have secretly supported the extremist faction, the "16 May group". Along with Yao Teng-shan, he is supposed to have been one of the people responsible for burning down the premises of the British Chargé d'Affaires in Peking. He is alleged to have criticised the formula of Revolutionary Committees based on the "triple union", seeing these (and not without justification, one is tempted to add) as a form of compromise devoid of a revolutionary character. The "Cultural Revolution" has not taken long to devour all its most zealous organisers. If the present trend continues, the encroaching purge may climb higher still and even end up by touching Yao Wen-yuan, Chang Ch'un-ch'iao, Hsieh Fu-chih and Ch'en Po-ta.

Second Half of March/April

The "Cultural Revolution" has developed a sudden and disconcerting fever.

At the beginning of March it seemed to be trying to redirect itself towards the cultural sphere. Purges such as that of the famous writer Pa Chin and even arrests (among others that of the painter Yeh Ch'ien-yü, a member of the standing committee of the Pan-Chinese Federation of Artists) have affected a number of literary, artistic, theatre and scientific personalities. Is it a diversionary manoeuvre — are the authorities trying to appease the extremists, whose revolution has been frustrated, by giving them a few intellectuals to devour? From the 22nd onwards vast demonstrations, the size of which recall the first days of the "Cultural Revolution", have taken place once again in the streets of Peking. The walls are covered with posters and the press has resumed its great attack against the "revisionist" threat. Since the 26th, the demonstrations and wall posters have specifically attacked three important military personnel: Yang Ch'eng-wu (who has been Chief of the General Staff since the purge of Lo Jui-ch'ing), Yü Li-chin (Political Commissar of the airforce) and Fu Ch'ung-pi (Commander of the Peking garrison and Deputy Leader of the Revolutionary Committee of Peking Municipality). Their disgrace has quickly been officially confirmed. On the 27th, Radio Peking broadcast the news several times that Mao had chaired an unexpected meeting of ten thousand military cadres. He was accompanied by his whole group of close assistants, who now form the united leadership nucleus of China: Lin Piao, Chou En-lai, Chiang Ch'ing, Ch'en Po-ta, K'ang Sheng, Hsieh Fu-chih, Yao Wen-yuan, Huang Yung-sheng, Wu Fa-hsien, Yeh Ch'ün and Wang Tung-hsing. During the course of the meeting Lin Piao made an "important announcement" giving official notice of Yang Ch'eng-wu's disgrace and his replacement by Huang Yung-sheng (Commander of the Canton military region and Chairman of the Kwangtung Revolutionary Committee — mention has already been made of him above).

At the same time demonstrators and wall posters in the streets of Peking have also attacked Chou En-lai's group of protégés, the higher civil servants: Li Fu-ch'un (Vice-chairman of the State Council and the person chiefly responsible for economic and financial affairs in the party, a member of the standing committee of the Politbureau and formerly number six in the supreme hierarchy), T'an Chen-lin (a former Minister for Agriculture) and Yü Ch'iu-li (previously Minister for the Oil Industry).

The lightning fall of Yang Ch'eng-wu (and the backwash which has surrounded it) is an event of considerable importance, and poses delicate problems of interpretation. We must wait for more complete disclosures, and these will probably not emerge for several years. But some basic information can be given now.

The first point to note is the state of complete ignorance in which the masses have been kept concerning the ins and outs of the affair. Until recently Yang Ch'eng-wu was still putting his name to a never-ending article in the *People's Daily* which condemned the crimes of Lo Jui-ch'ing, extolled the thought of Mao and was laying the foundations of the Lin Piao cult. He was promoted by the "Cultural Revolution" into second position in the military hierarchy, immediately below Lin Piao. (The decisive role which he played on the eve of the "Cultural Revolution" has already been pointed out in Section One. It was his support which enabled Mao to eliminate Lo Jui-ch'ing, take control of the capital again and launch the "Cultural Revolution".) He therefore had all the outward appearances of orthodoxy. But here he is, thrown off his pedestal overnight. At a moment's notice a hundred thousand demonstrators have mobilised in Peking to shout "Down with Yang Ch'eng-wu!" They do not do this on their own initiative: who, among the masses, would dare take a sudden groundless decision to denounce Lin Piao's right-hand man? If this huge crowd were roused by a spontaneous impulse and inspired by an autonomous will and an irrepressible desire for revenge, it would protest its grievances and give a hundred reasons which have driven it to demand Yang's head. But on the contrary, all we see is a bunch of people with walk-on roles, who are now a routine part of these spectacular demonstrations; they mechanically spout the handful of obscure clichés which the

prompter has just whispered to them. Yang is a "conspirator",
he "opposed Hsieh Fu-chih", he was trying to "rehabilitate T'an
Chen-lin".* He "sabotaged an exhibition dedicated to the victory
of the thought of Mao Tse-tung (!)". Yang's downfall would
seem to expose maoism's false claim to be the expression of the
"mass line". One thing stands out. The fall of Yang was decided
secretly, on the basis of a dossier unknown to the masses and for
motives which could not be revealed to them. It is the result of a
hidden struggle in which the masses have played no part and of
which they could know nothing. The only role which the "Cultural
Revolution" now requires them to play resembles that of the
unemployed and the beggars under the old régime, whom the
leading citizens hired in droves to bang cymbals in their bridal
processions and to carry wreaths in their funeral cortèges.

What can have justified Yang Ch'eng-wu's disgrace? Some
western commentators think his fall can be compared with that
of Lo Jui-ch'ing, his predecessor, and they therefore imagine
that he opposed Lin Piao. Others are confusing his case with
those of the left extremists who have recently been eliminated.
These interpretations are unanimously rejected by Chinese
observers in Hong Kong, and it seems to me that they are right.
Yang Ch'eng-wu was in fact Lin Piao's protégé. Ever since the
Long March, during which he acted as Political Commissar in a
division belonging to the First Army group led by Lin Piao, he
had always worked under Lin, and he eventually became his
right-hand man, someone Lin could rely on. It was by relying
on Yang that Lin succeeded at the beginning of 1966 in eliminat-
ing his most dangerous rival, Lo Jui-ch'ing, securing for Mao the
military control of Peking Municipality and thus opening the way
for the development of the "Cultural Revolution". Yang was
then rewarded for his decisive action with the post of Chief of
the General Staff. He thus became a cornerstone of maoist power.
In September 1967 he was even part of the four-strong retinue
which accompanied Mao Tse-tung on his tour of inspection of the
five Yang-tze River provinces. He proved to be the main person

---

* T'an Chen-lin was a close associate of Chou En-lai who in February
and March 1967 directly attacked the Cultural Revolution Group. He
denounced the muddle-headed initiative of Chiang Ch'ing and Ch'en Po-ta,
and even pleaded on behalf of Liu Shao-ch'i and Teng Hsiao-p'ing. The
"Cultural Revolution" turned T'an into one of its chief *bêtes noires*. Chou
En-lai tried several times to defend him, but was finally unable to save
him. T'an's last public appearance was on 31 July 1967. The recent attacks
this month seem to have sealed his fate. [*In fact he was rehabilitated with
Teng in 1977.*]

behind the Lin Piao cult. In the event of Lin Piao acceding to supreme power, Yang seemed already designated as his second-in-command. The idea that Yang is now supposed to have opposed Lin Piao seems particularly absurd, and shows complete ignorance of the past of the people concerned. On the contrary, Yang's disgrace must be seen as *a direct attack on Lin Piao's authority*, and consequently as a setback for Peking. This is confirmed further by the identity of the two soldiers who accompanied Yang in his fall. Both were trump cards in Lin Piao's game. Yü Li-chin, the Political Commissar of the airforce, was the organiser of a series of study sessions and meetings held in Peking for activist delegates in the army, the navy and especially the airforce (see above). The main objective of the meetings was to consecrate Lin Piao's role as the nation's model and guide. As for Fu Ch'ung-pi, who led the violent coup which had made Mao master of Peking Municipality in the spring of 1966, in his capacity as Commander of the Peking garrison, he guaranteed Lin permanent control of the capital and of the seat of government.

Among the leaks from official sources in these last few weeks there is one which merits particular attention. In his communiqué announcing Yang's removal Lin Piao is supposed to have indicated that one of Yang's main crimes was his "insane ambition" to eliminate the great regional commanders, Hsü Shih-yu (Nanking military region), Huang Yung-sheng (Canton military region) and Han Hsien-ch'u (Foochow military region and Commander of the front-line units in Fukien, opposite Taiwan). That the task of officially announcing Yang's disgrace should have fallen to Lin Piao should not come as a surprise, nor lead one to believe that the two men were opposed. In People's China, the usual custom is to entrust the task of publicly reading out the condemned person's sentence precisely to his close associate. This enables the victim to be isolated; it shows everyone that his natural allies have already broken their ties with him, and that he therefore no longer has any political potential. It will be noted that it is precisely Huang Yung-sheng who has now been promoted to Yang's former position at the head of the General Staff. In the struggle for power it is normal practice for the victor to get his adversary's spoils. Lin Piao had once become Minister of Defence in place of P'eng Teh-huai and Yang himself head of the General Staff in place of Lo Jui-ch'ing, in precisely this way. At the very moment when Yang fell, Hsü Shih-yu's regional power was officially confirmed when he became Chairman of the new Kiangsu Revolutionary Committee on 23 March.

I have already emphasised that Lin Piao's grip on the army is still far from complete. The great regional commanders whom the dismantling of the party has helped to make omnipotent, each in his fief and deaf to the orders of Peking, have formed a powerful coalition with their own demands. Peking is being forced to come to terms with this coalition. The Wuhan mutiny and its after-effects have already given a striking demonstration of this. It was because he had the full backing of his colleagues that Ch'en Tsai-tao dared to lock up the emissaries from Peking illegally. And the need to deal tactfully with this coalition of regional commanders has forced Peking to forego the temptation to intervene directly. The Wuhan crisis was cleared up through diplomatic channels. Ch'en Tsai-tao and his chief accomplice, Chung Han-hua, far from being given the exemplary punishment which their rebellion deserved, were simply subjected to a lengthy study session on the thought of Mao Tse-tung in Peking—a fate which was neither terribly enticing nor even dramatic in any way. By haggling over the price and the conditions of their support, the great regional commanders obtained a complete reversal of maoist policy. The order of 5 September 1967 gave each of them *carte blanche* to bring the revolutionaries to heel in their province. But this was not enough. They have gone on to demand the elimination of all the activist leaders of the "Cultural Revolution" in central positions of power, so that they can disperse and crush more conveniently the militants in their own provinces who have dared to challenge their authority. It seems very probable that it is these same commanders who have now demanded that Yang Ch'eng-wu be deposed and replaced by one of them — Huang Yung-sheng. In his position as head of the General Staff, Yang Ch'eng-wu — being Lin Piao's right-hand man — had to spend his time chiefly in uniting the army and making it a homogeneous instrument which would be entirely at Lin's disposal. He therefore had to eliminate all these small pockets of resistance, these networks of old loyalties which had a firm regional foundation and still clustered around several of the military personalities who had been victims of the purge. In the process, he inevitably ran up against the prerogatives and ambitions of the regional commanders. The ensuing trial of strength tipped the balance in favour of the regional commanders. With Huang Yung-sheng in Peking, they now have a representative of their interests at the top of the apparatus who is a direct counterweight to Lin Piao's authority. To say that China is now under the army's thumb is still only half the truth: the fact is that this army is itself fundamentally divided and disturbed by various currents. The outcome of the Yang Ch'eng-wu affair clearly shows the limits of Lin Piao's power. The prestige and sudden ratification of Lin appeared from the very beginning to be no more than an arbitrary propaganda device. And when events put it to the test, the artificial and precarious nature of his authority was exposed even more clearly.

"Without a people's army, the people have nothing." This famous remark of Mao's has been quoted, with a great deal of relevance, in the articles marking the setting up of the most recent Revolutionary Committees (Kiangsu on 23 March, Chekiang on 24 March, Hunan on 8 April, Ninghsia on 10 April and Anhwei on 18 April). Without a people's army the population undoubtedly would not have Revolutionary Committees. These are all chaired by the army. The case of Hsü Shih-yu, who heads the Kiangsu Revolutionary Committee, is particularly remarkable. Hsü, who commands the military region of Nanking (he also used to be Deputy Minister for Defence) has distinguished himself by his impertinent opposition to the "Cultural Revolution". If the Red Guards are to be believed, he still made his troops study Liu Shao-ch'i's little doctrinal handbook up until June 1966. He publicly stated that he did not know a thing about the developments of the "Cultural Revolution" and adopted an attitude of passive obstruction, even refusing several times to reply to the central authorities when they summoned him to Peking. Taking advantage of the order of 5 September 1967, which restored the authority of the army over the revolutionaries, he spent his time subduing the left wing in his province. That such a person can now be called upon to lead a Revolutionary Committee is simply a mockery. The ratification of his power coincides with Yang Ch'eng-wu's downfall. This, combined with the rise of Huang Yung-sheng in Peking and the promotion of a large number of "revisionist" cadres to the leadership teams of most of the new Revolutionary Committees, gives a good indication of how central authority has weakened and how provincial autocracies are continuing to spring up. This twofold phenomenon promises to make it particularly difficult to convene the party congress. (It appears to be getting increasingly doubtful whether the ninth congress can be held before this year's National Day. According to Chou En-lai, whose remarks were reported in a Red Guard publication, it is to be postponed till next year.) Conscious of the danger, Peking has used the pages of the *People's Daily* to launch an official alert against the danger of "revisionist" infil-

tration into the Revolutionary Committees. Several already established committees have come up against serious difficulties. In
Shantung in particular, the rebels are violently accusing the committee and the army of veering to the right. In Peking, three
members of the committee have just been eliminated. In Hunan,
Kweichow and Kwangtung, the committees are being pressured
by rebel factions trying to challenge their composition. In Shensi,
Szechuan and Tibet the disturbances persist, and are delaying the
setting up of the committees. In Liaoning, which does not even
have a preparatory group to set the committee up, Sung Jen-
ch'iung, who is First Political Commissar of the military region
of Shenyang, a deputy member of the Politbureau and a former
subordinate of T'eng Hsiao-p'ing (Sung is one of the main power-
holders in the North-Eastern provinces, where he hindered the
development of the "Cultural Revolution"), is supposed to have
attempted a violent coup in Shenyang backed by some armoured
units.

The very idea of the "Revolutionary Committee" has been so
discredited in the eyes of the left that official propaganda is now
having to use all the means at its disposal to give it some value
again. Thus on 20 March a joint editorial in the *People's Daily,*
the *Red Flag* and the *Liberation Army Daily* entitled "The
Revolutionary Committees are a Good Thing" recalled that this
Revolutionary Committee formula was Mao Tse-tung's own
creation, and it underlined the positive value of the "triple union"
as well as the revolutionary role of the army. We should note in
passing that the official propaganda organs have been suffering
from pathetic ideological deficiencies for several months. The
People's Daily rarely publishes editorials on doctrine. This
reveals the state of confusion and uncertainty into which the staff
have been plunged (today's truth is tomorrow's crime) and is a
result of the continual mowing down of the batallion of professional party scribes.

One remarkable phenomenon is that Peking is endeavouring
to revive the ghost of the Kuomintang. Mao's "most recent directives" have put forward an astonishing definition of the "Cultural
Revolution": "The present struggle is the continuation of the
struggle between the Communist Party and the Kuomintang" (!)
The first time this was reported was in a broadcast by Radio
Hunan on 5 April, and it was taken up again on 10 April in a
joint editorial in the *People's Daily* and the *Liberation Army Daily*
celebrating the birth of the Hunan Revolutionary Committee.
The same theme is still being frequently presented. On 26 April,

Radio Peking broadcast the results of a military conference held in the capital: "Although the Liberation is already more than eighteen years old, the remains of the Kuomintang have not yet been eliminated. The struggle to the death must continue, and preparations must be made for a long-term struggle". Acts of sabotage are officially attributed to the Kuomintang, and in several areas "Kuomintang agents" have been exposed and condemned. All this obviously pleases Taiwan, which never knew it wielded such influence and is very flattered to have forces attributed to it which it does not possess. But the significance of the phenomenon lies elsewhere. The maoists have come up against such large-scale opposition forces within their own régime, forces which are threatening to crystallise the centrifugal tendencies of discontent and anarchy latent among the masses, that they have decided to lance the abcess and undertake ruthless repression. The Kuomintang label is being used both to discredit the adversary and to justify the severity of the repression. By resorting to this old bogey they are demonstrating that the problems posed by the opposition movements have reached a national scale, and that the struggle will be merciless. The diagnosis advanced by several observers in Hong Kong of an approaching Reign of Terror seems justified, and is already beginning to be confirmed by the many executions which have been carried out in public, as an example, in various parts of the country.

In a speech made in February (and reproduced in a Canton Red Guard broadsheet), Hsieh Fu-chih is alleged to have stated that eighty per cent of the security organs are corrupted by supporters of Liu Shao-ch'i. This is very probable. Mao, confident of his direct appeal to the masses, has never been very interested in the work of organisation or the police, and preferred to leave such things to the bureaucrats in the apparatus — to the Liu Shao-ch'is, the Teng Hsiao-p'ings etc., who thus had all the time in the world to form themselves into a state within a state. In any case, since February the majority of jobs normally falling to security have been entrusted to the army, and this has brought with it a considerable relaxation of the political control of the masses. The army in fact is only capable of keeping law and order in the streets, and is not at all equipped to extend its investigations into the sphere of private life. This explains the recent reappearance and proliferation of all kinds of illicit activities — gambling, theft, prostitution, the black market, factional revenge etc. The ruthless and summary manner in which the authorities are now treating all troublemakers is evidence of their disquiet over this dangerous weakening of discipline, which may lead to the development of clandestine political activity.

The economic situation does not seem to be all that healthy either. In two separate speeches (17 January and 2 February) which have now at last reached us through Red Guard publications, Chou En-lai declared that sabotage and anarchy have produced disturbances in communications and a drop in industrial production; as a result, numerous economic objectives have not been achieved, and on the whole, production in 1967 was lower than in 1966. He added that the cost of the "Cultural Revolution" could to some extent be compared to that of the Civil War and the Korean War. How long can China go on subjecting itself to this kind of exorbitant waste? The régime has never been more vulnerable. China is like a gigantic open powder keg: a single spark, a single revolutionary slogan which could be launched by a handful of new men, would be enough to blow everything up. But failing such a spark, and given time, Mao can be relied upon: as long as there are no adversaries other than his own party dinosaurs, his superior tactical agility will always give him the last word.

May

On 1 May there was no parade in Peking, and the celebrations were restricted to fireworks in the evening. If one considers that 1 May is the most important celebration of the year after the National Day, this cancellation of the parade, which is unprecedented in the annals of the régime, comes as a real surprise, especially at a time when the leadership would have the country believe that the "Cultural Revolution" has already won its "decisive victory". Such a departure from established custom cannot have been decided on without a serious reason. It seems in fact that the maoist authorities are no longer sure that they can control the situation completely in the capital. Fu Ch'ung-pi, who was purged scarcely a month ago, was, remember, *Commander of the Peking garrison*. The sudden elimination of someone occupying a post of such essential strategic importance is an indication of the fragility of maoist power, which seems to have been undermined from the inside, directly beneath its most fundamental prop.

The list of those present at the fireworks on 1 May shows that the régime's eight most senior individuals were there in the same order as at the National Day celebrations of October 1967,

namely Mao, Lin, Chou En-lai, Ch'en Po-ta, K'ang Sheng, Chu
Teh, Li Fu-ch'un and Ch'en Yün. The Cultural Revolution
Group seems to have been cruelly decimated but, as a compensation, its last three survivors, Chiang Ch'ing, Chang Ch'un-ch'iao
and Yao Wen-yuan, have advanced to stage front, upstaging
several members of the central committee on the way. The central
committee itself has thinned out dramatically. Out of a theoretical
total of more than 190 members and deputy members, only
twenty-six were present. In other words, this organ hardly exists
any longer, except on paper.

The general political situation is unclear. Behind this amor-
phous curtain of uncertainty there is still the intensive struggle at
the top, but since it has so far not come to any decisive conclusion, the propaganda organs are still bereft of any firm and
coherent political orientation and are confining themselves to a
discreet silence. Meaningful news is becoming increasingly rare,
and seeps through to the outside world with increasing difficulty.
(The Kwangtung authorities have just strengthened this water-
tight bulkhead by taking strict measures to put an end to illegal
emigration to Hong Kong.) There is nothing of great importance
to be derived from the official sources, either in the doctrinal
sphere or in that of actual events. Observers recall that there was
a similar blanket over information in 1959, shortly after the famous
and crucial conference at Lushan, and they see in the silence of
the propaganda organs a sign of crisis.

The little that is known about the present trends of the
political situation points to an insoluble contradiction. Theoretically, there should be a swing to the left. The 1 May editorial
published by the *People's Daily* enlarged on Mao's new directives,
saying that there had to be a vigorous counter-attack against the
current rehabilitation of right-wing elements, which is threatening
to submerge the Revolutionary Committees. But the left does not
seem to have been strengthened by this. Ch'en Po-ta has had to
make a self-criticism and to disown Ch'i Pen-yü, while Chou
En-lai, Ch'en Yün and especially Ch'en Yi (who has been very
active in the last few weeks) and their technocrats seem to be still
firmly established. This does not fit in well with the directive
attacking the rehabilitation of the rightists.

In practice, the application of a new left line throughout the
country would be a difficult thing to achieve. The Revolutionary
Committees, far from forming a homogeneous whole, are a
political hotch-potch which extends from a nice shade of maoism
(this is the smallest number of cases — Shanghai is more or less

the only example) to centrifugal militarism (Hsü Shih-yu in
Kiangsu, for example) and traditional bureaucracy (such as Li
Hsueh-feng in Hopeh), via the orthodox military government of
Lin Piao's satellites (e.g. Li Yuan in Hunan). The degree of loyalty
and obedience which each Revolutionary Committee observes
towards Peking is therefore very varied. This regional diversi-
fication (corresponding to the old, irrepressible centrifugal aspirations of the provinces which People's China had succeeded in
stemming until the explosion of the "Cultural Revolution") now
prevents the country from responding docilely to the helmsman's
touch. Since the destruction of the party apparatus which used
to guarantee political homogeneity in the provinces, the central
power has only one transmission belt left: the army. I have
already pointed out how badly equipped the army is for this task.
Lin Piao has not succeeded in imposing his authority uniformly,
and still has only an extremely limited number of trusted men at
his disposal. In many regions he has had to be content with
ratifying the power of local commanders of dubious allegiance.
Elsewhere the cohesion and efficiency of the army have been
weakened by the purges and the rebellions. Even where Lin Piao
has managed to place men who are absolutely and unconditionally loyal to him, in most cases they have been recently parachuted to the summit of a regional hierarchy which is foreign
to them.

A more worrying phenomenon is that the army, which has
become the sole pillar of maoist power, has gnawed away its inner
substance. The antagonistic relations between the army and the
maoists have not degenerated into civil war for the simple reason
that the latter have been completely sacrificed to the former. Since
the purge of the extreme left, which was demanded by the army,
Mao has disowned the victims in order to keep up appearances;
they are accused of having acted on their own initiative, in contradiction to the directives of the "great helmsman". Neither the
disavowal nor the accusations can deceive anyone. The activist
elements of the "Cultural Revolution", who suddenly surged to the
fore in 1966-7 and have now no less suddenly been secretly
swallowed up by history, were Mao's creatures from top to toe.
They had no revolutionary past and no political credentials; they
had no support either in the party or in the ranks of the army. They
faced all the authorities and all the constituted powers with bare
hands. Even they could not delude themselves that they could play
the Lone Ranger, since their only strength came precisely from the
fact that they were directly expressing Mao's political designs,

acting on his orders and with his personal guarantee. The idea that they could have considered rebelling against Mao, from whom they received their semblance of a political existence, is obviously absurd. In fact it is through them that the army has now put Mao himself into check.

June

The present orientation — or rather disorientation — of the "Cultural Revolution" is marked by a mixture of intransigence and impotence.

The intransigence is expressed particularly in the "most recent directives of Chairman Mao" (*People's Daily*, 5 June): "Protect the masses or crush them: this is the fundamental difference between the Communist Party and the Kuomintang, between the proletariat and the capitalist class, the dictatorship of the proletariat and the dictatorship of capitalism". In this same vein, the *Wen-hui pao* in Shanghai (whose articles continue to be much further to the left than those of the Peking *People's Daily*) published an editorial on the 12th which, while recognising that serious disturbances were taking place, denounced the attitude of people who are prepared to buy order at the price of compromise with the enemy. Such remarks have had an inflammatory effect on the rebels, who in fact see them as a new justification for their efforts to challenge the order imposed by the army and the "Revolutionary Committees", which has been used precisely to "crush the masses". There have now, therefore, been renewed disturbances. Various Revolutionary Committees have come adrift on the stormy waters of factionalism and are threatened with disintegration and paralysis. The *Wen-hui pao* of the 21st devoted an article to these disturbances, which are described as "civil war" (in inverted commas in the original). The fate of the people who instigated the disturbances, who have conveniently been labelled "Kuomintang agents", has been settled promptly. The dozens of bodies which the flood tide has thrown up on the shores of Hong Kong in these recent weeks are a macabre illustration, on a local scale, of a drama which extends throughout the country.

From 22 June, a number of bodies which had been drifting at the mercy of the tides and currents were discovered on the beaches of Hong Kong, the New Territories and the small islands belonging to the colony. By mid-July the total number of bodies already amounted to thirty-four. For the most part, they were men belonging to the eighteen to thirty-five-year age-group, but also included a young girl aged between thirteen and fifteen and an older woman. Their clothes were those of labourers and peasants from the Kwangtung region. The majority of the bodies were bound hand and foot in what is known as the "great binding of five flowers" (*wu-hua ta-pang*), that is, by means of a rope tying the feet, the wrists and the neck successively, and indicating that they were not victims of random violence, but had been methodically put to death in a mass execution. Several massacres occurred in the Kwangtung region at the beginning of June, the biggest being on the Kwangtung-Kwangsi border, but it is difficult to determine to which of them these corpses belong. The first bodies to be discovered had already spent some time in the water, and the last ones to be found were in a quite advanced stage of decomposition. The number of bodies washed up on the shores of Hong Kong can only represent a very small percentage of the total number of victims, because the current of the Pearl River into which they must have been thrown flows straight into the sea, depositing only a small proportion of its silt on the shores of Hong Kong, which are situated on one side very far to the east of the estuary.

All revolutions are no doubt inevitably accompanied by massacres, but those which are taking place in China are of a fundamentally different nature from those which attended the establishment of the régime twenty years ago. Today's victims no longer belong to the minority class of exploiters and land-owners (who were put out of action long ago — the last survivors of this race have been completely inactive in the present struggles) but are, on the contrary, peasants, workers and students — the representatives of revolutionary youth, the very sons and daughters of the new China. The red sun of maoism is manifestly no more than a bloodstained, setting sun.

Considerable efforts are being made to boost the soldiers' morale. However privileged their situation, the ranks are after all recruited from among the masses, and they cannot be enthusiastic about the tasks which they are being given at the moment. In Peking on 3 June, twenty thousand military activists from the military regions of Nanking and Shenyang, who had come to take part in a study session on the thought of Mao Tse-tung, were treated to a collective audience with Mao. The propaganda machinery exploited the event in a hysterical fashion. Here are some examples of the cascades of prose which came tumbling out:

"Oceans will dry up, rocks will turn to liquid before our red heart, loyal to Chairman Mao, will ever change. The earth may tremble, the mountains move, but our will to conserve the revolutionary line of Chairman Mao will never shake! The love of our father and mother is not as deep as the love of Chairman Mao! The revolutionary fighters who have been received by our great Commander-in-Chief Chairman Mao and by his close comrade in arms, Vice-chairman Lin, are steeped in unrivalled happiness. Young soldiers are losing sleep — during the night they feverishly put down their resolve in writing, swearing Chairman Mao, O Chairman Mao, we are going to convert the audience which you granted to us into the most tremendous vigour. We are determined to keep to the pattern of the bright example of Vice-chairman Lin to remain eternally loyal to you and eternally loyal to your glorious thoughts, eternally loyal to your revolutionary line. Like comrade Men Ho we wish to think of you in everything, obey you in everything, follow you in every way, do everything for you and make the defence and the realisation of your revolutionary line the sacred mission of our entire existence . . ." (New China News Agency, 5 June)

Then this description of the actual meeting (*Liberation Army Daily*, 3 June):

"The happiest moment which we will never forget for the rest of our lives has arrived! The east is red, the sun comes out! Our great teacher, great leader, great Commander-in-Chief, great helmsman, Chairman Mao, his face rosy and radiant, his body sturdy, comes forward with resolute step and, he takes his place on the platform. At this moment enthusiastic shouts form like a tidal wave, thousands and tens of thousands of red hearts turn towards the red sun, thousands and tens of thousands of smiles of happiness welcome the red sun. . . . O supremely beloved Chairman Mao, ten thousand songs of praise would not be enough to sing of the boundless love which revolutionary fighting men feel for you. Ten thousand red pens could never finish describing the boundless trust which these revolutionary combatants put in you, ten thousand ocean waves would not suffice to extol the limitless adoration which revolutionary combatants have for you, the infinite expanses of space would not be sufficient to contain the feelings of boundless loyalty which revolutionary fighting men possess for you. . . ."

There then follows a description of the insomnia of the soldiers who, when they learnt that they would see Mao on the 3rd, were so excited that they could no longer sleep, etc., etc.

July

On 30 June, the forty-seventh anniversary of the foundation of the party, the *People's Daily*, the *Liberation Army Daily* and the *Red Flag* published a joint editorial. The *Red Flag* has just begun to reappear, and this corresponds to the slide to the left which has started in recent weeks. The *Red Flag* stopped appearing in November 1967, i.e. during the purge of the principal ideologists of the extreme left. In recent months, a bizarre phenomenon has appeared: several doctrinal texts have been published under the heading "joint editorial of the *People's Daily*, the *Liberation Army Daily* and the *Red Flag*", thus attesting to a theoretical survival of the latter publication without it in fact reappearing.

The joint editorial of 30 June deals mainly with the close links which the party should establish and maintain with the masses. It states that the struggle against the revisionist enemy will still be long and arduous, and underlines the importance of the Revolutionary Committees, analysing the main difficulties they face: sabotage, attempts to corrupt committee members and to isolate them from the masses, currents of rehabilitation, and factionalism. The article concludes by saying that, as far as party members are concerned, the "Cultural Revolution" is a test from which they should emerge stronger. Finally, it gives a new definition of the "Cultural Revolution": "The great proletarian Cultural Revolution is a great movement for mobilising the revolutionary masses to proceed to a rectification of the party."

A curious feature of this article (which in principle is supposed to celebrate the party's anniversary) is that it deals much less with the party than with the Revolutionary Committees. The task of reconstructing the party is no longer mentioned: this now seems a very distant objective. (In any case, most observers have increasing doubts about the possibility of the ninth party congress being convened this year. The "Cultural Revolution" is constantly behind schedule: for example, a speech made by Chou En-lai to the planning commission has revealed that it was initially anticipated that all the "seizures of power" would be finished by 1 May of this year.) All the energy is now required for a more urgent task: to impose and maintain the chaotic and disparate Revolutionary Committees, to which the neglect, paralysis and ruin of all the political, administrative and governmental machinery have given a vital importance. (It is an important sign that the adjective "temporary", which originally applied to the power of the committees, is no longer mentioned.)

On 1 July there was a cultural reception to mark the forty-seventh anniversary of the founding of the party. The list of those present leads one to think that it would be more appropriate to celebrate its death: the central committee was represented by only nineteen per cent of its available members, and more than half the audience was composed of soldiers. This cultural evening in fact took on the improper character of a personal homage to Chiang Ch'ing. A performance was given of Peking opera, modernised by her efforts, with the traditional instrumental orchestra being replaced by . . . a piano! This ridiculous story of the piano (a sad one for all lovers of Peking opera, which seems to have been condemned to death) would in itself not be worth mentioning were it not for the fact that official propaganda tried to blow it up into a political event. It is no accident that the piano, the petty-bourgeois fetish *par excellence* (Sundays in the suburbs, Laforgue, etc.) has been chosen as the symbol of the "revolution" in the artistic sphere. The fascination of the "proletarian headquarters" with the putrefied aesthetics of the European petty bourgeoisie of the nineteenth century, piously assimilated and retransmitted by the Soviet Union, is also manifested in painting: the masterpiece which has been presented for the admiration of the masses is a sickly oil-painting (one is tempted to call it a painting in margarine) representing "The Young Mao Tse-tung on the Road to Anyuan". Thus all good red families must in future hang a revolutionary Bouguereau above the revolutionary piano. The work is so affected, so sugary and so out-of-date that one of the countless reproductions sent to Europe got lost in the Vatican and was hung in one of the Pope's waiting-rooms by a priest, who in all good faith thought it was a picture of a missionary.

A dozen articles published one after the other in the *People's Daily* used the pretext of the revolutionary piano in order to celebrate the leading role of Chiang Ch'ing. The puerility and the poverty of the pretext does not detract from the seriousness of the symptoms: the recent emergence of Chiang Ch'ing indicates that Mao has chosen to spur on the "Cultural Revolution" once more. The denunciation of left extremists has now been followed by a struggle against right extremists. This movement has taken the form of a wave of purges among the various Revolutionary Committees, and of the removal of several high-ranking army officers. Even more seriously, it seems that Chou En-lai himself is beginning to lose ground. Not only is he indirectly affected by the attacks which are still being made against Nieh Jung-chen and Li Fu-ch'un but, as the duplicated tracts of groups of Red Guards reveal, he has been directly and sharply attacked by the extreme left, who are accusing him of playing a double game which benefits the revisionists. At a time when the general situation is unstable (there is an increase in violence in the provinces, but even in Peking the régime is no longer able to make itself heard to the various factions which are massacring each other freely, particularly at Tsinghua University), and when the army, the only bastion of order, seems more irresolute than ever, this turn to the left — if it continues — runs the risk of causing the disintegration of the régime.

Several interesting documents have reached Hong Kong during recent weeks. One of them is a military document concerning the new levies of troops in Kwangtung province. The total strength for the whole country is to be increased this year by an extraordinary levy of 600,000 men, 7.2% of whom are to be contributed by Kwangtung. This levy applies to young men between eighteen and twenty-five. For the army and the navy, the recruits are to be chosen as follows: 55% from students and the tertiary sector, 21% from the working class, 19% from the peasants, and 5% from the cadres. For the airforce, the proportion is 82% from the students and tertiary sector, 15% from the working class, 1% from among the peasants and 2% from among the cadres. As for the official reasons for this levy, Lin Piao has alleged to the military service commission that China is confronted by a triple threat — Soviet revisionism, American imperialism (which is still escalating the war in Vietnam, and eventually could even try to launch fresh, unprovoked attacks in Korea), and the remaining forces of the Kuomintang (which, from its exile in Taiwan, could attempt an attack against the mainland). The American threat to Vietnam must certainly be a serious cause for concern: but it is also very probable that because the military leaders have been defeated by their tasks as improvised guardians of order, they have finally judged that the simplest means of bringing the rebels to order is to send them to the barracks.

Another very remarkable document is the text of a speech made by Mao to a group of foreign visitors, on 31 August 1967. This text was printed in a Red Guard leaflet which recently arrived in Hong Kong, where it has been published in the *Ming pao*. Here is a translation:

"In 1962, I declared to the 'assembly of the seven thousand': 'The victory in the struggle between marxism-leninism and revisionism is still undecided — revisionism may well succeed and we shall be beaten.' In referring to the possibility of defeat, my intention was to arouse everyone's vigilance so as to guard better against the danger of revisionism. Inside the party, the struggle between the two classes, between the two roads, continues to exist; these facts cannot be denied. . . .

The Cultural Revolution began in the winter of 1965 with Yao Wen-yuan's article denouncing the essay 'The Dismissal of Hai Jui'. *At that moment the country was controlled by the revisionists; it was impossible to do anything, they had everything under their control.* At the time, I had initially proposed that comrade XX should try to have an article written criticising 'The Dismissal of Hai Jui', but *in this red metropolis* [i.e. Peking, *S.L.*] *we were reduced to impotence, and it was necessary for me to go to Shanghai to be able to begin to organise anything.* Finally, when the article had been edited, I read it through three times and thought it was basically acceptable. I instructed comrade XX to have it published, and I suggested to him that it be shown first to several leading comrades on the party's central organs. But comrade XX suggested it be published straight away as it stood, without letting the comrades (Chou) En-lai and K'ang Sheng read it first. [At this moment, Lin X intervened: 'There are some people who pretend that comrade Mao Tse-tung is waging a factional fight against another faction and that all the leading comrades, all those who today have prestige in the eyes of the revolutionary masses, had all been warned in advance by Chairman Mao about what the very basis of the Cultural Revolution would be, so that they could avoid making mistakes. As I see it, the Cultural Revolution has on the contrary been a sort of closed-book examination for us: all those who have closely followed marxism-leninism and the thought of Mao Tse-tung have naturally found themselves in the ranks of the proletarian revolutionaries again. For this reason, I say: you must apply the thought of Mao when you understand it, and even when for a moment you may not understand it.']*

After the article by Comrade Yao Wen-yuan had appeared, it was reproduced throughout the country *except in Peking and Hunan, which did not print it.* Afterwards I suggested that it be published as a pamphlet, *but this project was opposed and could not be put into practice.*

But Yao Wen-yuan's article was *simply the signal* for the Cultural Revolution. Consequently, in the central leadership we applied ourselves in particular to supervising the final touches of the '16 May Memorandum'. As our enemy was extremely subtle, the first signal had set him in motion, and therefore we too had to act. This 'Memorandum' took up clearly and explicitly the problem of the struggle between the two lines. *At the time, the majority was not in agreement with my outlook, at certain moments I remained absolutely alone, while everyone said that my outlook was out of date.* The only way open to me was to submit my opinions to debate at the second session of the eighth central committee. At the end of the debate, I eventually obtained a fraction over half the votes. And even then many did not support me: neither Li Ching-ch'üan nor Liu Lan-t'ao did so. Comrade (Ch'en) Po-ta went to look for them and discuss it with them, but they both answered: 'I did not support you in Peking; the same thing applies now.' When all was said and done, the only thing I could do was to push the experiment further and to see what could come of it! After the second session of the eighth central committee, the crucial moment came during the three months of October, November and December 1966. Because of the denunciation of the reactionary capitalist line, the internal contradictions within the party were publicly exacerbated. Let me just mention something in passing: the fact is that during the process

---

* This memorable fib indicates that "Lin X" must certainly be Lin Piao. (See the editorial of the *Liberation Army Daily,* 7 September 1967, which enshrined this pearl for the edification of the masses.) Besides betraying Lin's intellectual limitations, the argument in question also explains why Lin became for a while the sovereign's favourite. As for comrade XX (the double X indicates a name in two characters, and the context implies a very intimate and unofficial relationship), my hypothesis is that this is probably Chiang Ch'ing. "He" and "she" are homophones in Chinese, and the transcription does not necessarily reveal the gender of the personal pronoun.

of denouncing the reactionary capitalist line, the great majority of soldiers, peasants and rank-and-file cadres let themselves be led astray. If we now study how these comrades who went astray should be judged, I myself have always thought that the great majority of workers, soldiers and peasants were good, that the overwhelming majority of the party members were good. At all stages of the proletarian revolution they were the principal force, and there was no good reason why it should be any different where the Cultural Revolution was concerned. The great mass of the workers, peasants and soldiers, being involved in hard toil, can of course have only a limited understanding of what takes place in the superstructure. Add to this the fact that the rank-and-file party cadres have an ardent love for the party and its leaders. Thus, like the faction in power which follows the capitalist road while brandishing the red flag in order to fight the red flag, they went astray; and they were still unable to retrace their steps even after quite a long period of time. There are historical factors involved: if they made mistakes, so what! Once they are corrected, let bygones be bygones. They have again become the major force in the movement, which has always gone forward. The workers of Shanghai were responsible for the 'January tempest'. Following them, the workers and peasants of the whole country rose up; this is the law of development of every revolution. The democratic revolution was carried out in the same way. The 4 May movement was the work of the intellectuals, and it fully demonstrated the prophetic quality of the intellectuals' ideas; but when it was a question of carrying through the revolution to the end, with expeditions on a large scale like the 'Northern Expedition', this could only be done by relying on those who were the real masters in this period, i.e. the workers, soldiers and peasants, acting as the main force. Workers, soldiers and peasants can be reduced to workers and peasants, as soldiers are basically only workers and peasants in military uniform. The denunciation of the reactionary capitalist line was at first led by the intellectuals and the mass of the student youth. But in order to seize power with the 'January tempest', we had to rely on the real masters of our epoch. The intellectuals have very lively minds for analysing and perceiving problems, but they are victims of the very limitations of their specialisation; they are incapable of carrying the revolution

right through to the end, since they are unable to rid themselves of their hesitant nature.

In broad outline the Cultural Revolution can be divided
into four stages, from the point of view of strategy and
tactics. The first stage goes from the publication of comrade
Yao Wen-yuan's article to the second session of the eighth
central committee. Essentially, this was the stage of setting
the Cultural Revolution in motion. The second runs from
the second session to the 'January tempest': the stage of
the turning-point in the movement's orientation. The third
covers the seizure of power with the 'January tempest', the
'great alliance' and the 'triple union'. The fourth covers the
whole period beginning with the articles by Ch'i Pen-yü,
'Patriotism or treason?' and 'The essential harmfulness of
the *Spiritual Formation of the Communist* is that this
work denies the dictatorship of the proletariat'. The third
and the fourth stages were devoted entirely to the problem
of the seizure of power. The fourth stage is to strive to take
power from revisionism and capitalism at the ideological
level. This stage also marks a decisive phase in the struggle
to the death in which the two classes, the two roads, the two
lines confront each other. It concerns the major problem,
the real problem. Originally, after the 'January tempest', the
party leadership was very much concerned with the 'great
alliance', but did not achieve any tangible results. It was subsequently realised that these subjective desires did not correspond to the objective law of class struggle, because the
political forces of each class and of each faction still had to
appear in their pure form. The capitalist class and the petty
bourgeoisie have no strength, you unite them and they fall
apart; the attitude of the party leadership is now to try and
hasten the process and not to impose a premature cohesion.
Pulling at the stem does not help the plant to grow. The
subjective will of individuals cannot change this law of class
struggle. There are abundant illustrations of this which can
prove it to be true. In the municipality of XX there is an
assembly of workers' delegates, an assembly of Red Guard
delegates, and an assembly of peasant delegates; with the
exception of the peasant delegates, who still get on relatively
well, the workers and the Red Guards have heated brawls.
The way things are going, it will be necessary once again to
reconstitute the organisation of the Revolutionary Committee of the XX municipality.

Originally, I dreamed of training a certain number of men among the intellectuals who could take over from me; but now in the light of the present situation, my calculations were quite wrong. As I see it, the intellectuals, including young people who are still working at their studies, members and non-members of the party, have retained a bourgeois view of the world. The sphere of culture and education has been completely dominated by revisionism. Bourgeois thought flows in their veins; that is why the intellectuals who want to make revolution must take care to really reform their view of the world in this decisive phase of the struggle between the two classes, the two roads, the two lines. Without this they run the risk of starting on a course which runs counter to that of the revolution. At this point, I would like to ask you all a question. In your opinion, what is the goal of the great proletarian Cultural Revolution? [Someone in the audience replies, 'It is the struggle against the faction which follows the capitalist road inside the party.'] To struggle against the faction which follows the capitalist road within the party is the principal task, but it is not the goal. The goal is to resolve this problem of the world view, to tear out the roots of revisionism. The central authorities have continually emphasised the need for self-education, because a world view is not something which can be artificially added from the outside. Thought-reform is only effective when external factors have come into contact with internal factors, and it is the latter which are the most important. If we do not succeed in reforming the world view, the only result of the Cultural Revolution will be that some two thousand members of the faction following the capitalist road will have been eliminated, and next time perhaps four thousand will re-emerge. This time we have had to pay a considerable price for the Cultural Revolution. Although it has resolved the problem of the struggle between the two classes, the two roads, these problems will not be resolved by one or two, even three or four Cultural Revolutions. After the present Cultural Revolution, at least fifteen years will be required to consolidate its gains, and in the space of a century it will be necessary to start the process again twice or three times. We must see things from this angle — the need to tear out the roots of revisionism, and to increase our ability to block the road to revisionism at all times.

Now I would like to ask you another question. What is

the faction which follows the capitalist road? [Silence in the audience.] Well, the capitalist faction consists of people who, once they are in power, set out on the road which leads to capitalism! In other words, those people who actively participated in the struggle against the 'three giants' during the period of the democratic revolution, but whose enthusiasm waned when, after the Liberation, we had to eliminate the bourgeois class. They agreed with the elimination of the landlords and with redistribution of the land, but after the Liberation, when it was a question of collectivising the land, they no longer agreed. They do not follow the road to socialism and they are in power; therefore, should they not be called the faction in power which follows the capitalist road? Imagine, by contrast, an old revolutionary who faces new problems: if he has a totally proletarian world view, he will resolutely pursue the socialist road. A man who has a bourgeois world view will follow the capitalist road. The bourgeois class thus seeks to transform the world in the image of its bourgeois world view. In the Cultural Revolution there are some people who made mistakes in the line they followed; it could be said that some were old revolutionaries faced with new problems. But precisely because they made these mistakes, this indicates that — old cadres that they were — they had not yet succeeded in ridding themselves of their bourgeois world view. The old comrades will still have to face many new problems; the only way of guaranteeing their loyalty to the socialist road is to bring about a complete proletarian revolution in their thought. I ask you all, in your opinion, when all is said and done, how can we proceed concretely from socialism to communism? This is the great question facing our country, the great question facing the whole world.

In my opinion, the spirit of the Red Guards is full of energy. This is very good. Only you cannot go on stage; if you go on stage today, you will be chased off tomorrow. This argument has been repeated by one of the vice-chairmen of the governmental council; but it should not have been. The problem concerning the Red Guards is to train them. When they make certain mistakes, they should not be given a cold shower.

There are some people who pretend that elections are a good thing, very democratic. 'Elections', in my opinion, is a very fine phrase. I cannot believe that there are any true elections. Suppose that the Peking region elected me as a deputy to the National Assembly. In Peking, when all is said and done, how many people really understand me? There are people who maintain that the Chinese people passionately love peace. In my opinion, I do not believe that their love for peace has reached such a level, I rather think they are fond of a scrap.*

Regarding the cadres, in the first place we should get it into our heads that more than 95% of them are good or relatively good. . . . Even those who have followed the capitalist road should, when they have corrected their mistakes, be authorised to return and participate in the revolution after a long period of re-education. The fundamentally bad elements are not numerous. Among the masses, they represent at the most 5%; within the party, 1 or 2%. Those who obstinately follow the capitalist road are only a small handful, but they must be the main object of our attacks, because they are immensely harmful and influential. Thus our main task in the Cultural Revolution is to defeat them. The bad elements among the masses represent at most 5%, but they are dispersed and powerless. Yet for all that, 5% means 35 million individuals; if they were to organise themselves in an army and oppose us in an organised way, they would pose a serious problem; but they are dispersed and powerless. Therefore, they are the main target of the Cultural Revolution. But we must be increasingly vigilant and, especially during the decisive phase of the struggle, we must prevent the bad elements from creeping in. That is why the two fundamental premises of the 'great alliance' are: first, 'to eliminate the individual and to establish the collective', and second, that it is necessary to go through a period of struggle; without going through a period of struggle, nothing valuable can be produced. Now this fourth stage of the Cultural Revolution is the crucial stage in the struggle between the two classes, the two roads, and the two lines. Therefore sufficient time must be devoted

---

* From "In my opinion, the spirit of the Red Guards . . ." up to this point, the text seems to be rather disjointed and incoherent. I suspect that this is a corrupted version, and that at this point several fragments belonging to different speeches have been telescoped together. The final paragraph, "Regarding the cadres . . .", is a coherent whole, but I doubt that it belongs to the speech of 31 August, because the problem it deals with could only interest a Chinese audience.

to a criticism of it. This question has been discussed in the central organ of the Cultural Revolution; some people have proposed 1 May next year [1968—*S.L.*], but as far as the question of timing is concerned, the most important thing will be to submit to the laws of the class struggle."

August-September

The left zigzag which has taken place in the last few months, with the denunciation of rehabilitations and the fight against compromise with the enemy, was simply the last agonised spasm of the "Cultural Revolution". The death-knell began to sound for the last survivors of revolutionary activism at the end of July, when the order was given to the "groups of workers and soldiers for propagating the thought of Mao Tse-tung" to occupy the universities and carry out a general clean-up. In order to make this action quite unambiguous, Mao sent a parcel of mangoes at the beginning of August to the first of these repressive battalions occupying Tsinghua university. This is a symbol of the supreme leader's personal concern for the men charged with extinguishing the last sparks of the revolution, and has been celebrated enthusiastically throughout the country. The Red Guards have been given notice of an order to submit completely and definitively to the workers and soldiers, who are now alone entrusted with maoist orthodoxy. On 15 August, the *People's Daily* and the *Liberation Army Daily* published the "most recent directive of Chairman Mao": "Our country has seven hundred million inhabitants, and the working class is its leading class; its leading role in the Cultural Revolution and in all sectors of activity must be emphasised." On the 25th, the *Red Flag* carried an article by Yao Wen-yuan which again underlined the fact that the actions of the Red Guards had anarchist tendencies and had provoked the resentment of the masses.

Between May and July the hesitation of the maoist authorities, who at one moment seemed to want to leave things in the rebels' hands again, hampered the foundation of new Revolutionary Committees. The rebels, who were expecting a new endorsement from the top, took heart for a moment and put up a desperate resistance to these puppet committees. The local authorities, who were themselves uncertain of Peking's intentions, remained watchful and prudent. As a result, only three new committees appeared in three months: Shensi, Liaoning and Szechuan (all formed in May). The first two have a quite unexpected proportion of new men among their deputy leaders: six out of ten in Shensi, and five out of fifteen in Liaoning. Of course, each of these committees is as a rule chaired either by a bureaucrat (Shensi) or a soldier (Liaoning and Szechuan); and in the case of Szechuan, where the chairmanship has been conferred on Chang Kuo-hua, a notorious butcher of Red Guards, any participation by the rebels among the deputy leaders is naturally out of the question. But although the Shensi and Liaoning committees could not claim to be genuinely revolutionary, they nevertheless began to differ from the routine of the previous committees, and to acquire a pinkish hue. Was there going to be genuine revolutionary participation in the formation of future committees? It is easy to imagine how uneasy the authorities must have been in the face of such a development. This dangerous tendency has therefore been repressed: no Revolutionary Committees were established in June and July. The maoists hastily set their house in order, Mao sent his gift of mangoes and the rebels were finally disowned.

Any ambiguity has since disappeared, and the "Cultural Revolution" has found the right road again. The last five Revolutionary Committees were founded within the space of barely three weeks, one after the other (Yunnan, 13 August; Fukien, 19 August; Kwangsi, 26 August; Sinkiang, 5 September; and Tibet, 5 September). This formally marks the "total victory" of the "Cultural Revolution". The last five committees are most reassuringly orthodox: they are composed exclusively of former soldiers and bureaucrats, and they include *no* representatives of the revolutionary masses. In Sinkiang and Tibet, the committees were set up with particular alacrity: they merely named the military commander of the region and his political commissars as leader and deputy leaders of the Revolutionary Committee, without even resorting to the collaboration of party bureaucrats. In Tibet in particular, this means that the leadership of the Revolutionary Committee is entirely in the hands of the army of occupation, as the Tibetans themselves are denied any representation.

The double farce of Sinkiang and Tibet on 5 September completed the establishment of Revolutionary Committees throughout the country; all that remained was to celebrate the "total victory" of the "Cultural Revolution" with a big rally in Peking on 7 September.

Chiang Ch'ing cut an incredible figure at this rally. It isn't usual for the régime's officials to express their private anger and frustration in their public speeches. Chiang Ch'ing's short improvised speech (it lasted scarcely five minutes) was a memorable exception to this rule. The abrupt and disconnected speech began thus: "*It was only this morning* that I learned of the decision to convene this large meeting to celebrate the establishment of Revolutionary Committees throughout China. At very short notice, I have been asked to say a few words. . . ." It would have been very difficult to convene such a vast rally on the morning itself; the fact that they neglected to inform Chiang Ch'ing about it beforehand (she is the deputy leader of the central Cultural Revolution Group!) displays a quite remarkable degree of insolence and says a lot about the political credibility of the activists of the "Cultural Revolution". She went on for a few more sentences, asking the victors to show mercy to her former troops, and trying to sweeten the bitter pill of defeat for them:

"Among the young fighters, some individuals may have made this or that mistake. It is our duty to help them to correct their mistakes. . . . On the orders of our great leader, Chairman Mao, the working class has now, since 27 July, entered the arena of struggle-criticism-transformation of the superstructure. The People's Liberation Army is supporting it. The young Red Guard fighters and all the teachers and cadres who are ready to make the revolution must welcome this working-class action and follow its directives. . . . Being the leading class, the working class should at all times strive to protect the young Red Guard fighters, to help them and educate them. . . . We still have much work to do, we have to consolidate and reconstruct the party, and to purge the class ranks. We are still going to encounter many things which we do not understand. We must therefore follow the teachings of our great leader, Chairman Mao, and be on our guard against arrogance and impulsiveness. Raise aloft the glorious red banner of Mao Tse-tung thought and go forward to victory! That is all I have to say."

In contrast to Mao's wife, Chou En-lai seemed very relaxed and completely in his element, like the "cat who offers his warm sympathy to the mouse".

Now that this formality of the "Cultural Revolution" has finally come to an end, it will be necessary to get down to the real job: reconstructing the party. This enormous task is still at the stage of pious vows, and no specific plan is yet visible. The ninth congress was supposed to have taken place before the National Day, but it stood no chance of being able to meet this date and seems to have been put off until doomsday. But the whole tenor of current propaganda, re-emphasising as it does the leading role of the working class, is certainly the prelude to a reconstitution of the apparatus — of an apparatus free from "rebel" influences. Obviously an enterprise of such scope cannot be carried out within a few weeks. It will be a long time before the party has an effective hold over the country again, if it ever does. Meanwhile it is the countryside which is profiting most from this lack of authority. The traditional clans in the villages have never been so free, while the lower cadres, having already burned their fingers, are prudently abstaining from any action that might provoke the wrath of those under their command. The peasants are using their new and temporary autonomy to consume as much as possible and to deliver as little as possible to the state. While Peking is religiously celebrating the victory of its "revolution", in the villages the pigs are being slaughtered and they are playing cards, very cynically. Such a state of demobilisation in the countryside is unprecedented in the history of the régime. Ironically, it is precisely this kind of situation which proves in the long run to benefit agriculture the most.

While the régime has gained nothing by the "Cultural Revolution", it is a personal victory for Mao Tse-tung. He has eliminated his opponents, recovered the power which was gradually taken from him after 1959, and obtained a decisive confirmation of his position as supreme leader. He has paid a heavy price for this, for the old potentate reigns over nothing but a formless political wilderness. In fact, this kind of situation has its advantages for Mao. The great leap backward of the "Cultural Revolution" has brought China noticeably nearer to the ideal "blank page" which the incorrigible artist has always dreamed of bringing it to.

The particular domain which Mao is now undertaking to make into a desert is education. I have already shown above how in the past all Mao's attempts to destroy the universities were sabotaged by his opponents. In 1959, under the joint influence of Lu Ting-yi (director of the Department of Propaganda of the central committee, subsequently purged in 1966) and Yang Hsiu-feng (Minister of Education until 1964, purged in 1966, attempted suicide in January 1967), Mao's proposed reforms of the preceding year were gradually eliminated. The level of studies rose again, and the normal duration of the study cycle was re-established. After 1961 nothing remained of Mao's reform, and Ch'en Yi could tell the students calmly, "Your first task at school is to study." In 1965, on the eve of the "Cultural Revolution", Mao once again showed a desire for reform, but once again he was effectively

opposed. Now at last he has some elbow room, and can give
free rein to his obsessive hostility towards the "specialised
disciplines" and "scientific authorities". One aspect of this
obsession, which observers have perhaps not emphasised enough,
is its essentially traditionalist and conservative character. Mao
Tse-tung is imbued with the Confucian mentality, even more
deeply than he realises. The maoist primacy of the "red" over the
"expert" echoes the *chün-tzu pu ch'i* of Confucius (literally, "a
gentleman is not a vessel": i.e. his talent is not limited to a
determined capacity, nor enslaved by a specific function). Revolutionary "virtue" should alone suffice for maoist man, just as
humanitarian virtue (*jen*) should in itself be enough for Confucian
man. The possession of this virtue makes any specialised technical ability unnecessary. Mao's statements about "paper tigers"
must also be understood in the Confucian perspective; this idealist
conception, attributing to man's revolutionary will alone a force
superior to that of nuclear arms, is entirely derived from the
Book of Rites: "What virtue accomplishes is superior, what
technique accomplishes is inferior." Maoism shows many uncon-
scious relics of Confucianism. One of the most remarkable
is its optimistic faith in the perfectibility of man, and its
belief in the omnipotence of education. The way in which the
thought of Mao Tse-tung is sanctified and utilised by the ruling
class as an instrument of power is a faithful reproduction of the
scholastic fate of Confucian thought and of its transformation
into an ideology serving the imperial bureaucracy. Mao's selected
writings are learnt by heart and religiously recited just as the
"Four Books" used to be. (Note further that the *Quotations from
Chairman Mao* are designated in Chinese by the term *yü-lu*; this
term, which goes back to the Buddhist literature of the T'ang
period, subsequently became essentially associated with the neo-
Confucian philosophy of the Sung, who sanctioned its use.)

October

The National Day was rather dull, and this merely confirms the
recent course: the workers are placed stage front, the army
appears as pillar of the régime, and the Red Guards are reduced
to the role of extras. People are still talking about reconstructing
the party, but nothing substantial has been accomplished yet in
this direction. Anhwei province has made December its deadline
for completing the selection of new candidates for the party. So
far, to my knowledge, it is the only province which has done
anything concrete.

Knowledgeable observers reckon that the ninth party congress will probably be held at the beginning of next spring, so as to finish before the 1 May celebrations.

On 16 October, the *Red Flag* published a sensational article entitled "Absorb new blood from the proletariat". The importance of this text lies not so much in the news that the "Chinese Khrushchev" has been stripped of all his posts both inside and outside the party" and that "he has been finally swept into the dustbin of history" (since the "Chinese Khrushchev" has already been dragged through the mud, the news has rather lost its impact), as in the denunciation of the democratic voting procedures which are theoretically the rule in the party. "A really revolutionary power should get rid of this formalistic and superstitious respect for the voting system, the methods of which cannot correspond to the requirements of proletarian democracy." More precisely, that means (but didn't we know this already?) that Mao and his supporters are still in a minority in the legal organs of the party. The injection of new blood, therefore, would not take place from the base — this would be much too dangerous for the maoist authorities — but from the top, with the small leading group selecting "delegates" who are unconditionally loyal to it. The new party thus formed will then officially sanction Mao's personal power. This sudden scorn for the democratic expression of majority opinion is rather amusing, since it goes directly against a principle enunciated by Mao himself — a principle considered so important that it was thought worthy of inclusion in the "little red book":

> "One of the principles of discipline in the party is that the minority obeys the majority. After the minority has had its opinion rejected, it must rally to the motion adopted by the majority. If need be, it is possible to propose a new debate at a subsequent meeting, otherwise it is forbidden to show the least opposition at the level of action." (*Mao chu-hsi yü-lu*, ch.26, p.220).

Needless to say, Mao himself has always avoided observing this rule. His practical principle of action, which is well illustrated by the "Cultural Revolution", had always been: "When the majority is of my opinion, one must submit to the majority; when the majority is against me, one must obey the minority" (and when the minority is really very weak indeed, you bolster it with the army — Shanghai, February 1967).

Who is governing the country while it waits for the party to rise from its ashes? At the very top, for form's sake, the slogans

issued to the country are generally being put out in the name of
the central committee of the party, the state council, the Cultural
Revolution Group and the military commission. In reality,
the first two of these organs are paralysed or three-quarters
destroyed, and the third has been almost completely purged.
Actually China is now ruled by a mere handful of individuals —
fourteen, to be precise — of whom half are not even members of
the central committee. They derive their authority either from
the personal links which connect them to Mao or Lin, or from
the pressure groups which they represent. Politically they are a
disparate group. Far from being monolithic, they seem to be
more a temporary alliance which is based on unstable compromises and temporarily held together by force of circumstances.
The composition of the group will certainly be subject to alteration, depending on what happens in the power struggle. Here
is a list of the fourteen individuals, in the hierarchical order which
the official communiqués always assign them:

1. Mao Tse-tung: chairman of the central committee, member of the standing committee of the politbureau, chairman
of the military commission.

2. Lin Piao: vice-chairman of the central committee, member
of the standing committee of the politbureau, vice-chairman
of the military commission, Defence Minister.

3. Chou En-lai: member of the standing committee of the
politbureau, chairman of the state council (head of the
government).

4. Ch'en Po-ta: member of the standing committee of the
politbureau, head of the Cultural Revolution Group, director
of the *Red Flag*, Mao's private secretary.

5. K'ang Sheng: member of the standing committee of the
politbureau; adviser to the Cultural Revolution Group; responsible for the secret service.

6. Chiang Ch'ing: Mao's wife, deputy leader of the Cultural
Revolution Group.

7. Chang Ch'un-ch'iao: Mme. Mao's protégé, deputy leader
of the Cultural Revolution Group, leader of the Shanghai
Revolutionary Committee, first political commissar of the
Nanking military region.

8. Yao Wen-yuan: Mao's son-in-law(?)*, member of the

---

* It seems certain that Yao enjoyed some kind of direct, private link with
Mao and Chiang Ch'ing, but the "son-in-law" theory has now generally
been abandoned.

Cultural Revolution Group (the movement's scribe), deputy leader of the Shanghai Revolutionary Committee.

9. Hsieh Fu-chih: alternate member of the politbureau; vice-chairman of the state council, Minister of Security, leader of the Revolutionary Committee of Peking municipality.

10. Huang Yung-sheng: alternate member of the central committee, chief of the general staff of the People's Liberation Army; secretary of the military commission; leader of the Kwangtung Revolutionary Committee.

11. Wu Fa-hsien: first deputy chief of the general staff, deputy secretary of the military commission; commander-in-chief of the airforce.

12. Yeh Ch'ün: Lin Piao's wife, responsible for the administrative organs of the defence council.

13. Wang Tung-hsing: Vice-minister of Security, director of the administrative organs of the central committee (Mao's former bodyguard).

14. Wen Yü-cheng: deputy chief of the general staff, responsible for the administrative organs of the defence council, commander of the Peking garrison.

The presence of several survivors from the "Cultural Revolution" tendency (4, 6, 7, 8) should not be allowed to create any illusions about how much influence this group has left. They are now generals without an army, and have only been rescued from the massacre because their intimate personal relationships with Mao guarantee immunity. The massive presence of the military (who make up half the group) does not necessarily imply that Lin Piao's power is prevailing; with the exception of his own wife, none of Lin's close collaborators are among them. Chou En-lai represents the bureaucratic and governmental apparatus, Huang Yung-sheng the interests of the great regional commanders. K'ang Sheng embodies the hidden influence of the secret services and the intelligence network, Hsieh Fu-chih has authority over the police. Each of these four occupies his own isolated but powerful citadel. They make up a fluid coalition whose leader seems to be Chou. This coalition (the "faction playing a double game", to use the expression forged by its opponents) controls the key sectors and really seems to have the wind in its sails; but the last waves of the "Cultural Revolution" have not completely died down, so it can still move only slowly and prudently.

At the head of this odd little band, which is plagued by jealousies and secret rivalries, Mao seems increasingly like an old emperor surrounded by his private court. The cult of Mao has now been imposed on the whole country and one significant (and bewildering) phenomenon must be pointed out: the resurrection of the old feudal concept of *chung* (literally, "faithfulness" or "loyalism") to describe the feelings which the populace must cultivate towards the supreme leader. It may be difficult for the Western reader who is unfamiliar with the context of Chinese history to appreciate the full importance of this. The notion of *chung* was a specific product of the old imperial despotism; it describes the feudal bond of unconditional personal loyalty which unites the subject with the sovereign and the servant with the master. The fact that the "Cultural Revolution", by way of an epilogue, has had the audacity or ignorance to pick this dubious relic out of the dustbin in which the republican revolution of 1911 thought it had buried it for ever, tells us a lot about the "revolutionary" nature of the present régime.

The effectiveness with which the army transmits the will of the little group of fourteen to the nation varies from one province to another. As I have already said, Lin Piao's authority is to a large extent counterbalanced by the confederation of big regional commanders: Huang Yung-sheng (Canton), Hsü Shih-yu (Nanking), Han Hsien-ch'u (Foochow), Ch'en Hsi-lien (Shenyang). The power of the army is spreading and consolidating. The leading role which has in theory been assigned to the workers is in reality a cover for the universal grip of the military. Thus soldiers are always being added to the "workers' groups for propagating the thought of Mao Tse-tung" which have taken charge of the schools, and these soldiers in fact take over the leadership. The "detachments of support for the left" (*chih-tso pu-tui*) are shock troops, directly dependent on the central military authorities. They are sent into all parts of the country at very short notice, and are authorised to re-establish order by any means the situation might require, with authority over local administrations and garrisons. The attitude of the army towards the people has changed noticeably, and become harsher. This was inevitable from the moment when policing responsibilities were handed over to the army. The previous stoicism displayed towards agitators and Red Guards has given way to ruthless repression.

November

The event of the month has been the publication (in the *People's Daily*, 2 November) of the "communiqué of the twelfth enlarged session of the eighth central committee of the Chinese Communist

Party." This session took place between 13 and 31 October, under Mao's chairmanship. On the whole, the communiqué simply ratifies Mao's policy and its course since 1966, in the "Cultural Revolution" — but it does make one salient point. In the passage about Liu Shao-ch'i, he is mentioned by name for the first time:

> "The plenary session has ratified the report on the rebel, traitor and renegade Liu Shao-ch'i presented by the commission of inquiry formed by the central committee. . . . The plenary session has unanimously decided to expel Liu Shao-ch'i from the party forever, and to deprive him of all his official positions inside and outside the party."

Some remarks on this "twelfth enlarged plenary session": several features strike one immediately. Nineteen days is a long time for a session to bring forth just this one decision. We are told that both Mao and Lin gave important speeches during the session, but *not one word of their contents has been revealed.* The communiqué is laconic to the point of emptiness. Not a single photograph of the session has been published in the press. There is no mention of the number of participants. In fact, this session seems to display enormous irregularities which violate the party constitution. Upon examination, it shows itself to be not only curiously "enlarged", but also very restricted: according to the official communiqué, the participants at this session were (1) *some* members and alternate members of the central committee; (2) *all* the members of the Cultural Revolution Group; (3) the main leaders of the Revolutionary Committees in the provinces, municipalities and autonomous regions; (4) the leaders of the army. As for the central committee, it seems likely that the number of members present cannot have reached a quorum. Of the 120 or so members of the committee, more than forty have been denounced by name during the "Cultural Revolution". Of the remaining eighty, more than half have been attacked. The elements who are acceptable by maoist criteria can represent at most only a third of the membership of the central committee (as some indication, only a quarter of the members showed up in public at the National Day celebrations). The "restricted" character of this session therefore invalidates its decisions. Its "enlargement" is also a violation of the party constitution. In theory, individuals who are not members of the central committee may be present at meetings, but they cannot take part in the voting. Normally a terminological distinction is made between "participants" (*ch'u-hsi*), i.e. members of the committee, and mere "observers" (*lieh-hsi*), who are non-members and therefore non-voters. This time the distinction has been abolished, and non-members of the committee have taken part in the voting. Finally, the power to deprive Liu of his positions inside the party belongs not to the central committee but to the party congress alone. As for his position as head of state, only the National Assembly has the power to take this away.

All these legal objections were brushed aside in advance by the famous article in the *Red Flag* (16 October, see p. 146) denouncing the bourgeois superstition of democratic voting procedures. The motives for this article can now be understood more easily. By discrediting the procedures laid down by the party constitution, it was preparing public opinion and muzzling the critics who might have been scandalised by this violation of the constitution. It announced on the 16th (when the second session had only been in progress for three days) that the "Cultural Revolution long ago deprived Liu of all his positions both inside and outside the party and has thrown him into the dustbin of history", and thereby confronted the twelfth session with a *fait accompli*; this immediately disheartened the opposition and dictated in advance the "conclusions" which the twelfth session was to arrive at a fortnight later by "unanimous vote".

The aim of this comedy was to ward off all the opposition elements in the apparatus, and to finally give Mao's power a semblance of legality again. The maoist minority has used this conjuring trick to assume the mantle of legitimate authority, while the majority group opposing it has been passed off as a tiny handful of traitors. By resorting to such an exceptional procedure, Mao has confirmed that he is still in a minority and is not yet in a position to confront the legal organs of the party. The latent threat posed by the opposition is still so considerable that in order to meet it he has had to improvise this parody of legality, without being able to wait for the ninth congress to be convened. The preparations for the ninth congress are bound to run up against considerable obstacles: if the maoists have to resort to the lame formula of an "enlarged session" of the central committee in order to carry out something for which the congress is responsible, it is because the convening of the congress is still a mere hypothesis. The communiqué from the twelfth session rightly says that "the conditions are now ripe for convening the ninth congress", and that it "will be convened at an opportune moment": but no date has been fixed.

On the 25th, the *People's Daily* republished the text of the report which Mao Tse-tung presented to the second plenary session of the seventh central committee on 5 March 1949. The publication of this text has been greeted with a fanfare throughout the country, and the population invited to study it. This long document, which was first published on the eve of the change of régime (the Liberation Army had not yet crossed the Yang-tze), defined the main policy lines to be followed by the party as soon as it controlled the whole country.

This text is today being held up as proof of the fact that the conflict between Mao and Liu is an old one, and that it dates from the establishment of the People's Republic. In reality, although this point is underlined in the commentaries, it is far from apparent upon reading the report itself. It would be easier to use the report to demonstrate the opposite.

Why, then, has it been chosen for distribution now, with all the additional publicity? The most remarkable thing about the text is its pragmatism and realism. Several lessons can be drawn from this, which might well be applied to current problems and provide a justification for abandoning the doctrinal imperatives of the "Cultural Revolution".

The first paragraph of the report emphasised the major political role that the *army* would be called on to play once the whole country had been liberated. Since the party did not have sufficient personnel at its disposal to organise the population immediately, this fundamental task of political organisation of the nation had to devolve temporarily on the military. This is now reality once again.

The report then indicated that the initial phase, when the countryside had encircled the towns, was to be followed by an opposite phase, and that it would be necessary to transfer the centres of political action to urban China. Moreover, it stated that "contrary to what certain confused people believe" the motive force of the revolution *was not supplied by the masses in the broad sense, but by the proletariat alone.* Again, this coincides exactly with current policies.

It analysed the policy that was to be adopted towards heterogeneous, neutral or theoretically hostile elements, whose collaboration was needed by the party: the intellectuals and the national bourgeoisie. It condemned both the rightist error in this respect, which consisted in giving full rein to these various elements, and the leftist error, which was to shut the door on them. It laid down a policy that was rigid in its strategic objectives but supple and realistic in its tactics.

Are they trying to establish a parallel between the tasks of reconstruction which China faced at the time of the Liberation and those which she faces following the "victory" of the "Cultural Revolution"? Undoubtedly one of the main lessons they intend to draw from the 1949 report lies in their dual condemnation of "right opportunists" and "left adventurists"; the central idea is that absolute intransigence of principles must at times be accompanied by certain transitory compromises with various individuals whose abilities the party cannot afford to lose.

December

An interesting document has reached us: the text of a speech made by Wen Yü-ch'eng in about March or April of this year to a group of soldiers from the shock brigades providing "support to the left". This speech contains a calendar of operations for the "Cultural Revolution". By comparing this calendar with the developments which have actually taken place, we can measure how far Peking has once again deceived itself in its estimate of the situation:

> "The provinces which have not succeeded in establishing a Revolutionary Committee by 1 May will be placed under military administration. [This is in fact what did eventually happen, although a sense of decency demanded that these military administrations be decorated with the title of "Revolutionary Committees"—S.L.] The current situation cannot drag on any longer; all activity has been paralysed. In May and June a vast rectification campaign will begin, particularly in the spheres of education and defence. In July preparations will begin for the ninth party congress, which will be convened in August or September. Thus, according to the plans laid down by the central committee and by Chairman Mao, the new forces will occupy the platform during the National Day celebrations."

We saw what actually became of these plans.

All over China, certain strata of the urban population are in the course of migrating to the countryside on an unprecedented scale. This has happened intermittently in the past, but the solemn publication of the "latest instruction of Chairman Mao" (21 December) has given it a new impulse, and seems to be the first phase in a basic remoulding of the Chinese economy and society. At first sight Mao's "latest instruction" does not seem very striking:

"It is extremely important for young intellectuals to go into the villages to be re-educated by the poor and lower-middle peasants. The cadres and other inhabitants of the towns will have to be convinced of the necessity of sending their sons and daughters to the countryside in mobilised masses when they have finished their studies at the secondary or university level. The comrades of the villages must make them welcome."

The *People's Daily* has echoed this directive from the Chairman, describing the start of an exodus by the urban population to the countryside. In the example described (in Kansu), it is no longer just a question of young students staying in the countryside, but of the transplantation and permanent settlement of entire families. An editorial urges young intellectuals and town-dwellers who are not productively employed to follow this example, and hopes that "instead of remaining in the town to eat the bread of sloth, they will respond with enthusiasm to the great appeal of Chairman Mao and go to the front line of agricultural production."

The New China News Agency reports that the whole country is feverishly echoing the Chairman's appeal. Revolutionary Committees everywhere have spent all night studying the new instruction, and are immediately taking measures to apply it in practice (New China News Agency, 22 December). The very first results seem to be relatively modest. In Lanchow, 18,000 middle-school pupils have left to settle in the villages. In Wuhan, the departure of 20,000 adolescents was celebrated with a big rally; parents everywhere were putting their children forward as candidates for the departure, as a sign of their loyalty to Chairman Mao. In Tientsin, more than 40,000 high-school pupils and more than 10,000 students have left for the countryside. But to grasp the real dimensions of the movement we must look at the numbers for the province of Kiangsi, which has been held up as a model (New China News Agency, 23 December). More than 720,000 persons (including 130,000 cadres, teachers and doctors) have gone to settle in the countryside in order to turn themselves into simple peasants; they have been shared out among 12,000 production brigades.

From all the information available on this large movement, we may single out the following characteristics. It is not a temporary period of re-education but a permanent migration. The groups chiefly aimed at are young students (from the age of fifteen upwards); intellectuals in general, and particularly teachers, doctors and hospital personnel (already, according to certain eye witnesses, there is a serious shortage of staff in urban hospitals); and unemployed and independent workers (those who have stuck to their small artisan trades in the towns, dubious political elements or people of bourgeois origin).

The motives for this movement seem to be both economic and political, a response both to a certain philosophy and to certain specific problems. Chinese society as a whole has to be taken back to the primitive-peasant stage, which is the only stage where it is receptive to Mao's thought and where this thought can be applied fully. The tertiary sector which, because of its level of education and the very nature of its activities, has developed specific demands and a critical attitude and has therefore rejected emphatically the simplistic dogmas of maoism, must be eliminated. The formation of urban élites must be prevented. The tension between town and country must be reduced. The problem of urban unemployment and of supplying the towns with agricultural products must be solved. The number of unproductive urban consumers must be reduced, by transforming them into manual agricultural labourers. The opposition cells in the towns must be broken up and dispersed, and the old social framework must be shattered by breaking the bonds of family and soil. A considerable number of reasons can be found for this movement; far from being mutually exclusive, they all in fact converge.

The town-dweller regards this emigration with no hope of return, to distant villages where living conditions are still very primitive, as an exile and a punishment. The peasants who have to welcome them are also extremely discontented. These demoralised and inexperienced newcomers, instead of helping, are at first extra mouths to feed, parasites who have to be housed and supported: in short, an increase in expense for the villages. In the short term, the respective grievances of the new arrivals and the peasants tend not to combine: they neutralise each other through mutual hostility, which the authorities play upon. Yet in the long term, the countrywide contact between hundreds of thousands of intellectuals and frustrated activists, and peasant masses who have remained to a large extent on the political sidelines, may turn out to be an explosive mixture; perhaps the critical bitterness of the former will act as a revolutionary ferment on the dormant political consciousness of the latter.

More than half the provinces have held or are holding their provincial assembly of party delegates, in preparation for the ninth congress. We now have texts of the decisions taken by three provincial assemblies: Honan (in session from 8 November to

30), Hunan (from 12 to 25 November) and Kweichow (from 8 to 22 November). These three texts are quite similar in their main outlines: they pay homage to Mao, to Lin Piao, to the Cultural Revolution Group and to the People's Liberation Army. The Honan text is the most interesting, because it analyses in sufficient detail the types of difficulty and obstruction which the Revolutionary Committees are currently running up against. Here is an extract:

"The enemy refuses to admit defeat and continually seeks to take advantage of the circumstances to make counter-attacks. The enemy consists on the one hand of the bad cadres, leaders of the 'February opposition', and on the other hand of sceptics. Faced with a new situation, the enemy has modified his tactics and is now appropriating revolutionary slogans and distorting their meaning, so as to cause trouble in our ranks. Thus, quite recently, the class enemy has used the revolutionary slogan 'Struggle against the restoration of the past' to divert the orientation of the struggle, and to turn the spearhead against the workers' groups for propaganda of the thought of Mao Tse-tung, against the Liberation Army and against the new members of the Revolutionary Committees, thus scheming to take power out of the hands of the proletariat. Under the pretext of opposing the 'restoration of the past', in reality they are opposing the seizure of power carried out by the Revolutionary Committees. In claiming to support the revolutionary line, they are in fact opposing the principle that the working class should be in complete command. They falsely claim that the rebels are oppressed, but in reality they themselves are sheltering all the bad elements. The main barrier to the activity of the Revolutionary Committee is 'polycentrism'. This is the work of extreme-left egocentric individuals: so as to avoid making any contribution now, they arrogantly boast of their former revolutionary merits. They fight on behalf of their little personal cliques, substituting sentiment for politics, and a capitalist factional spirit for the proletarian spirit of the party; they build up independent strongholds for themselves and fraternise with the enemy. When the masses seize a bad element, they plead in his favour, saying that 'such an old companion in the struggle should not be treated in such a way'. They sow dissension in the revolutionary ranks, incite the masses against the masses, and disorient the struggle. 'Polycentrism' is the worst enemy of the headquarters of Mao Tse-tung. A correct attitude towards the masses must be adopted; it is intolerable to support one faction in order to smash another, and especially intolerable to bully the masses and to carry out reprisals against them. In places and in units where the great revolutionary alliance has not yet been consolidated, it is absolutely necessary to be patient and to carry out careful ideological work to unite the revolutionary masses. . . . Some comrades, who are resting on their laurels, underestimate the enemy and are only concerned with developing production, thus neglecting the importance of the class struggle. They remain passive because of threats from the right and the extreme left, or lay down their arms and dare not fight. The most important current tasks are: to purge our ranks so as to construct a solid base for the rectification and reconstruction of the party; to support and consolidate the army, to strengthen the bond between the army and the masses, to be inspired by the example of the army."

This remarkable text gives such an enlightening description that it makes all commentary superfluous. Like the "Cultural Revolution" as a whole, it could be simply subtitled "maoism versus the revolution".

A retrospective glance at 1968

The course of the "Cultural Revolution" in 1968 was essentially determined by the decisive turning-point which took place the previous year, after the attempted mutiny by the army at Wuhan (end of July 1967). This serious incident showed that if the anarchy of the revolutionary rebels was not stopped quickly, the army would for its part no longer remain a passive witness. Peking did succeed in allaying the threat of sedition by peaceful means, but in order to conciliate the army it had to make concessions, and the following months revealed the extent of these. The army was given *carte blanche* to re-establish order and put the Red Guards back in line; then, to further appease the military, the ideologues of the extreme left (the theoreticians of the "Cultural Revolution") were purged.

Formally, the "Cultural Revolution" continued; during 1968, the provinces continued one by one to equip themselves with Revolutionary Committees. But these successive "seizures of power" had very little in common with those which had taken place right at the beginning of 1967. In fact, the theoretical "triple union" (the military, rehabilitated cadres, and revolutionary rebels) was replaced by a dual alliance (soldiers and bureaucrats). In most of the provinces, the "Revolutionary Committee" formula thus amounted eventually to the army (the regional military command) taking over the whole of the political and administrative machinery. The "rebel" organisations were practically excluded from power or even brutally crushed, and the "Cultural Revolution" was thus deprived of its original content.

But this process went through a series of oscillations which reflected the internal divisions of the maoist general staff. The latter was divided between its desire to set the "Cultural Revolution" back on its initial path, and its obligation to fall in line with the army's demands for order. It faced the impossible task of improvising a substitute for the specialised abilities of the old bureaucratic apparatus, and the need to bring the anarchy to a rapid halt. Throughout the first half of 1968 it followed an erratic course, veering from right to left and back again. The various oscillations were as follows.

In January-February, a right turn. In the provinces, the army obtained wide powers to suppress the rebels; doctrinal texts denounced the misdeeds of "factionalism", i.e. revolutionary rebels who, seeing their revolution betrayed, refused to recognise the authority of the Revolutionary Committees or tried to prevent them from being set up. Ch'i Pen-yü, one of the star turns of the "Cultural Revolution", was viciously attacked and then disappeared from the political scene. (Wang Li, Kuan Feng, Mu Hsin, Lin Chieh etc. had been purged in the final months of 1967, and so the "Cultural Revolution" had succeeded in devouring its own élite.) The cult of Lin Piao increased to remarkable proportions. The army ran off with the honours.

From the end of March to May: a left turn. The purge of Yang Ch'eng-wu, Lin Piao's chief assistant and architect of the Lin cult, should not be imputed to the left but rather to the pressure of the regional commanders; however, it was accompanied and followed by renewed attacks against Chou En-lai's collaborators (Li Fu-ch'un, Yü Ch'iu-li, T'an Chen-lin). The 1 May editorial of the *People's Daily* brought a halt to the movement for the rehabilitation of the bureaucrats from the old party apparatus. The maoist general staff seemed to be shielded from this. Because of the state of uncertainty in the capital, there was no parade in Peking to celebrate 1 May (an unprecedented phenomenon in the history of the régime).

From the end of May to June: a thick fog surrounded any

information. In the ideological domain, there was a total absence of doctrinal editorials. Factional struggles continued to rage in the provinces.

At the end of June, the misdeeds of factionalism were denounced, and there was an attempt to patch up the Revolutionary Committees, which had become increasingly discredited in the eyes of the rebels.

At the beginning of July Chiang Ch'ing used her operatic reform (the famous piano) to gain an advantage. Because of her, the Cultural Revolution Group had the wind in its sails again. Li Fu-ch'un and Nieh Jung-chen were attacked, and the line of fire seemed to be nearing Chou En-lai himself. The Revolutionary Committees were hit by a wave of purges of rehabilitated cadres. The *Red Flag*, the forum of the extreme left, began to reappear after a silence of eight months. Were we about to witness a renewal of the "Cultural Revolution"?

But the country was getting dangerously embroiled in anarchy and violence. The revolutionary rebel factions continued to tear each other to pieces as well as to challenge the authority of the Revolutionary Committees continually. The "Cultural Revolution" was desperately behind schedule (according to the initial plans, all the provinces should have had a Revolutionary Committee by 1 May). There was only one way to get it out of the rut: to strike at the left.

This was done at the end of July by setting up "groups of workers and soldiers for propagating Mao Tse-tung's thought", shock brigades which were ordered to wipe out the last nuclei of activism (mainly in the universities). At the beginning of August, Mao sent a gift of mangoes to one of these brigades stationed in Tsinghua university, using this symbolic gesture to express his support and approval for the repression. This was the death-knell for the Red Guards and the revolutionary rebels — subsequently these disturbances would no longer be tolerated. (The reader who is remote from the reality of China today will no doubt be astonished to see me harking back to these stories about the piano and the mangoes. Contrary to what he or she might believe, they are not pointless anecdotes but *political events*. On each occasion the masses were mobilised throughout the country to celebrate them: the oscillations of power are expressed in this symbolic language.) On the pretext of restoring the working class to its leading role (the workers' groups for propagating Mao Tse-tung's thought were in fact organised and led by the army), the extreme left was disowned and disarmed. In these conditions, the last Revolutionary Committees which still had to be established as a matter of form could quickly be set up, and at the beginning of September (the rally in Peking, 7 September), the "total victory" of the "Cultural Revolution" could be celebrated: all the provinces, municipalities and autonomous regions of China had finally been blessed with Revolutionary Committees.

What did this victory mean? If we recall the movement's initial plans, and if we examine its whole evolution from the famous "January tempest" (Shanghai 1967) onwards, the final balance seems singularly deceptive. As the first initiatives in Shanghai testify, Mao Tse-tung had at first dreamed of an entirely new type of revolutionary power, inspired by the Paris Commune. When this proved to be unrealisable, he was forced to fall back on a less radical formula: the Revolutionary Committees. It soon became quite clear that while the rebels were capable of seizing power, they were incapable of administering it. In order to compensate for their inexperience and their lack of discipline, it was necessary to invent the formula of the "triple union". Theoretically, the rebels should have supplied its motive force, backed by the muscle of the soldiers and the specialist skills of the former cadres. But the triple union soon showed that the requirements of rebellion on the one hand and of order and efficiency on the other were incompatible. In the end it was rebellion which was sacrificed to order — the order of the gun. But the rebels did not give up without a fight, and their stubborn resistance succeeded in a number of provinces in delaying the setting up of Revolutionary Committees for several months; and even after they were set up, these committees continually found that they were exposed to sabotage and attacks from extremist factions.

After this purely formal victory of the "Cultural Revolution", the National Day celebrations of 1 October were rather dull. The celebrations and slogans reflected the new situation: the army was consecrated as the pillar of the régime, the workers were given star billing, and the Red Guards were silenced. The country's new mission was to reconstruct the party. Specifically, this meant that a start had to be made on preparations for the ninth congress.

On 1 November, the communiqué from the enlarged twelfth plenary session of the eighth central committee announced that Liu Shao-ch'i had been deprived of all his posts inside and outside the party. This improvised and irregular procedure indicated that the maoists were still in a minority inside the current party apparatus, but they could no longer wait for the hypothetical ninth congress to cut off their opponents' retreat and to give their own power the appearance of legality.

While the "Cultural Revolution" misfired in the political sphere (it did not manage to give the rebels power, and was of definite benefit only to the army), its activity in other sectors continued to develop.

In the sphere of education, Mao was finally able to carry out his old dream of reform, which the apparatus had torpedoed on two previous occasions (in 1958 and 1965). Priority was given to "red artisans" over scientific experts. The specialised disciplines were discredited and "make-do and mend" (*t'u fang-fa*) put forward as an example; theoretical education was largely reduced to the study of Mao's "thought", courses were replaced by "productive activities".

The administration was rearranged and simplified. In certain branches of the administration the staff was reduced to one fifth of its former number; the excess were sent to the fields.

A considerable percentage of the urban population was sent into the countryside, where it came under the responsibility of the people's communes.

The people's communes, which after the failure of the "Great Leap Forward" were in practice reduced to the role of mere administrative departments, were reactivated; the state withdrew from the greatest possible number of financial burdens (primary education, medical care etc.) in order for the communes to take them over.

The "Cultural Revolution" is a personal victory for Mao Tsetung; he has eliminated his enemies, recovered the power which was gradually taken from him after 1959, and temporarily averted the threat of de-maoisation which began to emerge in the early sixties. Otherwise, neither the country nor the régime has gained anything from the adventure. The party apparatus, which used to guarantee the country's political stability and enabled it to survive the most testing circumstances without any real setbacks, has been almost entirely ruined and discredited, and for the time being it has been replaced only by the improvised disparate and temporary formula of Revolutionary Committees. The fundamental principle that the party commands the army has been reversed. Not only are the military leading the majority of the Revolutionary Committees but they are ruling the country at every level; they are present in every sector of activity, in the schools, the fields, the factories and in the administration. But the army does not have the ability to deal with all the administrative and policing tasks it is now saddled with. And it is a long way from the monolithic unity which was the party's strength. Lin Piao has endeavoured to put the greatest possible number of his men at the head of the Revolutionary Committees, but this was not possible everywhere; in numerous provinces Peking has had to come to terms with military commands which are not devoted to Lin Piao, and are so strongly entrenched that Peking has to be content with ratifying their authority. Thus the influence of Lin Piao, which was already limited at the beginning, is now counterbalanced by a group of big regional commanders who, in their own provinces, have concentrated military and political power in their own hands; in fact they are threatening to push China back into a situation where the regional authorities would be relatively free of the control of the central power.

Peking's most urgent task is therefore to reconstruct the party; this presents enormous difficulties — witness the delays in convening the ninth congress. Will the army allow itself to be stripped of the powers which have so dangerously been conceded to it? Or will it get a decisive confirmation of its privileges? 1969 will give us the answer.

1969

January

The New Year editorial published jointly by the *People's Daily*, the *Liberation Army Daily* and the *Red Flag* is rather mild. It tends towards moderation, especially over the attitude to be adopted towards cadres. It should be realised that "the enemy is only a very small minority", and where the great majority of cadres are concerned, everything must be done to help them mend their ways and resume active service within the framework of proletarian orthodoxy. The editorial makes an urgent appeal for unity and denounces the poisonous deviation of "polycentrism". This desire to conciliate, to bridge gaps and level differences in a single fellowship of the thought of Mao Tse-tung and under the unified command of the Chairman's general staff (the editorial is entitled "Let everything be directed by the thought of Mao Tse-tung") betrays a very real and urgent need: a large number of the Revolutionary Committees are still paralysed, and their authority is still being questioned by the local revolutionary rebels. As a broadcast on Hupeh provincial radio rather cynically put it last month, the Red Guards must finally understand that their role in the "seizure of power" *consists only in seizing power from the revisionist faction, not in exercising it themselves.* But despite Peking's safety guarantee, the reinstated cadres have learned from their recent experiences and are not very willing to take against the rebels measures which will perhaps be considered criminal again tomorrow. They have therefore withdrawn into a state of prudent apathy, which does not make it easy to normalise political and administrative activity.

The army has been brought into play more than ever before. Its ubiquitous presence in civilian life has led to some friction with the people. One of the big propaganda themes is therefore that "the army loves the people", with much insistence on the harmonious relations of support and affection which must be established between the military and the masses.

The centre of political attention now seems to have transferred from the town to the country. The "Cultural Revolution" has so far been a purely urban phenomenon, and because of the widespread anarchy the countryside has largely been left to itself. This, ironically enough, accounts for the favourable position of agriculture after the last two years of political chaos. In Kwangtung, the province on which we are best informed, numerous villages have spontaneously renewed their age-old traditions of autarky, and have barricaded themselves against all the raids of the itinerant rebels, isolating themselves almost entirely from the outside world. This state of isolation cannot last much longer. The forced migration of certain strata of the urban population to the countryside, which began at the end of last year, is still taking place on a large scale. Remember that we are not talking about periods of re-education, but rather of permanent settlement. In the town of Canton alone, 100,000 people — of whom 75,000 are school pupils and students (according to figures given by Kwangtung provincial radio) — have already been affected by this movement. As one can imagine, this movement is encountering opposition from two sources: the emigrants themselves, who dread exile (the aim of it, as far as student youth is concerned, is to smash the revolutionary activism of the Red Guards), and the peasants, whose burdens have been added to by these newcomers. The difficulties the movement is encountering are indirectly confirmed by the special propaganda efforts being made to try and persuade those concerned of the great political significance of their adventure. At the same time, there are increasing signs of an attempt to reinvigorate the people's communes. Private land is being confiscated and free markets suppressed, while the poor and lower-middle peasants are being mobilised to launch a campaign of "struggle and criticism". These political agitation campaigns are encountering some difficulties, and it is often necessary to make use of the military. For example, Chekiang provincial radio announced on the 22nd that army detachments have been sent into the villages to help the peasants root out the remains of Liu's forces and put Mao Tse-tung's directives into practice.

Likewise, the reorganisation of the production brigades into larger and more powerful units (an experiment which is currently taking place in Kiangsi) is also aimed at reactivating the people's communes. The combination of these various measures has led certain observers to believe that some kind of new "leap forward" is perhaps being prepared. The very phrase "Great Leap Forward" clearly has no propaganda value, because it is still linked in the minds of the population with some rather unpleasant memories; but very recently we have begun to notice that official sources are frequently using quite similar expressions, such as "economic take-off" (*ching-chi fei-yueh*). Now that Mao is once more in power and unimpeded, he must be strongly tempted to revert to his old obsessions. At any rate, to propose a new "leap forward" at this moment would be even more dangerous than in the past. The catastrophic consequences of the "Great Leap Forward" were mitigated before by the discipline of the party, which had the whole country in control. But if the adventure is repeated now, the tightrope-walker will have no safety net.

The New China News Agency has issued a communiqué on the publication of the works of Mao Tse-tung during the "Cultural Revolution". From 1966 to 1968, 150 million copies of the *Selected Works* were printed, 740 million copies of the *Quotations* and 96 million copies of the *Poems*. (This last statistic is rather amusing, when one considers that the poems are rather archaic in form, written in an abstruse language and stuffed with literary and historical allusions, and are therefore quite unintelligible to the man in the street.) One district on the Tsinghai province has set a record: every inhabitant of the province between the ages of seven and seventy owns a copy of the *Quotations*, and every family owns a set of the *Selected Works*. (In western publishing, perhaps only *Tintin* can pride itself on reaching such a wide age-range.) "One can go without food or drink for a whole day, but one could not go for one single day and not read the works of Mao Tse-tung without the ears becoming deaf, the eyes dimmed and the mind losing its sense of direction."

February

There have been no outstanding events in recent weeks. The death on 31 January of the former statesman Li Tsung-jen (he was seventy-eight years old) cannot be considered a noteworthy event: Li had been a marginal figure in history and politics for almost twenty years. He distinguished himself in the military field during the "Northern expedition" and then in the war of resistance against Japan; those were the glorious years of his career. He was elected Vice-chairman of the Republic after victory, and began negotiations with the communists in 1949. Then a few months later, when the Liberation took place, he took refuge in

Hong Kong and finally reached the USA. He tried in vain to interest the Americans in a project for a "third force". The isolated ex-statesman had no prestige, no audience and even no social acquaintances (he did not speak English), and his long stay in the USA became a dreary exile. In 1965 he decided to return to China to end his days there. Peking exploited his return to the full for propaganda purposes, and in the autumn of 1965 organised a big press conference to which numerous journalists from Hong Kong and abroad were invited. The value of the propaganda to be gained from Li Tsung-jen proved to be very limited in any case. Had he chosen to return to his mother country earlier, the decision might have had far-reaching repercussions. But the date and circumstances of his return indicated all too clearly that he had been guided by purely personal considerations. These were understandable, but hardly remarkable. Thereafter, Li Tsung-jen led a retired life; from time to time he was exhibited among the lower ranks on some official platform like an antique porcelain vase, for decoration. The "Cultural Revolution" could hardly have affected his destiny; it has been just as merciless towards the old heroic revolutionary élite as it has been merciful towards retired Kuomintang men and fossils of reaction.

The slogan "let us prepare to welcome the ninth party congress" is being repeated continually by the radio and the press. The congress will no doubt be convened before 1 May. We have had the opportunity to read the draft of the new party constitution before its release.* Compared to the 1956 constitution, this text seems more like a manifesto than a constitution. The way it sanctifies the authority of the thought of Mao Tse-tung is particularly remarkable. The 1956 constitution, by contrast, made no mention of Mao's name, and even went so far as to state that "no political party *or individual* can be free of failings and mistakes". The 1956 constitution's notion of collective leadership and its condemnation of the personality cult were essentially Teng Hsiao-p'ing's initiative, and counterbalanced the 1945 constitution, in which the thought of Mao Tse-tung had been men-

---

* The definitive version, officially published on 28 April, fully confirmed the authenticity of this document, which was initially put out by Taiwan. Taiwan's propaganda and interpretation of political events may be preposterous, but its intelligence is often valuable when it concerns the publication of original communist documents reserved for internal party use. These documents sometimes come clandestinely from China via Hong Kong, and are sometimes captured during commando raids on the coast of Fukien.

tioned for the first time ("The Chinese Communist Party is guided by the thought of Mao Tse-tung, which has united marxist-leninist theory with the practice of the Chinese revolution"). In the draft of the new constitution, the reference to Lin Piao as the heir-apparent seems particularly incongruous, since in theory this type of document is only supposed to deal with abstract principles which are capable of being applied universally and permanently. The party secretariat is no longer mentioned: is it going to be suppressed? Likewise, the control organs are passed over in silence. The central power seems to be strengthened at the expense of the local levels, which used to be allocated specific areas of authority. As far as the conditions of admission to the party are concerned, candidate membership is no longer required. Social origin has become a determining factor in candidates' qualifications (entry is virtually barred to intellectuals). Finally the predominant position of the army has been ratified: the style of work which Lin Piao has imposed on the army has been extended to civilian life, as a model to be universally applied.

All political life seems to have been suspended in the waiting period for the ninth party congress. The cadres are particularly anxious to have it convened, because in the present confused situation they have no definite orientation, and do not always know which compass to steer by. This feverish expectation is being nurtured by the propaganda organs. The revolutionary hymn-book has just been enriched by a new song entitled "Let us prepare to welcome the ninth congress!"

A conference was held in Peking between 7 and 9 February, assembling the cadres from the provinces (including observers from Hong Kong and Macao) to work on the preparations for the ninth congress. Peking would like to speed up the process of admitting new party members who show complete loyalty, but here it is running up against resistance from the local authorities. At first it was thought that the ninth congress would be convened in March, but it has now been postponed till the beginning of April.*

Publication of the thoughts of Teng Hsiao-p'ing: a Red Guard pamphlet (*Tsinghua Ching-kang shan*, nos. 17 and 18), has put together Teng's most criminal ideas. It is interesting to

---

* We shall see later that the congress did finally open on 1 April.

recall these texts now, when the Mao cult is being solemnly consecrated:

"Another fundamental question in the system of the democratic concentration of power in the party is that of collective leadership at all levels of the apparatus. On all the important questions facing the party, leninism requires that decisions be taken by an appropriate group and not by an individual. . . . Loyalty to a leader is essentially a matter of showing an attachment to the interests of the party, to the interests of the class, to the interests of the people, and not of making a myth out of the individual concerned. One important contribution made by the twentieth congress of the Soviet Communist Party has been to alert us to the fact that the personality cult can lead to all kinds of disastrous consequences. Our party has always reckoned that any party and any individual can, in respect of their own actions, have deficiencies and make mistakes. This point is now explicitly noted in the new draft of the party constitution. In this way, our party also repudiates the personality cult." [Report on the new draft constitution presented on 16 September 1956 to the eighth party congress.]

"Our duty is to continue to apply the policy of the central committee regarding the struggle against emphasising and glorifying the personality." [Remark made at a meeting of the central committee, no date.]

"Only the party leads, it is the party which is our only leader." [1958. The commentary adds: "Here Teng Hsiao-p'ing viciously denies that Chairman Mao should be our glorious chief."]

"All it talks about is the thought of Mao Tse-tung. Where is marxism-leninism? It is not necessary to issue this report. . . . Young people must be encouraged to study certain basic things in the works of Mao Tse-tung, but we cannot make them do this the whole year round." [Comment on a report drawn up by a commission of the central committee on the study of Mao Tse-tung's thought.]

"Regarding the 'four essays' [i.e. the three most widely read of Mao's texts — lao san p'ien — plus his short article 'Against Liberalism'], they can be studied, but there would be little point in going over these few texts the whole year long. If the same things are discussed over and over again, how can you expect people still to be interested? . . . [in the Selected Works of Mao Tse-tung] there are texts which

have already been studied a great number of times — why
go over them indefinitely? This formalism is deadly!"
[Speech to a meeting of the secretariat of the central committee, 1965.]

In 1961, Teng ratified a report from the central committee's
propaganda department ("Examination of certain questions raised
by propaganda on the thought of Mao Tse-tung"), a report
which described the methods of studying the thought of Mao
Tse-tung used by peasants, workers and soldiers as "a vulgar
devaluation", "simplistic" and "formalistic". In 1962, he ratified
and circulated a report by Chou Yang on material for teaching
literature in schools — a report in which it was said that "artificial attempts to compose school books based on the thought of
Mao Tse-tung simply aggravate the tendencies to vulgar devaluation and over-simplification." He forbade local organisations to
publish the works of Mao on their own initiative, and stated in
1964 that "every edition of selections from Mao Tse-tung first
requires an authorisation from the central authorities." In March
1966, when "the revolutionary masses were begging to be supplied with the texts and quotations of Mao", Teng vetoed any
new publications: "The fifth volume of the *Selected Works* is
going to come out soon; wait until the fifth volume appears
before printing new volumes."

In domestic affairs, Teng is accused of avoiding the class
struggle. The proof:

"The preceding stage was a revolutionary one. Now the
revolutionary objectives are practically achieved. Today and
in the future, the task is one of construction." [1956]

"Classes have already disappeared in China and have been
replaced by internal contradictions. The internal contradictions cannot be resolved by adopting the methods of class
struggle without the risk of making mistakes." [1956]

"In recent times, the situation has fundamentally changed;
workers and employees represent only a division of labour
within one class. Poor peasants and rich peasants have all
become members of co-operatives. Very soon, the differences
between them will be of historical significance only." [1956]

"Most Chinese capitalists started from nothing and have
succeeded through their own efforts and talents. We are not
equal to these capitalists; go to Shanghai and see how they
used to organise medium-sized and small enterprises."

"With regard to bourgeois intellectuals, given our requirements, we cannot use marxism-leninism as a criterion. At

the moment we need them, and even if they spend their time grumbling, the essential thing is that they can teach."

On the "Great Leap Forward" and its results:

"When Chairman Mao says that the situation is excellent, he is referring to the political situation. It cannot be said that the economic situation is excellent; in fact it is very bad." [Working conference of the central committee, 1962]

"It seems to be difficult for us to open our mouths now; not only the League of Communist Youth but also the party has this impression. People are badly clothed, badly fed, standards are falling. There have been too many turgid speeches; we have been too sure of ourselves, we have bluffed too much." [Speech to the central assembly of the Communist Youth League, 1962]

"The improvement in the country's agricultural situation will not take three or five years, but seven or eight." [Working conference of the central committee, 1961]

"The agricultural question must be resolved at the level of production. We now have the commune system, the brigade system: Anhwei still has the system of fields for which the peasants are responsible — in fact this amounts to an illegal restitution of land. . . . In each area we must adopt whichever system is most suited to ensuring the development of production. We must adopt the system which the peasants themselves are most inclined to adopt and, if necessary, legalise illegal acts. [Teng was thinking of emergency measures to save the population from the famine which had followed the catastrophe of the 'Great Leap Forward' — S.L.]. . . A large number of peasants are asking for the land to be redistributed; the peasants have lost confidence in the collective economy. . . . Since 1957 the party as a whole has been imprudent and has developed a complacent attitude; our good traditions are lost or are getting weaker. . . . The atmosphere of our society was still a good one until 1958, or the beginning of 1958 [i.e. until the 'Great Leap Foward' — S.L.]; in recent years it has become spoilt." [Speech to the central assembly of the Communist Youth League, 1962]

"In China our mules are slow, but this has its good side. Cars are fast, but if you lose control, you get killed. If the mule goes slowly, at least it goes surely." [1957 speech to the students of Tsinghua university]

"The most important issue now is to increase the production of food supplies. It does not matter whether the mode of production is individual or collective, what is essential is that it helps to increase food production; it doesn't matter whether the cat is black or white, the cat which catches mice is a good one." [Speech to a conference of the secretariat of the central committee, 1962]

"Priority can be given sometimes to politics and sometimes to economics, as the situation requires." [Speech to the central assembly of the Communist Youth League, 1957]

On foreign policy:

"The USSR has the atom bomb. Why? To make the imperialists afraid of them. Are the imperialists afraid of us? I hardly think so. If the Americans have troops in Taiwan, it is obviously because we don't have the atom bomb. But the USSR has the atom bomb, and if the USSR did not have it, the imperialists would dare to attack us." [Speech to the students of Tsinghua university, 1957)

"We do not entirely agree [with the twentieth congress of the Soviet Communist Party], but we do not completely deny its validity either. We recognise that it includes a large number of good things which will be profitable for the internal development of the Soviet Union and the international situation. . . . It cannot be said that the denunciation of Stalin is entirely mistaken." [1960: source not given]

The commentary adds:

"In 1966, a delegation from the Japanese Communist Party came to China to ask the Chinese Communist Party to fix a common policy with the USSR towards Vietnam. In defiance of principles, Liu and Teng wanted to issue a joint communiqué with the Japanese revisionists. . . . In July 1966, at a meeting in Peking of the conference of Afro-Asian writers, Teng criticised the organisers of the conference and gave them the following advice: 'Don't get carried away', 'Keep your feet on the ground', 'The tone of the conference should remain simply anti-imperialist and anti-colonialist'." [i.e. it should not mention revisionism]

March

The armed clashes between Soviet and Chinese frontier guards on Chen-pao island, on the Sino-Soviet frontier, are monopolising everyone's attention for the time being. Although this affair has no connection with the "Cultural Revolution", which is what we are concerned with, it is serious enough to require a few lines of commentary.

For a better understanding of the degree of sensitivity of Chinese opinion on the conflict, it is first of all worth recalling some historical facts. Of all the foreign imperalist powers which China fell prey to in the past, Russia was the most important — both in length of time (Russian pressure on the Chinese borders began at the end of the seventeenth century) and in the rapacious nature of its territorial annexations. The Kazakh, Kirgiz, Uzbek and Turkmen Soviet Republics in central Asia were carved from the ancient territory of the Ch'ing empire: the territorial annexations to the north of the Amur on the north-eastern border of China covered an area of more than 600,000 sq. km., and those to the east of the Ussuri more than 400,000 sq. km. Unlike other foreign imperialist powers Russia never returned them, and despite Lenin's noble declarations of principle denouncing tsarist annexations, the Soviet Union simply consolidated its hold over the spoils it had inherited from imperial Russia. The first Chinese republic was weakened and absorbed by internal problems, and was in no fit state to discuss the border problem with the Soviet Union. As far as People's China is concerned, history will reproach Mao Tse-tung for not asserting China's rights in Moscow during the régime's early years. Putting the interests of the party before those of the country, Mao thought it wise to rely totally and unconditionally on the "Soviet elder brother". To a certain extent, the bloody conflicts which took place on the Ussuri were made possible by the terms of the Sino-Soviet friendship pact ("free use of the border river") signed by Mao in Moscow in February 1950.

Immediately after the Sino-Soviet split (the way in which the Soviet Union brusquely disowned its commitments in the field of technical assistance was quite rightly regarded by the Chinese as a despicable act of sabotage and treachery) the Soviet Union actively resumed the old tsarist policy of expansion, and serious incidents — revolts and the flight of national minorities at the instigation of the Soviets — took place in 1962 in Sinkiang, which was the main object of Russian attention.

In 1964, China initiated negotiations with the USSR on the border question. It was even willing to recognise in principle the borders which had been laid down by the unequal nineteenth-century treaties, in return for certain amendments in the detail. The proposal was a generous one, and there was no reason to doubt China's good faith. (In fact, it was by this same principle that China had settled all its old border disputes with various neighbours, entirely to the satisfaction of the parties concerned. India was the only exception, but here again the conclusions of impartial observers — and these are universally accepted today — show there had been bad faith on the Indian side: the Chinese attitude, on the other hand, was marked first of all by naiveté and then by the inflexibility of outraged good faith.) The negotiations broke down. If the Chinese version is to be believed — and it does seem plausible — the Soviets first of all refused in principle to recognise the annexationist character of the old treaties. (In 1858, when Tientsin had just fallen to the Anglo-French expedition, Russia used China's desperate position to force her at gunpoint to sign the Treaty of Aigun. This treaty cut China off from the territories to the north of the Amur, and placed the territories to the east of the Ussuri under a joint Sino-Russian administration. In 1860, after the Anglo-French forces had seized Peking, Russia rushed for the spoils, and the Treaty of Peking ceded outright the territories to the east of the Ussuri.) And secondly, they put forward new territorial claims which China could not accept.

Chen-pao island, which is now the scene of clashes between Soviet and Chinese frontier patrols who both claim that they are conducting manoeuvres on their own territory, is a tiny islet; it is probably uninhabited (whenever Chinese sources refer to eyewitness reports by the population, the expression used is "the inhabitants of the Chen-pao island *area*" — the inhabitants of the island itself are never mentioned), and it sees little more than the occasional passing hunter or fisherman. We may assume that the Soviets have taken advantage of the more or less abandoned state of this unimportant islet to carry out occasional patrols there under cover of winter (the river is then entirely frozen, and this allows motorised units to cross). They are undoubtedly using these discreet, intermittent acts of occupation to give the impression that the law is in their favour.

Which country owns Chen-pao island? Chinese opinion states unanimously (this includes the Chinese communities overseas and all the different political tendencies) that Chen-pao is undoubtedly Chinese territory: not just for moral and historical reasons (until the unequal treaties were imposed on China by force, the Ussuri was a river *inside China*) but also for legal reasons. Even if we adopt the perspective of the Peking treaty of 1860, Chen-pao is under Chinese sovereignty, and was moreover recognised as such by the Soviets themselves at the time of the 1964 negotiations. The Peking treaty ceded all the territory east of the Ussuri to Russia. As far as the islands in the river were concerned, where no explicit stipulation was made, the dividing line between the territories was to be determined by the main navigable channel. According to the map now published by the *People's Daily*, Chen-pao is to the west of the channel, and during low water it is linked directly to the Chinese bank. In comparison with the Chinese, who have produced a complete dossier, it is worth noting that the Soviets have evaded the objective issue of sovereignty, and are content merely to make strident protests on the passionate but vague theme of "provocations" and "atrocities" committed by the Chinese frontier patrols.

Aside from the problem of insignificant little islands like Chen-pao, the Ussuri border is clearly drawn and hardly lends itself to the possibility of big territorial disputes. In fact the really big border problems are more likely to arise in Sinkiang, a vast area which is rich in natural resources and is the centre of the Chinese nuclear industry. Its borders are unclear, and its scattered population is largely composed of ethnic groups related to those in the Soviet Republics of central Asia. Sinkiang has always excited Russian ambitions, and if a serious confrontation were to take place between China and the USSR, Sinkiang would be the location and the object. On the other hand, if the opponents simply want to test each other and to exploit the tension for purely political ends, the little islands of the Ussuri offer a relatively closed arena and allow the conflict to be kept within strictly local limits.

It is superfluous to add that the political capital being made out of the incident is quite disproportionate to the real dimensions of the event itself. On 12 March, the New China News Agency announced that the anti-Soviet demonstrations which have been taking place all over China for a week have already mobilised four hundred million participants (i.e. slightly over half the total population of China!) There is every reason to believe that this time the demonstrators are marching with sincere conviction. Chinese crowds are constantly mobilised for political demonstrations on various themes, and in varying numbers: sometimes to welcome an unknown African politician, sometimes to denounce some tyrant who rules on the other side of the world and whose name they cannot remember. Even the demonstrations of hate for America are curiously unreal and abstract. An anti-Russian or anti-British demonstration, on the other hand, obviously arouses feelings: those who are demonstrating in the streets know very concretely why they are marching, and they

do so all the more willingly because they suffered a great deal in
the fifties when Peking burdened the nation, against all the lessons
of history and all current evidence, with the image of the "Soviet
elder brother" who was well-intentioned, generous and loved.
(This article of "unshakeable Sino-Soviet friendship" was particularly difficult for the population of the North-East to accept,
since they had witnessed the looting and the dismantling of
industrial equipment in their region by the Soviet army at the
end of the war; it gave rise to much heart-searching on the part
of the local militants.) Coming at this point, the Chen-pao incident
is a real blessing for Mao Tse-tung: it is allowing him to create
unanimity. (It is a unanimity which, incidentally, transcends
frontiers: an editorial in a right-wing Hong Kong daily has
applauded the way in which the People's Army defended the
soil of the motherland.) It comes just when Peking is doing its
utmost to impose the principle of "unified command" on the
provinces, which are still racked by the anarchist currents of
the "Cultural Revolution". It has given the army a halo of glory
and given it complete immunity, at a time when military intervention in all spheres of national life was becoming a constant
source of friction and tending to make the army unpopular with
the masses. It justifies the new agricultural and industrial mobilisation; peasants and workers are being asked to redouble their
activity and to exceed the norms in the direct interest of defending
their country. In the delicate process of preparing for the ninth
congress, it has suddenly created a valuable unanimity which will
enable certain thorny questions of internal policy to be
conveniently evaded.

While it appears obvious from all this that Peking is deriving
considerable advantages from the Chen-pao affair, it would be
wrong to infer that Peking has deliberately staged the incident.
China is too poorly equipped to be able to view with equanimity
the risk of a military confrontation with the USSR. Furthermore,
China is far from machiavellian in its foreign relations in general,
and with its neighbours in particular. On the contrary, it has
always behaved with strict and lofty honesty, and this had been
unscrupulously abused by countries like North Korea, India and
the Soviet Union. The Soviet Union may imagine that applying
external military pressure will enable it to aggravate the internal
splits in the maoist régime. In fact such action can only lead to the
opposite; but the Soviet Union is perfectly capable of such an error
of judgement — didn't the Czechoslovak invasion of 1968 show that
its political clumsiness is on a par with its brutality?

The main preoccupation in domestic policy at the moment is to quickly reinstate the greatest possible number of experienced cadres, in order to speed up the normalisation of political and administrative activity. This problem, which in the jargon is being called "the liberation of the cadres", has already given rise to a large number of statements (an editorial in the *Wenhui pao*, an editorial in the *Honan jih-pao*, provincial radio broadcasts in Anhwei, Kiangsi, Honan, a report from the revolutionary committee of Kweichow). The same themes are constantly repeated: the bad cadres are only a tiny minority, the majority of cadres can be cured, only a small number need to be re-educated by force, the experienced cadres are "a treasure to the party and to the country", those who oppose their reintegration are ambitious troublemakers who do not understand the political problems and are motivated by factionalist zeal, etc.

Another great topic of the moment is the reform of university teaching. For the time being, instead of being revolutionised, teaching is simply being paralysed. Students and teachers are unwilling to resume their courses, especially in social science subjects. Such activity either seems useless, since in the end it will only lead to work in the fields (many young people now avoid the universities, the most sought-after position being that of a factory apprentice — politically it is sheltered from events, materially it is better paid than any other job, and above all it makes it possible to remain in the town), or dangerous: in the absence of precise directives or of a new and clearly established programme, anyone who takes action is running the risk of having it rebound on him.

Under the heading "How should socialist universities be organised?" the *People's Daily* published on 29 March three reports from groups of workers and soldiers stationed at the Tsinghua, Futan and Liaoning universities respectively, to indicate the starting-point and general orientation of a new campaign. When one reads through these three reports, it becomes immediately obvious that despite the stagnation of university activities, the maoist authorities have no intention of liberalising their attitudes in this respect. In fact, the reports underline the fact that the revolution in university teaching can certainly not be confined to a simple reform which will enable the teachers, in return for various modifications of the programme, to resume their former activities on the strict basis of their "scientific authority". The reports bring up several basic principles: admission to the university has to be made on the recommendation of a revolutionary committee, which selects students from the poor peasants, the workers and the soldiers. The old examination system is abolished, the study period is restricted to two or three years, and university work is to be closely associated with the tasks of production (the report of Futan university criticises the department of biology, which spends its time splitting hairs "instead of being concerned with horses, cows, sheep, cotton, oil and cereals"). The students, having come from the fields and factories, must pass through university simply in order to return eventually to these fields and factories. Finally, and most importantly, the universities are, and will remain, firmly under the leadership of the peasants, workers and soldiers. The idea that this is purely and simply a matter of ideological and political leadership is refuted: the competence of the peasants', workers' and military leadership must also extend to specifically academic questions, and there is no question of abandoning the latter to the discretion of "specialists". It is the present state of inactivity at the universities which has forced the authorities to pay attention once more to the problem of higher education. But the intransigence with which the most radical principles of university reform are now being reaffirmed hardly seems favourable to the resumption of normal activity in this sphere. Peking's attitude to the universities strongly resembles that of a restaurant customer who orders a shrimp omelette and specifies that he would like it "without shrimps". It would be more logical to get rid of the universities altogether; but this suggestion, which was put forward by the left, has been officially condemned. Keeping the universities on the one hand, but replacing biology classes with desultory chats by old peasants about cows and sheep on the other, is a contradictory scheme and it is inevitably going to prolong the deadlock.

1-24 April: the Ninth Party Congress

The ninth party congress opened on 1 April. Theoretically, the congress is the supreme source of power in the party. In practice, it is subordinate in importance to the central committee, which is drawn from it and serves as its executive organ. The central committee itself is handled by the politbureau, and the politbureau in turn is led by a standing committee, composed of a handful of individuals who are the real masters of the régime.

It was initially envisaged that the congress would be held yearly, but in fact this principle has never been observed, and between the foundation of the party in 1921 and the revision of its constitution in 1956 the congress was convened only eight times. The new constitution of 1956 provided for the congress to be held once every five years. In fact, the mandate of the eighth congress (1956) extended over thirteen years! The Chinese Communist Party has never been very concerned about respecting its constitution, and one wonders why it feels the need to have one.

The birth of this ninth congress was a difficult and slow one. It had to be postponed several times. A circular from the central authorities to the provincial party organisations stated that it would be held at the end of 1967. A speech by Wen Yü-ch'eng then indicated that they aimed to hold it in May 1968. Then it was expected for September: it was supposed to have preceded the National Day celebrations of 1 October 1968. Finally, during October, instead of a congress there was the peculiar "twelfth enlarged plenary session of the eighth central committee" which, under irregular conditions, announced the removal of Liu Shao-ch'i. The bastard device of a "twelfth enlarged plenary session of the eighth committee", to carry out a task which is the business of the congress alone, was an admission of impotence, and indicated that the maoists, despite their wishes, were still unable to convene the congress. Such delays and obstacles in convening the plenary assembly are unprecedented in the party's history.

The plenary assemblies of the party usually last two or three weeks (the eighth lasted thirteen days, the second session of the eighth — in 1958 — lasted nineteen days; the seventh — at Yenan in 1945 — was exceptionally long, lasting forty-eight days). In principle, then, the ninth should end before the 1 May celebrations.

1,512 delegates have assembled for this ninth congress. This is a big increase on the eighth (1,021 delegates), but it is very much what one expected. The procedure for electing delegates seems to have been rather curious. The official communiqué described it in a remarkably obscure fashion:

> "The delegates have been chosen unanimously in accordance with the decisions of the twelfth enlarged plenary session of the eighth central committee [which rejected the bourgeois superstition of democratic elections by majority vote — S.L.], after being submitted to complete and democratic consultation at various levels of the party organisation and after gathering the broad opinions of the masses."

Chosen "unanimously"? The unanimity of which voters? If the masses (in the jargon, "the masses" always refers to those who are not members of the party) have expressed an opinion on an internal party matter, it is a remarkable innovation. In plain language, what the communiqué seems to imply is that the central authorities were forced to make their own selection of delegates, but that in doing so they came up against the opposition of the provincial army men and local bureaucrats who wanted to present their own selection. This led to bargaining between the centre and the regions.

There are 176 members on the presidium of the ninth congress (a considerable increase: the presidium of the eighth numbered only 63). It is worth noting the composition of the presidium because it usually enables us to anticipate by and large the composition of the future central committee.

While the list of the presidium of the eighth congress was in *pi-hua* order (Chinese lexicographical order, equivalent to alphabetical order), so that Mao's name only came after that of some obscure second fiddle, the list for the presidium of the ninth congress is regulated by a hierarchical game whose subtle complexity is worthy of some Byzantine ritual. The list is divided into four ranks, and within each of the first three ranks there are two levels.

First rank, first level: Mao Tse-tung. In his lofty isolation, he has the right to be wished "the limitless long life of ten thousand years" (*wan-shou wu-chiang*) traditionally reserved for emperors.

First rank, second level: Lin Piao. He merely has the right to be wished, in more down-to-earth fashion, "eternal good health" (*yung-yuan chien-k'ang*).

Second rank, first level: Chou En-lai, Ch'en Po-ta, K'ang Sheng, Chiang Ch'ing, Chang Ch'un-Ch'iao, Yao Wen-yuan.

Second rank, second level: Hsieh Fu-chih, Huang Yung-sheng, Wu Fa-hsien, Yeh Ch'ün, Wang Tung-hsing, Wen Yü-ch'eng. (Between Mao and Wen, in fact, we encounter the complete list of fourteen supreme power-holders whom I described above.)

Third rank, first level: Tung Pi-wu, Liu Po-ch'eng, Chu Teh, Ch'en Yün.

Third rank, second level: Li Fu-ch'un, Ch'en Yi, Li Hsien-nien, Hsü Hsiang-ch'ien, Nieh Jung-chen, Yeh Chien-ying. (This third rank is made up both of father figures who no longer have any real power but retain a certain decorative function on official platforms — Tung Pi-wu, Chu Teh — and of men discredited by the "Cultural Revolution" but then helped out of their difficulties and exhibited to the crowds in order to give heart to the old cadres — Ch'en Yün, Ch'en Yi etc.).

Fourth rank: the common herd. Here the impartial order of *pi-hua* rules.

The make-up of the presidium shows several special features. Contrary to custom, it includes only a small number of members of the former central committee. The presidium of the eighth congress was composed largely of members of the seventh central committee; but now, only 43 of the 170 members and deputy members of the eighth central committee are on the presidium of the ninth congress. There is a huge number of regular soldiers (over 60), who are mainly high-level cadres from the military regions and leaders of the provincial Revolutionary Committees. Many of them are supporters of Lin Piao. On the other hand, there is also a considerable number of new men. This is something new: in the past, seats on the presidium were usually reserved for men who had long-service medals with the party. Among these new men there are activists who distinguished themselves during the "Cultural Revolution" (including some Red Guards) and what might be described as a "corporate" delegation of workers, peasants, soldiers, (revolutionary) opera singers and even some scientists. The presence of these new men may point to an intended renewal of the party through the promotion of lower cadres, and therefore an attempt to eliminate mandarinism. On the other hand, prejudiced minds like mine cannot help noticing that a large number of these newcomers have a very low level of education (some of the peasants — as we learn from official sources — are completely illiterate, others semi-literate): the majority of them therefore have no political experience and, being new to the party, have hardly any knowledge of the mechanisms of power. This very ignorance means that they can only be a captive audience, hired to applaud the maoist juggling act.

If we compare it to preceding congresses, the ninth presents us with a number of anomalies. It is shrouded in secrecy. Its venue has not been revealed to the public. No texts of the speeches have been published yet. Apart from the first day's laconic communiqué, the press has not published any accounts of the various sessions. There are no foreign observers (at the eighth congress, forty-six foreign communist delegations were present as observers). There has been no mention of the examining commission which normally has to be appointed to verify the delegates' mandates. We know that a secretariat of the presidium has been formed, but a list of its members has not been published. The agenda is curiously skeletal: (1) a political report by Lin Piao; (2) a discussion on this report and on the draft reform of the party constitution, in committee; (3) the election of the central committee. The speaker on the reform of the constitution is not named. There are no economic issues on the agenda.

14 April: a press communiqué from the secretariat of the presidium of the ninth congress. The ninth congress has unanimously approved Lin Piao's political report and the party constitution. Mao made a speech which "won all hearts". Lin Piao made "an important speech". Chou En-lai, Ch'en Po-ta, K'ang Sheng, Huang Yung-sheng, Wang Hung-wen, Ch'en Yung-kui, Sun Yü-kuo, Wei Feng-ying and Chi Teng-k'ui "spoke in turn". Lin Piao's report and the constitution were sent to the secretariat of the presidium so that the latter can "revise the formulation". They will be published later. On the fifteenth of the month, the congress will take up the third point on its agenda: the election of the central committee.

Some comments. This is the second speech by Mao which has been mentioned without being published. We have been promised that Lin Piao's report and the constitution will be published later, but not the speeches. Why this censorship? As for the various delegates who spoke, it is important to note the silence of Chiang Ch'ing and her acolytes, Chang Ch'un-ch'iao and Yao Wen-yuan. Has the "Cultural Revolution" been struck dumb?

24 April: closing session of the ninth congress, in the presence of Mao and under Lin's chairmanship. The final communiqué describes in some detail the process which governed the election of members of the new central committee:

"Every delegation freely proposes a series of names: the presidium gathers all these suggestions together and proposes a draft list of candidates which it sends to the delegations. After a discussion with the delegations, the presidium produces a new list of candidates, following which there is a pre-election, by secret ballot. The same process is repeated several times in succession, allowing for consultation from the top to the bottom and vice-versa. Eventually, the presidium draws up a final list of candidates and presents it for the final vote of the congress, which takes place by secret ballot."

Finally, it gives the composition of the new central committee (which numbers 170 members and 109 deputy members).

Some comments. Ten days is rather a long time just for electing the central committee. The birth of this committee seems to
have been a difficult affair, and the congress as a whole was a
lot more troublesome than anticipated. Contrary to what we
imagined, the assembly did not let its hand be forced, and far
from blindly countersigning a list prepared in advance, it seems
to have haggled bitterly over the proposals made by the
presidium. And this time the communiqué no longer mentions a
"unanimous vote". The "delegations" mentioned by the communiqué are a puzzling phenomenon. This term has never been
employed at previous assemblies. Do they represent the various
pressure groups or regional strongholds? The total number of
members and deputy members of the new central committee is
considerable: 279, as against 170 for the eighth central committee. The most noticeable feature about its membership is the
spectacular preponderance of regular soldiers: a quick preliminary count indicates about 110 (and this is according to the
strictest count, i.e. excluding political commissars in the army
who have civilian functions too — such as Li Hsueh-feng, Chang
Ch'un-ch'iao, Wang Hsiao-yü and Liu Ke-p'ing — as well as
former soldiers such as Chu Teh, Li Hsien-nien and Teng Tzu-
hui). The three armed forces are represented as follows. (1) The
airforce is represented by all the principal members of its general
staff (Wu Fa-Hsien, Liu Hsien-ch'üan, Wang Hui-ch'iu, Wang
Ping-chang, Ts'ao Li-huai, Lo Yuan-fa, K'uang Jen-nung and
Tseng Kuo-hua); by comparison only two members of the eighth
central committee were from the general staff. The airforce
played an important part in the "seizure of power", and in general
seems to be a trump card in Lin Piao's strategy. (2) The navy is
also well represented (Hsiao Chin-kuang, Li Tso-p'eng, Wang
Hung-k'un, Wu Jui-lin, Chang Hsiu-ch'uan, Chao Ch'i-min and
Liu Hao-t'ien) — on the eighth central committee, however, it
had only one representative (Hsiao Chin-kuang). (3) Every section
of the army is represented: the engineers (Ch'en Shih-chü), tanks
(Huang Chih-yung), artillery (Ch'en Jen-lin) and communications
(Huang Wen-ming). Finally, and most importantly, the high
command of the various military regions is present in force. Each
of the large military regions is represented by at least three or
four of its leaders (for example, the Nanking military region is
represented by Hsü Shi-yu, commander of the military region,
Chang Tsai-ch'ien, second-in-command, Tu P'ing and T'ang
Liang, political commissars); on the eighth central committee,
several military regions were not even represented by their com-

manders. The provincial military regions are similarly represented: Kwangtung beats all records with *six* members, while on the eighth central committee it had only one representative, a deputy member. The new party which is supposed to have sprung from this ninth congress thus seems to be a radically militarised one. This is a quite faithful reflection of the situation of military government which prevails throughout the country at the moment.

It may be noted that the central committee contains various people whom the "Cultural Revolution" attacked violently, and who made themselves famous by the way they crushed revolutionary activities: for example, Chang Kuo-hua and Wang En-mao, who were accused of sabotaging the "Cultural Revolution" in Tibet and Sinkiang respectively, and T'an Ch'i-lung (ex-secretary of the East China bureau), the *bête noire* of the Red Guards of Shantung. I pointed out above, with a certain degree of surprise, that there are a lot of new men on the presidium. *But the central committee, generally speaking, remains closed to them*: nearly forty of them have failed to gain admittance.

We should note in conclusion that the national minorities are sparsely represented. This reflects "Cultural Revolution" policy which, on the question of national minorities, annulled all the relatively liberal measures which had previously been in operation (the principle of an indigenous administration under Chinese tutelage rather than direct Chinese administration; tolerance of traditional, social, cultural, and religious customs, etc.). In a crude and short-sighted fashion, it imposed measures which were inspired by Sinocentric chauvinism and were likely to alienate the loyalty of the minorities.

27 April: publication of Lin Piao's political report, which was presented on the 1st and unanimously approved on the 14th. We shall analyse this document later.

28 April: a press communiqué from the ninth central committee. The ninth central committee held its first session on the 28th under the chairmanship of Mao, who made a "very important speech" (once again not a word of it has been revealed). Mao was elected chairman of the central committee and Lin vice-chairman. The central committee elected the standing committee of the politbureau: Mao Tse-tung, Lin Piao and then, in lexicographical order, Ch'en Po-ta, Chou En-lai and K'ang Sheng. It then elected the politbureau: Mao Tse-tung, Lin Piao and then, in lexicographical order, Yeh Ch'ün, Yeh Chien-ying, Liu Po-ch'eng, Chiang Ch'ing, Chu Teh, Hsü Shi-yu, Ch'en Po-ta, Li Hsien-nien, Li Tso-p'eng, Wu Fa-hsien, Chang Ch'un-ch'iao, Ch'iu Hui-tso, Chou En-lai, Yao Wen-yuan, K'ang Sheng, Huang Yung-sheng, Tung Pi-wu and Hsieh Fu-chih; alternate members, Chi Teng-k'ui, Li Hsueh-feng, Li Teh-sheng and Wang Tung-hsing. I shall attempt later on to interpret the new balance of forces in the politbureau.

28 April: publication of the new party constitution. This text essentially conforms to the October 1968 draft which was leaked out of China, and which I mentioned previously.

May

The composition of the new politbureau which was announced at the end of April is worth examining closely. The current balance of forces is in fact crystallised in the politbureau.

All the observers have of course emphasised the massive presence of the military on the politbureau (a majority, in fact — thirteen members out of twenty-five). But it would be a serious mistake to infer from this that Lin Piao has a determining influence. In fact the opposite is the case. Let us look at who these military men are. Apart from Wang Tung-hsing, who is one of Mao's men, there are Chu Teh, a retired octogenarian, and Yeh Chien-ying, who now seems very much a marginal figure. Lin Piao has in fact only three allies: Li Tso-p'eng, Wu Fa-hsien and Ch'iu Hui-tso. In contrast to this, there is an opposing group remarkable for its coherence and power, which is sponsored by the old Marshal Liu Po-ch'eng. It consists of veterans of the former fourth front army: Ch'en Hsi-lien, Hsieh Fu-chih, Li Teh-sheng and Hsü Shi-yu. The People's Liberation Army was historically split into four groups of influence: the Lin Piao group, the Ho Lung group, the group of the fourth front army (under the command of Hsü Hsiang-ch'ien) and the group of the new fourth army (which was reconstituted under the command of Liu Po-ch'eng). The third group had acquired such influence at the beginning of the war that Mao became uneasy about it and eventually disbanded it. One half was incorporated with Lin Piao's troops, the other became the core of the new fourth army under the command of Liu Po-ch'eng. Chen, Hsieh, Li and Hsü all belonged to this third group and forged solid links before it was disbanded. Because of his great age and very bad health, Liu Po-ch'eng is definitely a non-starter in the power struggle, but his old team is quite capable of acting as a counter-weight to the authority of Lin Piao. And through Hsü Shi-yu, Ch'en Hsi-lien and Li Teh-sheng, this group (to which Huang

Yung-sheng must also be added) represents the insolent power of the large military regions which are bold enough to defy directly the authority of the central government. The victory of these regional barons is confirmed by their massive presence on the central committee.

With the exception of Mao's secretary, Ch'en Po-ta, and of the two intimate followers of Mao's wife (Chang Ch'un-ch'iao and Yao Wen-yuan), the "Cultural Revolution" has nobody to speak for it on the politbureau.

Chou En-lai's team has been completely disbanded; his allies — Ch'en Yi, Nieh Jung-chen and Li Fu-ch'un — have all been eliminated from the politbureau; and Li Hsien-nien almost certainly owes his survival to his well-established military connections rather than to Chou's support. Individually, Chou is unsinkable: he is the eternal and irreplaceable servant of power — any kind of power.

The main conclusion, therefore, which it seems can be drawn from the membership of the politbureau is that no faction has succeeded in gaining a decisive advantage. This subtle balancing of contradictory forces is to Mao's personal advantage: this way, he is still the sole arbiter of power. An exemplary illustration of this situation can be found at the highest level, the standing committee of the politbureau: Mao is surrounded here by four men (Lin Piao, Ch'en Po-ta, Chou En-lai, K'ang Sheng) who are *each linked with him personally but otherwise do not have any links with each other.*

In order to preserve the existing balance and to prevent any of the present factions scoring points over others, a climate of uncertainty is deliberately being maintained. Thus, for example, no *hierarchical* list of the members of the politbureau has been drawn up, and its members are always named in lexicographical order. Contrary to custom, the *People's Daily* did not publish any doctrinal editorial for the first of May, and thus avoided having to support any particular tendency.

If we now turn to Lin Piao's political report hoping to get a clearer picture, we shall be disappointed. It is a long text which is altogether dull, insipid and banal. If it really is the version that was presented to the ninth congress on 1 April, why did its publication have to be put off for such a long time? What are the "formal revisions" which the secretariat of the presidium has carried out in the meantime? Is this an emasculated version? What was the original content and what kind of corrections have been made? All these questions remain unanswered for the moment. Whatever the reason, the colourless nature of the document testifies once again to the situation of political uncertainty which the central authorities wish to maintain for the time being.

Let us therefore be content with a few marginal comments on this report. The denunciation of Liu Shao-ch'i is couched in language of unprecedented violence. Liu has not been dealt such vehement abuse since he was denounced by name in the communiqué from the twelfth enlarged plenary session of the eighth central committee. There is no point in flogging a dead horse. Is Liu still such a formidable opponent? As an individual, undoubtedly not (although his obstinate refusal to confess his crimes — despite threats and blandishments — must exasperate Mao beyond all measure); but everything he represents — his prestige, the reluctance of his faithful supporters to forswear their old allegiances or to make an act of unconditional submission to a new, unstable authority — all this must surely still arouse serious anxiety among the maoists.

Lin Piao makes a reminder that the task of struggle-criticism-rectification must continue. The "Cultural Revolution" is not over. A while ago, its "decisive victory" was announced, then its "total victory", but now we are told that it is still going on. The "Cultural Revolution" is like a bad public speaker who wants to bring his speech to an end but does not know how: he tries to stop, announces twenty times that he is about to, and in doing so embarks on a whole new paragraph. The "Cultural Revolution" has failed to establish its proposed new form of power; it cannot accept defeat, but at the same time it no longer has the means to return to the attack. This is the fundamental contradiction of maoism, which tries not to sacrifice either order or the revolution but ends up by overturning one and crushing the other; it comes out clearly in Lin Piao's report. On the one hand the report fans the flames of the "struggle-criticism-rectification" movement, and on the other hand it insists on the urgent need to rehabilitate former cadres. In practice, these two requirements seem largely incompatible, and in fact priority has now been given to the latter. The case of someone like T'an Ch'i-lung is typical: this former first secretary of the provincial party committee of Shantung, who was considered too revisionist to be tolerated in the Shantung Revolutionary Committee, has been promoted to the central committee! And on the very day the ninth congress ended, the New China News Agency announced that the Heilungkiang Revolutionary Committee has just rehabilitated en bloc a large group of leaders from the former provincial party committee. This action has been put forward as an example for the whole country. On 5 May the *Red Flag* published a very significant article by the "workers' and soldiers' group for propagating the thoughts of Mao Tse-tung" stationed at Tsinghua university. The article preaches leniency: the sinners must be helped to redeem themselves. "If these reactionaries don't carry out any sabotage, and don't stir up trouble, that will be enough; they will be left with a way out, so that they understand that under our socialist system it is enough to correct one's views to discover a new future for oneself." Then came this extraordinary remark: "All errors, whether they are of the right or of the left, are enormously harmful to our party's undertakings, and at certain moments *mistaken ideas from the extreme left blind the masses more easily than mistaken ideas from the right*: what is extraordinary is that some comrades have still not recognised their destructive character." Then the article criticises the view that "on the whole, it is much better to be a leftist than to let oneself be dragged to the right", and it condemns the attitude of the leftists who advocate following the will of the masses on every point — this is a mistake, and for the proletarian class it amounts to "an abdication of its authority". The mistakes of the left are more pernicious than those of the right, the will of the masses only has a relative value and cannot play a leading role: this is what you can read in the *Red Flag* today, after three years of "Cultural Revolution". The total victory of the movement? You would think you were reading its obituary.

June

The big theme now being orchestrated by the official propaganda organs is one of *unity*. It is particularly well illustrated by an important joint editorial in the *People's Daily,* the *Liberation Army Daily* and the *Red Flag,* published on the 8th. This editorial is very interesting, because it gives us a number of disclosures about the exact nature of the current difficulties.

The editorial points out that "the enemy is not yet disarmed", and that it is also important to "consolidate and develop the Revolutionary Committees". Let us note in passing that the *temporary* nature of these organisations (referred to when they were first established) is no longer mentioned; the reconstruction of the party is still at such an elementary level that the central authorities are now reduced to complete reliance on this one semblance of local authority. But the effectiveness of the Revolu-

tionary Committees is still very limited, because they still suffer
from internal disunity. The left forces are the principal factor in
this disunity. They are the rebels who were the first to build the
committees but have now been excluded from them in favour of
the military and of the "revisionist" bureaucrats. On this point,
the editorial is quite explicit:

> "Among those who were the first to rebel against the
> capitalist faction, there are those who during the tortuous
> course of the revolutionary movement have themselves made
> mistakes. . . . Their way of thinking 'we alone are revolu-
> tionary, we alone are the left' is erroneous, does not conform
> to reality and is prejudicial to unity and to the revolu-
> tion. . . . To make the revolution is to unite the greatest
> number."

But for the leftists, "to unite the greatest number" means
simply to do deals with the enemy and, what is worse, to
relinquish the power which they conquered with such difficulty to
those very same people whom the "Cultural Revolution" was
meant to defeat. We can therefore deduce that "in the tortuous
course of the movement" the revolutionaries are not executing
this pirouette very gracefully. A second problem is the lack of
co-operation between the new cadres and the old, rehabilitated
cadres. The new cadres consider the old ones to be incorrigible
mandarins, and that it would be better to get rid of them once and
for all; the old cadres regard the new ones as incompetent
fanatics. The need to establish respect, confidence and mutual
reliance between the old and the new cadres has already been
dealt with in several articles in the *People's Daily,* and the
editorial on the 8th of the month came back to this question.
The "movement for release of the cadres" has been taken further
and extended even to those cadres who have committed "serious
mistakes", as long as they are not "enemy agents" or "counter-
revolutionary elements" (*People's Daily,* 31 May). But in practice
the effects of this movement have been cancelled out by the
obstructionism of the left, which is constantly questioning the
validity of these rehabilitations. The editorial also issued an
appeal: "Regarding the cadres who have already been freed, it
is necessary to be bold in trusting them with work; when they
make the slightest mistake it is not necessary to settle all the old
scores again or to try and overthrow them again. . . . They should
be given the opportunity to correct themselves, so do not
immediately begin crushing them without respite." The problem
is further complicated by the fact that those concerned do not at

the moment seem very interested in resuming their normal activities. Their experience of the "Cultural Revolution" has inflicted a deep trauma. In the past they were completely devoted to the party, and they did not hesitate to make themselves unpopular with the masses in order to serve it better. Then during the "Cultural Revolution", the party coldly abandoned them to the wrath of the people. Their former privileged position has become as thankless, as undesirable and as dangerous as it could possibly be. Until Peking succeeds in reconstructing and reimposing a unified and coherent régime, and in formulating a clear and stable political line that follows well-defined criteria, these cadres feel they have no guarantees; they are paralysed by their fear of making fresh mistakes and of being delivered once again to the fury of the crowd, and so they try to take the least possible risk by confining themselves to prudent inaction.

The editorial ends by referring to the switchback effect, which is something the régime has never been able to control and is an inevitable consequence of its autocratic methods of government: "Every movement with a given orientation harbours its opposite. Just as a campaign against rightism is being conducted, leftism develops; when one is struggling against leftism, rightism emerges." The key to the problem is the fact that, despite Mao's claims to incarnate the "line of the masses" and to "liberate the spontaneity of the masses" (I have already described the value which the *Red Flag* attaches to the will of the masses!), political initiative operates unilaterally from the top down, and the internal logic governing the helmsman's contradictory changes of direction remains unintelligible to the galley-slaves below. The various directives which periodically fall on the confused masses from the sky tend to evaporate as soon as they touch the ground, and are reduced to an empty formalism. A good illustration of this is the development of the two theoretically complementary movements, one for "purging the class ranks" (the elimination of the "class enemies" still existing among the cadres), the other being the "release of the cadres" (i.e. the exoneration of the great majority of cadres, who can be rescued once the small irrecoverable minority is eliminated). In the field, the activity of these two movements has led to inextricable confusion. When they receive the first directive ("purging of class ranks"), the peasants are concerned to show their maoist zeal and do not want to be thought lukewarm — so they immediately expel all the brigade and commune cadres from the collective. This is followed by a

fine state of anarchy which requires the intervention of the
"military groups for propagating the thought of Mao Tse-tung".
The military gets the situation under control; the peasants are
accused of "extreme left adventurism" and of "sabotaging the
concrete application of the thought of Mao Tse-tung". They
are told that they must now "release the cadres". Anxious to be
pardoned for their previous error and to show their good will and
enthusiasm, the peasants hasten to reinstate, immediately and
en bloc, all the cadres they have just eliminated. But in doing so,
they bring a new disaster on themselves. This time they are com-
mitting the sin of "right opportunism" and "lack of principles":
the cadres should not be released at random. At this point, the
perplexed peasants realise that zeal can be more dangerous than
passivity. They prudently leave it to the army to stage the comedy
— they are now quite content just to provide the chorus. The
soldiers know their catechism, but they are strangers to the region.
The peasants choose some village idiot to play the role of "class
enemy" for the army. This class enemy is duly criticised and
unmasked at an open meeting. Once this formality of "criticism"
has been carried out, the cadres can resume their positions and
life goes on again as normal. Every dynasty has its ritual: this
is how it has gone on for centuries.

July-August

The editorial jointly published on 30 June by the *People's Daily,*
the *Liberation Army Daily* and the *Red Flag* to commemorate
the forty-eighth anniversary of the founding of the Chinese Communist Party endeavoured to re-establish theoretically the party's
former leading role, and recalled that the party's authority should
take precedence over the army's. In line with this recollection of
former principles, propaganda articles on the army have grown
muted. But in practice at any rate, the power of the army is far
from diminished and is being increased by discreet but significant
measures. Quite recently, for example, several Revolutionary
Committees have increased their number of leaders — in the
majority of cases, by including regular soldiers. Similarly, inside
the army there has been a series of changes and promotions,
whose general significance is clear enough: Lin Piao is trying
to dislocate and reduce the main cells which are still impervious
to his influence. At the same time, he is installing men loyal to
him in various key posts. This is a long-term enterprise, but
until it is successfully completed Lin Piao's power will be based
on fragile foundations.

A huge campaign has been launched to prepare the country to "tackle war and famine". All the communes have been urged to stock up with provisions, so that in case of necessity they can be self-sufficient, without having to appeal for aid from the central government. This campaign has brought new austerity measures; the population is psychologically prepared to accept them because it is now living under the threat of war. There are few details on the recent border incidents (at Pa-ch'a island in Heilungkiang on 8 July, and more particularly the one in Sinkiang on 13 August). The Chinese seem to be in an unfavourable position militarily, and Peking is aware of the danger. Since the skirmish in Sinkiang, the Chinese communiqués have concentrated on describing patriotic reactions inside the country, the mass demonstrations etc., while remaining rather laconic about the actual fighting; it is no longer a matter of Chinese counter-offensives victoriously sweeping the invader away, but only of the stoic "patience" of the frontier guards who fell back before the Soviet raids "in order to avoid bloodshed". The communiqué of the 15th commented on the Chinese masses' demand that "the USSR immediately withdraw its troops from Chinese territory", and this leads one to suppose that the battlefield of this incident is still in Soviet hands. The Soviet threat to Sinkiang must worry Peking very seriously; in this sparsely populated region, with its vast, ill-defined frontiers, the Soviet armed forces have the tactical advantage. Among the USSR's military clique, whose political influence is certainly increasing, the hard-line faction must be sorely tempted to take advantage of the disorder of the "Cultural Revolution" in order to try and annihilate the Chinese nuclear installations in a lightning operation. China's defensive strategy of the guerrilla and the people's war is obviously no defence against this kind of rapid operation, with its precise and limited objectives.

The exodus of young people into the country continues. For example, in the town of Tientsin alone 174,000 young intellectuals and Red Guards have been sent to the fields. The New China News Agency adds the following interesting information: "Among them are members of the Revolutionary Committee of Tientsin municipality, leaders of the general assembly of Red Guard delegates, leaders of the students' Revolutionary Committees, and leaders of various groupings of Red Guards." In other words, the brains of the revolutionary youth, the activist élite of the "Cultural Revolution", are being sent to "the remote reaches of the country, to the most primitive regions, in order to be re-educated by poor and lower-middle peasants." The revolutionaries of Tientsin are thus destined to shovel manure or plant cabbages in far-off deserts for the rest of their careers, and the bureaucrats and the army, who lead the city's Revolutionary Committee, are finding their task very much easier. But this is not happening everywhere; in many provinces, the factions which are still armed continue to put up a desperate resistance. A very remarkable document had just reached us concerning the nature and the extent of this unrest: this is a "warning" addressed by the central committee to the province of Shansi on 23 July. Here is a complete translation:

"Approved by President Mao. This must be followed!
Central Committee of the Chinese Communist Party.
Warning!
Since the ninth plenary assembly of the Chinese Communist Party, under the stimulating effect of the slogan put forward by our great leader Mao Tse-tung 'Let us unite, let us win a greater victory!', the situation in the whole country is excellent. This applies to the province of Shansi and to the rest of the country, where the situation is excellent too ['the situation is excellent': a conventional expression normally used to denote a serious or disastrous situation — S.L.]. However, in T'aiyuan municipality and in parts of the central and southern regions of Shansi, a tiny handful of class enemies and bad elements have penetrated the mass organisations, have resorted to the methods of capitalist factionalism to blind a section of the masses, are refusing to carry out the orders, communications and repeated warnings of the central committee, and have committed the following series of very serious counter-revolutionary crimes:

(1) They organise groups who specialise in armed struggle, who beat, loot, arrest and damage the safety of individuals and goods, and who sabotage revolutionary order.

(2) They refuse to put into effect the great revolutionary alliance or to carry out the policy of triple union decided on by the central committee. They have sabotaged those great alliances which have already been formed as well as the Revolutionary Committees based on the revolutionary triple union; and they establish autonomous strongholds. They create divisions, put forward the counter-revolutionary slogan 'the seizure of power must be carried out by arms' and have effected a counter-seizure of anti-proletarian power.

(3) They forcibly seize the installations of the People's Liberation Army, take possession of arms and equipment belonging to the army, commit atrocities and abductions, and kill and wound fighters of the People's Liberation Army.

(4) They sabotage railways, roads and bridges, make armed attacks on convoys, seize means of communication, loot travellers' goods and threaten their safety.

(5) They loot or occupy state banks, warehouses and shops, and establish their own banks, taking away considerable quantities of goods belonging to the state.

(6) They occupy and forcibly control areas of territory, establishing combat bases or creating counter-revolutionary dissent, persecuting the population and subject them to blackmail and ransom demands.

(7) They stir up or threaten workers so that they interrupt work and stop production, incite the peasants to come into the towns to create disturbances, and sabotage agricultural and industrial production and the state plan.

The central committee considers that the crimes of this small handful of class enemies and bad elements are sabotaging the application of the various orders for struggle given by the ninth congress, are sabotaging the dictatorship of the proletariat, the great proletarian Cultural Revolution and the construction of socialism, go counter to the interests of the mass of the population and arouse the anger of the great majority of the masses of Shansi province. Therefore the central committee is taking the following decisions:

(1) The central committee reiterates its previous directives: all these directives must be carried out resolutely, radically and completely, by all organisations and individuals.

(2) There must be an immediate and unconditional cessation of hostilities between the two camps, all special fighting groups in any form and under whatever name must be dissolved; all the combat bases must disappear, all arms and equipment must be returned. All those who have laid down their arms will either resume their original posts or be collectively subjected to an educational session organised by the army. As for those who forcibly occupy a territory and who refuse to carry out the present order: (a) those who resist — the army will surround them militarily and will attack them by political means in order to induce them to lay down their arms; (b) those who escape — the army will pursue and arrest them, and they will be handed over to

justice. The act of hiding, exchanging or transporting arms, and of using the state's workshops and supplies to make arms for personal use, is a serious crime and will be punished in accordance with the law.

(3) It is forbidden to appropriate arms, munitions, vehicles or other equipment belonging to the People's Liberation Army. All appropriated military goods must be returned unconditionally and in full. As regards the class enemies who create dissension between the army and the people, their deeds will be firmly checked.

(4) Road and railway communications must be immediately and unconditionally re-established; the 19-3 convoy illegally organised on the southern section of the T'ung-P'u line must be abolished. Attacks on stations and convoys, the sabotage of road and railway transport, the appropriation of goods in stations and vehicles is banditry. The tiny minority of bad and counter-revolutionary elements will be taken into custody and handed over to justice.

(5) No one may occupy or loot the banks, depots and shops, or other state property. Those who incite the looting of state goods must be severely punished and made to hand back the goods and liquid assets.

(6) As regards those criminals who are found guilty of the extreme crimes of murder and arson: the masses must be urged to hand them over. As regards those among them whose crimes have been formally established, there will be a public statement of their crimes which will be submitted to the masses for discussion, and they will be punished in accordance with the law.

(7) Depraved individuals who incite or threaten workers to desert production and their place of work will be punished in accordance with the law. As regards the masses who, blinded by lies, have left production and their places of work: we must proceed to educate them and impel them to go back to work. As from the day this warning is published, those who have let more than one month pass without resuming their work in office or factory will have their wages suspended. If they continue their obstinate refusal and are permanently absent, the Revolutionary Committee of Shansi province, having examined the concrete circumstances of each case, will decide on disciplinary sanctions which may lead to dismissal. As for those who start work again; they must be welcomed and their personal safety guaranteed. To burden

them with discriminatory measures, to bully them, or to inflict reprisals on them is forbidden. If they are persecuted, those responsible must be sought out and severely punished.

(8) All activity tending to divide the great alliance, to sabotage the triple union and to establish autonomous strongholds is illegal, and is repudiated by the central committee.

The party's policy has always been as follows: anyone of good faith will be treated with magnanimity; anyone who is obstructive will be treated severely. The leaders will be punished, the followers pardoned. Anyone who has been led astray will be acquitted, anyone who changes over to the right direction will be rewarded. The bad elements of the two factions must be purged by the masses of each of the two factions. The proletarian policy of Chairman Mao must be put into practice, the two different kinds of contradiction must be clearly distinguished and all the possible forces must be rallied. The small handful of class enemies must be ruthlessly attacked, and Chairman Mao's proletarian policy of always leaving a door open must be put into practice.

The central committee is convinced that the two factions are equally dedicated to the revolution. The central committee appeals to the working class, to the poor and lower-middle peasants and to the revolutionary masses of Shansi to raise higher the glorious red banner of the thoughts of Mao Tse-tung and, under the direction of the provincial revolutionary committee and with the support of the People's Liberation Army, to carry out conscientiously the tasks laid down by the ninth party congress, developing and consolidating the great revolutionary alliance and the revolutionary triple union in order to win a greater victory in the great Cultural Revolution and the construction of socialism."

This remarkable document needs no commentary. What is most striking is the extent of the troubles referred to: the occupation and armed control of whole territories, the training of combat groups, the occupation and looting of stations, banks and military installations, the interruption of communications, even the organisation of autonomous lines of communication — all these can hardly be the work of a "tiny handful of individuals", as the text would otherwise have us believe. The authorities' impotence is no less astonishing: the mildness of the sanctions against workers who have left their posts, the indulgence promised to all those who are willing to lay down their arms — all this indicates that the authorities are faced with a movement of such breadth and popularity that they cannot and dare not meet it head-on or suppress it by force.

In Kwangtung, the authorities have begun a stock-taking of all the losses and damage inflicted on the belongings of individuals during the "Cultural Revolution". Those concerned are being urged to make a statement to the administration listing all the goods which have been confiscated, stolen or destroyed during the "Cultural Revolution", and indicating where possible the names of those responsible or of the groups to which those responsible belong. When these instructions were first issued, about a month ago, the public response was practically nil. Many people were afraid that their complaints would rebound against them if they revealed that they had bourgeois possessions; but in the meantime the authorities have insisted on this directive actually being followed. The chances of getting the confiscated goods back are minimal (at least for non-proletarians), but it is possible that this information is being gathered in order to compile dossiers which will incriminate the leaders of the Red Guard movement.

September-October

On 16 September, the New China News Agency published the twenty-nine official slogans which are to be used at the National Day celebrations on 1 October (which is also the twentieth anniversary of the founding of the People's Republic). Every year, the list of official slogans for the National Day celebrations gives an interesting indication of the current political line, the priorities, innovations etc. In this year's list, a sharp decline in Mao's personality cult is immediately obvious; his name is only at the bottom of the list (no. 23, "Long live the victory of the revolutionary proletarian line of Chairman Mao; no. 28, "Long live the invincible marxist-leninism and the thought of Chairman Mao"; no. 29, "Long, long, long live our great leader Mao"). The tone is less hysterical, the theme less overwhelming. Lin Piao's name is not mentioned. There is a striking insistence on the problem of the war which China now feels threatened by. Slogans 10, 11 and 12 deal with the themes "Expand preparations against war", "Prepare to confront war, to confront famine", "Increase your vigilance — defend the country, be ready at any moment to annihilate the invading enemy". Note in particular slogan 22: "Peoples of all countries, unite and oppose all wars of aggression launched by imperialism or by social imperialism, especially those wars in which the atom bomb is used! If such a war does break out, the peoples of the world must annihilate the war of aggression by means of revolutionary war — preparations must begin right now!" (Slogan 22 was taken up separately and developed in a long commentary by the New China News Agency on 17 September, which shows that special importance was attached to it.) As opposed to the majority of foreign commentators, I do not think that this is mere rhetoric; rather, it betrays the real and justified fear, the awareness of a definite threat, that the Soviet Union might strike unexpectedly using nuclear weapons.

At the political and ideological level, no compromise with the revisionist, social imperialist USSR is envisaged: it is placed on exactly the same plane as American imperialism (slogan 16). Slogan 9, "Forge ahead with all your strength, aim to surpass it, build socialism more extensively, more quickly, better and more economically", is an old saw; it dates from the period of the "Great Leap Forward", and has not been heard for a long time. Over the past few months I have noted some reminiscences of the phraseology of the "Great Leap", but it is still too soon to draw any conclusions. The new Chinese economic policy has still not been clearly defined; certain outlines have emerged (the decentralisation of industry, priority for agriculture, the drive to eliminate free agricultural markets), but there are still some uncertainties: the move to reactivate the communes as basic units, and to reconstitute and extend the production brigades, has still not been followed up. Mao must surely be obsessed by his desire to return eventually to the "Great Leap Forward", but he cannot entirely ignore the objective conditions of the current situation: you don't leap across an abyss on one foot.

The National Day celebrations on the first of October went off quietly. The twentieth anniversary of the founding of the People's Republic has been celebrated, although it still has no Chairman. The national assembly, the only body competent to elect a new Chairman, cannot be convened yet.

In the ideological sphere, nothing very much can be gleaned from the joint editorial published on 30 September by the *People's Daily*, the *Liberation Army Daily* and the *Red Flag*, nor from Chou En-lai's speech of the same day, nor from Lin Piao's speech of 1 October. Let us note merely that Chou En-lai and Lin Piao

took up the old slogan of peaceful coexistence based on five
principles: there was a time when Liu Shao-ch'i was accused, as
if it were a crime, of using this slogan — it was seen as proof of
his desire to collaborate with the enemy. . . .

But one passage is worth picking out from the joint editorial:
"American imperialism and social imperialism are busy plotting
closely together, and impudently cherish the dream of launching
a war of aggression against our country; *they are going to the
extent of leaking all sorts of rumours in order to bring nuclear
blackmail to bear on our country.* . . . You impudently dream
of organising insurrections in our border territories. . . . You
impudently dream of unleashing armed aggression, etc." This
passage indicates that Peking is taking the Soviet Union's blackmail seriously. Several planned leaks to foreign press agencies in
Moscow have allowed it to be understood that a nuclear raid on
China is being considered as a theoretical possibility.* The
organised subversion of the national minorities of Sinkiang is
another specific threat to which Peking is very sensitive; the
Russians still dream of taking advantage of the periods of political
disorder in China in order to try and detach these border territories from her and eventually turn them into puppet republics.

The Chinese position on the Sino-Soviet conflict is set out in
two documents. On 7 October, the Chinese government published
a statement on the border question. This relatively brief text is
a clear summary of the problem. The tone is cool, measured and
free from hollow rhetoric. The main points can be summarised as
follows. The problem must be solved peacefully, but if a military
adventure against China's strategic centres is undertaken, China
is determined to defend them. As for the borders, the treaties
imposed on China by tsarist Russia were unjust, but China is
prepared to settle the whole problem on the basis of the borders

---

* *Note* (1971): This is in fact the basic source of the "ping-pong
diplomacy" we are now witnessing. It would be childish to see this as a
sudden, improvised volte-face. It follows in a straight line from the
threat of war, which is generally underestimated, if not ignored in the
West, and which the USSR imposed brutally on China in 1969. As for
the future of Sino-American relations, once the Vietnam affair is settled,
the ease with which Washington and Peking find grounds for agreement
will be a source of melancholy surprise both for the USA's old clients
and for the honest maoists of the West. In reality, the Sino-Soviet confrontation is deep and irreconcilable, to the same extent that the reasons
for the hostility between China and the USA are relatively artificial and
minimal. Mao Tse-tung had the nerve to express his warm friendship
for Yahya Khan: why should he be more disgusted by Nixon?

laid down by them; the Chinese government has never intended to reclaim the territories which Russia took from it by means of these treaties. The territories actually in dispute are territories which the USSR is today claiming *in addition* to the borders laid down by the unequal treaties. The border problem apart, China reserves the right to pursue its ideological denunciation of the USSR. There is an irreconcilable divergence of principle between the two countries, and the ideological struggle will therefore continue to be pursued for a long period. But this should not prevent China and the USSR from getting down to the task of establishing normal relations with each other, on the basis of the five principles of peaceful coexistence. Various concrete measures of détente have already been adopted, following the discussions between Kosygin and Chou En-lai. The status quo is to be maintained on the border, pending a settlement; in order to avoid new armed clashes, the two camps are to withdraw from the disputed zones or to give up trying to enter them; negotiations are to take place in Peking at vice-ministerial level.

The tone of this declaration is reasonable and moderate. By clearly stating that it is surrendering its right to the territories taken from it by tsarist imperialism, China is making an enormous concession even before sitting down at the negotiating table. The appeasement formula (maintenance of the status quo, mutual withdrawal of troops outside the disputed zones) goes well beyond previous declarations; in fact on 24 May China was demanding the immediate and unconditional return of the zones illegally occupied by the USSR.

On 8 October the Chinese Minister for Foreign Affairs published a long declaration refuting the Soviet statement of 13 June. The New China News Agency graciously published the two texts side by side. The Soviet document cuts a poor figure alongside this bitingly effective refutation. The Chinese text is long but sharp, and is set out in a highly rational and pertinent manner; what is remarkable is that *it contains not a single quotation from Mao*. It begins by recalling some historical facts. In the past, was it China that committed acts of aggression against Russia or vice-versa? On the historical issue, the Chinese position is obviously unassailable. Coming to the present: is it China or the USSR that is guilty of expansionism? Again, China has a good hand. The text points out that China does not have troops stationed outside its frontiers, while the USSR has bases in Mongolia, has conducted a military occupation of Czechoslovakia, and sends its fleets into the Mediterranean, the Indian Ocean etc.

On the border question, the Chinese position can be summarised in five points. (1) The USSR must acknowledge that, historically speaking, the treaties imposed by tsarist Russia on China were unjust. (2) For its part, China surrenders the territories it lost under these treaties, and accepts them as the basis for determining the frontiers. (3) The territories occupied by the USSR exceed the borders laid down by the unequal treaties, and must be restored; detailed amendments to the borderlines may be made, by common agreement, in the interests of the local population and in line with local conditions. (4) A new, just treaty will be signed to replace the old, unequal treaty. (5) The status quo will be maintained pending a settlement, and the forces of the two camps will withdraw from the disputed zones so as to avoid armed clashes.

The Chinese demands thus appear to be very moderate; what China mainly wants is the honourable satisfaction of righting the historical record. But the Soviet Union has obstinately refused to make this gesture of good faith, which would not mean sacrificing any territory; it wants China to promise to give up its ideological offensive, as a preliminary to any agreement on the border. China cannot accept such a condition — it believes that the questions of territorial conflict and ideological conflict should be clearly separated. Generally speaking, the Soviet Union's approach to the problem of China seems to be based on very dangerous premises. On the one hand it is overestimating — as it did in Czechoslovakia — the influence of the Moscow-oriented wing of the Chinese Communist Party and does not understand that if there is a conflict, these pro-Russian tendencies, far from being strengthened by the approach of the Soviet army, would on the contrary be swept away by a wave of nationalism which would unite even Mao's most unyielding opponents around him. On the other hand, the Soviet Union is blinded by its crushing superiority in arms and technology; when faced with political obstacles, it is irresistibly tempted to substitute crude military blackmail for any real effort at negotiation.

Foreign observers are still making great play of the rise of Chou En-lai and his increasing influence on Chinese politics. I am still very sceptical about the real importance of this. However spectacular the role Chou En-lai is now playing, this in no way means that his real power has increased correspondingly. Chou is the highest administrator in the régime, *but he is not and never has been anything but an administrator*: he may sing well, but we should not confuse the singer with the librettist. Mao is capable of executing tactical withdrawals when necessary, but in general he arranges things so that his name is not linked with any such inglorious manoeuvres. He prefers to leave their execution to his subordinates.

Three Postscripts

Successive events have confirmed the analyses of this diary of the "Cultural Revolution" in the years since it was written: first the disgrace of Ch'en Po-ta, then the violent elimination of Lin Piao, and finally the purge of the "Gang of Four" (Chiang Ch'ing, Chang Ch'un-ch'iao, Yao Wen-yuan and Wang Hung-wen) — the last bunker of the "Cultural Revolution" which, granted an extra lease of life through Mao's personal protection, fell as soon as the Great Helmsman had breathed his last. Alongside this gradual burial of the "Cultural Revolution" the movement of "revisionist restoration" has continued, culminating in Teng Hsiao-p'ing's rehabilitation. These events have been briefly considered in these three postscripts to the various editions of this book.

It is difficult to say whether or not the new leadership will ever start to undertake an overt "demaoisation" (such a course is fraught with dangers: the example of Khrushchev who, in trying to remove the Stalin idol, dropped it on his foot, is there to remind China's leaders that no totalitarian system can lightly dismiss its former gods), or if Liu Shao-ch'i will ever be formally rehabilitated. Both moves are perhaps unnecessary: it may seem more convenient to practise Liu's policies under Mao's label, now that this label has safely been deprived of any meaningful content.

1971 postscript

More than eighteen months have already passed since the end of this diary of the "Cultural Revolution". The events of this period have simply given us formal confirmation of the tendencies which I described in the diary. For example, the draft of the new constitution now sanctions the peasants' right to cultivate private plots of land. What is there left to criticise Liu Shao-ch'i for?

The extreme "left" has been ruthlessly hunted down: Yao Teng-shan, the "red diplomat" who was welcomed triumphantly in Peking when he returned from Indonesia and then led the revolutionary rebels in the assault on Chou En-lai's bureaucratic citadel, has been publicly tried in Peking and condemned to an exemplary sentence. (In the liquidation of the extreme left, Peking has now gone to the point of enlisting the services of foreign journalists in order to disown in the eyes of international opinion the "revolutionary" aspect of the "Cultural Revolution". During recent weeks, the lesson has been tamely transmitted not only by the usual stars such as Edgar Snow and Wilfred Burchett, but also by much smaller fry mobilised for the occasion, such as Jack Chen in the *Far Eastern Economic Review* and K. S. Karol in *Le Nouvel Observateur*.)

The purge of Ch'en Po-ta is even more remarkable. Ch'en has been absent from the political scene since August 1970, and the official press began to attack him violently from 1 May this year (the *Red Flag*, which he used to edit, opened fire, and the *People's Daily* soon began to echo it). These attacks were at first phrased in a cryptic manner, but they have become perfectly clear since the joint editorial published on 1 July by the *People's Daily*, the *Liberation Army Daily* and the *Red Flag*. As I write, Ch'en has not yet been denounced *by name*; but the 1 July editorial mentions him by way of a periphrasis which leaves no room for doubt (*hsiao-hsiao lao-pai-hsing*) — a "modest, ordinary little man", a famous expression used by Ch'en of himself and now turned against him: "A certain individual who has said that he is a 'modest, ordinary little man' and who is in reality dangerously ambitious".* He has been called a "charlatan claiming to be a marxist, of the Ch'en Tu-hsiu, Wang Ming and Liu Shao-ch'i variety." Ch'en Po-ta! For more than thirty years he has been Mao's modest and devoted shadow, his scribe and his mouthpiece, the man who carried out the highest and lowest jobs, who never claimed an existence or a personality separate from that of his master, who at Mao's inspiration and on his precise instructions organised and supervised the arrangement of the whole "Cultural Revolution" step by step, and who in return for such loyal service was finally promoted to fourth place in the hierarchy (immediately after Mao, Lin Piao and Chou En-lai). Here he is

---

* Chiang Ch'ing herself, as is logical, is indirectly attacked in these articles. But in her case at any rate, the settling of accounts will be purely academic — as long as her husband remains alive.

THE CHAIRMAN'S NEW CLOTHES

now, quite incredibly associated with Liu Shao-ch'i, whose fall he organised. Western supporters of maoism are used to undergoing the most extraordinary mental contortions and were even capable of finding good *a posteriori* reasons for the purge of Wang Li or Ch'i Pen-yü. Will they have the decency to observe a minute's silence this time? Let us for our part be content with recognising the rigorous logic of a development which is in the nature of things and could have been predicted three years ago. The pseudo-left joins with the pseudo-right again, the circle is complete. The "Cultural Revolution" was simply the revolution of a wheel : like the serpent which eats its own tail, it seems to form a perfect circle. What more can one say? The reconstruction of the party throughout the country has been for the benefit of the bureaucratic old guard, which has been rehabilitated everywhere, and for the benefit of the army, which is increasingly influential on all sides. In the few provinces where the left initially gained representation on the Revolutionary Committees it has now been forbidden access to the new provincial party committees. Shantung is a good example. This province is always given special attention by Mao and his wife (Chiang Ch'ing is originally from Shantung), and at the beginning of the "Cultural Revolution" it was one of the first to carry out a maoist-type insurrection. Wang Hsiao-yü took power there in February 1967, with Mao's personal blessing. Subsequently Wang ran into stormy weather, but at the beginning of 1969 Mao once again intervened personally to get him out of his difficult situation. But the composition of the new provincial party committee shows that Wang has today finally been eliminated. The new committee is led by a soldier, assisted by two of his colleagues and two veterans of the former local bureaucracy (Yang Teh-chih, Yuan Sheng-p'ing, Chang Chih-hsiu, Pai Ju-ping and Su Yi-jan). All the "revisionist" cadres whom the "Cultural Revolution" seemed to have swept away are coming forward one after the other, arrogant and triumphant. Take a man like Chao Tzu-yang, the ex-first secretary of the Kwangtung provincial party committee: in February 1968, when the Kwangtung Revolutionary Committee was set up, he was publicly denounced as the "agent of the Chinese Khrushchev and of the counter-revolutionary T'ao Chu, frantically engaged in a criminal plot to restore capitalism in Kwangtung". (These epithets were published at the time in an official statement from the New China News Agency.) The Kwangtung Revolutionary Committee even sent a telegram to Mao announcing the irreversible fall of this sinister enemy of the people. Irreversible fall? He has now surfaced as secretary of the new party committee in Inner Mongolia. Examples like this could be multiplied indefinitely. In Kwangsi, for example, Wei Kuo-ch'ing, who was personally responsible for the great massacres of revolutionary rebels in this province (massacres which in 1968 caused 100,000 deaths and destroyed most of the town of Wuchou), has now become first secretary of the new provincial party committee. In Kweichow, on the other hand, Li Tsai-han — who chaired the province's Revolutionary Committee and who showed himself to be a faithful maoist — has no place on the new provincial party committee.

"The Chinese Communist Party is now no longer a child, nor even an adolescent, it is an adult. Men become old and die. The same goes for the party. . . . The young comrades who have just entered the party and who have not read Marx and Lenin are perhaps unaware of this truth," wrote Mao Tse-tung in 1949 (*Mao Tse-tung hsuan-chi,* Peking, 1960, vol. IV, p.174). I would be prepared to bet that today's "young comrades" will find it difficult to stay unaware: the huge corpse is sprawled out across the country, and it already stinks.

1974 postscript

On re-reading this book four years after it was first published, all I can find to pick at is the occasional typographical mistake. As in geometry, where one's knowledge of a single segment of a circumference enables one to deduce the whole circumference, the events which have taken place since — far from invalidating the description which we have just read — only confirm it, and can be set firmly into the trajectory marked out at the beginning. The main part of the book described two developments: the gradual elimination of the artisans of the "Cultural Revolution" and the successive rehabilitation of all their opponents. These two complementary and opposed movements at first affected only the second fiddles; then they began to mount the hierarchy until they have now reached their apotheosis: the first with the solemn damnation of Lin Piao, the closest-comrade-in-arms-of-Chairman-Mao without whose support the "Cultural Revolution" could not have been conceived, the second with the glorious reinstatement of Teng Hsiao-p'ing who, along with Liu Shao-ch'i, had previously been taken for the grand guignol archtraitor, the absolute monster who for several years had been the object of the frenzied fury of hundreds of millions of militants.

On many specific points, the highest authorities in Peking have provided an incessant and striking confirmation of the description which I put forward then. For Western maoists, the bloodshed and violence which I mentioned were nothing but slanderous lies; Chairman Mao, on the other hand, told Edgar Snow in a famous interview that the foreign press had been quite right when it spoke about the violence. (This is not the first time, nor will it be the last, that a god snubs his own worshippers.) In my description of the ninth party congress I underlined the fact that signs of squabbling were drifting out from behind the closed doors and that there was wrangling about Lin Piao's report. This diagnosis was confirmed precisely and explicitly by no less a person than Chou En-lai in his report to the tenth congress. Rather than insert all this supplementary and largely redundant information in the margins of my book now, I prefer to keep it in its original form, without any cuts, additions or alterations. The experience of the past four years makes me confident of the book's ability to confront the test of time, and it leads me to think that in the future it will, just as it stands, be a historical testimony.

1977 postscript: maoism mummified

Ignazio Silone, who was for a time a leader of the underground Communist Party in Mussolini's Italy, recalled a dialogue he had in Moscow, during the early days of Stalin's rule, with Shatskii, the head of the Soviet Communist Youth. As Shatskii confessed his disappointment at having been born too late and not having been able to participate in either the 1905 or 1917 revolutions, Silone tried to comfort him: "There'll still be revolutions, there'll always be need of revolutions, even in Russia." Pointing to the mausoleum of Lenin which was still made of wood at that time and before which every day an interminable procession of poor ragged peasants was slowly filing, Silone continued: "I presume you love Lenin. I knew him too and have a very vivid recollection of him. You must admit that this superstitious cult of his mummy is an insult to his memory and a disgrace to a revolutionary city like Moscow." Silone then jokingly suggested to his terrified Russian friend that they should get hold of a tin of petrol and make a "little revolution" of their own by burning the totem-hut. (Shatskii was to commit suicide ten years later at the height of the Stalinist purges, while Silone, out of fidelity to socialist values, felt compelled eventually to break away from the communist movement.)

The Peking authorities have announced their decision to embalm Mao's body and to display the mummy permanently for the devotion of pilgrims. Will any young Chinese revolutionaries pick up Silone's idea some day?

Exceptional people need exceptional circumstances to give their full measure. The only trouble is that, after the storm, when they find themselves in a more routine situation, their very genius can prove extremely disruptive of the essential fabric in the everyday life of the nation. The advantage of the democratic system is that it makes provisions for shelving away Men of Providence once they have fulfilled their role and outlived their usefulness (remember Churchill, de Gaulle, etc.). After 1959 (the Lushan conference) the Chinese leadership constantly endeavoured to find some way of forcing Mao into a back-seat: the idea was to enshrine him as a supreme totem — thus reducing him to the paralysed status of a wooden image, and neutralising once and for all, in this glorified manner, his frighteningly inventive talent with all its potential destructiveness. Mao repeatedly succeeded in foiling their attempts — in this respect, the launching of the "Cultural Revolution" was his last masterstroke — but, in the long run, the bureaucracy's efforts were largely successful, so much so that one might well in fact say that maoism died even before Mao. Mao himself was aware of it, and this turned him in his last years into a truly tragic figure. Not long before breathing his last, he observed sarcastically to his entourage that a good number of them must have been all too eager to see him on his way to meet Marx.

Now at long last, taxidermy seems to have provided the Chinese leaders with the ultimate solution to the problem of what to do with Mao. Similarly, maoism itself is to be stuffed and relegated to the innocuous position of a formal State Religion — to serve the purpose of Confucianism as utilised earlier this century by warlord governments. The fact that it has become inoperative as a political recipe was dramatically illustrated by the downfall of Chiang Ch'ing and the whole group of the maoist radicals — an event so welcome to cadres and masses alike (it was the first time that rulers and ruled found themselves in spontaneous harmony) that it sent almost everyone dancing with joy in the streets. Such a reaction was quite understandable: for the people, radical maoism meant the substitution of an austere and fanatical political mysticism for the legitimate material, intellectual and emotional demands of human nature, the imposition of a permanent state of quasi-military mobilisation, the ruthless destruction of all traditional values, an all-pervasive drabness of life, the creation of a cultural desert, universal bigotry, aridity and boredom, relieved only by periodic explosions of violence and hysterical activism. For the cadres, constantly exposed to criticism, harried, scared, worn out, maoism meant permanent menace and uncertainty, continuous struggle, tension and insecurity, and they aspired to a stabler, safer and more conventional system of government.

Mao's posthumous fate might thus prove quite similar to that of his historical model, Ch'in Shih-huang, the 3rd century B.C. despot who first unified the Chinese empire. Ch'in Shih-huang's achievements were both ephemeral and long-lasting: the inhuman character of his rule provoked a popular reaction on the very morrow of his demise and turned his dynasty into one of the shortest-lived of all Chinese history; but at the same time, he laid the ground for the next two thousand years of imperial China.

However dramatic and sudden this dismissal and dismantling of the maoist orthodoxy might have appeared, with the disgrace of Mao's own wife and all his most dedicated followers and ideologues — while the rehabilitation of their opponents and, first of all, of Teng Hsiao-p'ing can be expected any time — it nevertheless fitted logically into a process which began with the end of the "Cultural Revolution". Though repeatedly interrupted by various accidents and setbacks in recent years (the death of Chou En-lai, the fall of Teng Hsiao-p'ing on the one hand, and on the other, the promotion of Wang Hung-wen, the anti-Confucius campaign, the continuing control by the radicals of the propaganda, culture and education sectors), the process never-theless kept its course. It can be roughly summarised as a drastic questioning of the philosophy of the "Cultural Revolution", global restoration of the former bureaucratic apparatus, a gradual elimination of all radical elements and, in particular, of all the new leaders who had gained eminence through the "Cultural Revolution" — in one word, a global veering away, in fact if not in theory, from all the basic tenets of maoism.

To understand why the party bureaucrats came to develop such a holy fear of maoism, one has only to consider what kind of life Mao's policies concretely entailed for them. Mao's political conception — a strange mixture of half-digested marxism and murky old taoism — was that of perpetual change, ceaseless metamorphoses, constant flow, alternation of opposites; to him, routine and stability were abhorrent, a middle-of-the-road course was anathema. He wished to institutionalise his own inner contradiction: he was at once a man of vision and a man of action — thus, he would in turn allow those responsible leaders whose efficiency satisfied the pragmatic half of his mind (the Chou En-lai type) to operate freely for a spell and achieve a certain amount of prosperity and material development, and then, on the strength of this accumulated wealth, he would indulge in a wild radical binge by letting loose all his favourite ideologues and whirling dervishes who would enact for a while his visionary fantasies at great cost to the country. Having thus squandered his resources, he would again find himself in need of the pragmatists, and temporarily dismiss the extremists . . . and so on, ad infinitum.

Mao thought — and wrote — that this was the proper way of running the country: "one measure of Yin, one measure of Yang, this is the Tao", one step to the right, one step to the left, this is the way of Mao. By this method, he could keep the bureaucratic establishment in a state of perpetual alert, constantly off balance, never allowing it to sink complacently into any set routine.

Such a "dialectical" process, albeit increasingly disruptive, remained viable as long as Mao himself was alive: he — and he alone — could uphold the principle of unity and continuity through all these turns and twists, switches and shifts. However, as old age and illness weakened his ability to supervise the whole process, and forced him to loosen his control on the political life of the nation, each faction, weary of playing only a precarious half-part in this game of maoist "dialectics", aspired once and for all to achieve a "synthesis" — at the expense of the other players. Chiang Ch'ing reached for a short while the peak of her power when Mao, though still alive, became almost completely incapacitated: by isolating the half-paralysed, half comatose, practically speechless old man, and making maximum use of her own privileged access to him, she could interpret and manipulate Mao's cryptic sputters to engineer Teng Hsiao-p'ing's downfall. But she over-reached herself in this exercise, lost balance and toppled after her one asset disappeared with Mao's death.

In maoist sailing, each lurch of the boat meant spilling half of the crew overboard: in the end, after having been repeatedly thrown in the water and fished out, then thrown in again and fished out, the wretched cadres, exhausted and terrified, just kept hanging on for dear life to the slippery ideological bulwarks without daring a single move, or attempting the slightest initiative. This state of paralysis, uncertainty and fear, so damaging to the basic functioning of government, further confirmed the new leadership in its determination to eradicate the last active remnants of maoism, while on the other hand confining the doctrine itself to the safe and prophylactic isolation of a glass showcase in a holy museum.

You can turn any man into a Cyclops by painting him with one eye only. This seems to have been the mistake of these analysts who choose to see only the "anti-bureaucratic" and "populist" character of maoism. By emphasising this single facet, while neglecting to observe that Mao was at the same time *the* ultimate totalitarian despot, they failed to grasp his central contradiction, and thus condemned themselves never to understand the essential dynamics of maoist policies. For all the emphasis Mao always put on the "mass line", it should be remembered that this "mass line" was encouraged and allowed to develop only insofar as it remained directed against Mao's enemies. Once he had obtained the supreme control over the party and the army (1935), for the next forty years Mao *never*, in any circumstances, allowed anyone to voice any criticism of himself or his policies, in whatever form. The few individuals who, on the strength of their own revolutionary credentials and intellectual integrity, ever dared to infringe upon this basic taboo, all met with a tragic fate.

Thus, as we have seen, Mao's heirs were in a hurry to bury once and for all the "populist" and "anti-bureaucratic" element of the maoist legacy; as for its despotic and totalitarian aspect, they might well prove all too eager to salvage it. While we can expect a measure of liberalisation to take place in the cultural sphere — nothing ever could conceivably be worse than Chiang Ch'ing's philistine, venomous and obscurantist rule in this field, and now that she is gone, one imagines that the irrepressible creative talents of the Chinese people will at long last find their outlets once again — in other areas, however, the new leadership may in fact apply increasingly authoritarian pressures: the sequels to the violence and anarchy of the "Cultural Revolution", especially among the youth, have brought the country to the brink of a general breakdown of law and order: in this situation, the new masters of China, with their Public Security background and enjoying the full support of the army, may well be only too tempted to impose strict disciplinary measures.

APPENDICES

1

Open letter from P'eng Teh-huai to Mao Tse-tung (14 July 1959)

Chairman,
The present conference of Lushan is an important one.

I have already made several speeches to the reduced Committee of the North-West, but I did not have the opportunity to present all my ideas during the meetings of this Committee. I want to set them down here in writing, for your information. I am a simple man, somewhat after the style of Chang Fei*; I have his unpolished side, but not his subtlety. And I do not know whether these lines are of any interest: that is up to you to decide. If my opinions are not apposite, please advise me.

A. *The accomplishments of the Great Leap Forward* of 1958 are self-evident. According to the Planning Commission, verification of various norms shows that the overall value of industrial and agricultural production rose by 48.4% in 1958 on the previous year; industrial growth was 66.1% up and agricultural growth was 25% up (for grain and cotton it must have been 30%). The resources of the state have grown by 43.5%. Such a rate of growth is unprecedented anywhere in the world, and beats all the established norms of socialist construction, especially if we consider that our country has only a weak economic base and an underdeveloped technology. This experiment of the Great Leap Forward has demonstrated the correctness of the general line, "more, quicker, better, cheaper". This is not only a great achievement for our country, but will exercise a positive long-term effect on the whole socialist camp.

However, when we re-examine the construction at the base which took place in 1958, it appears that in various spheres

---

* A hero of the Three Kingdoms (third century) who became legendary for his loyalty, rough appearance and outspokenness.

there was excessive haste; we tried to do too much, we wasted part of our investments, we deferred certain essential tasks, and that is a mistake. This mistake comes basically from lack of experience; the problem was not understood in its depth, and was only noticed at a late hour. And in 1959, far from holding back and exercising the necessary control, we have continued with the Great Leap Forward. As a result the imbalance has not been rectified in time, while new difficulties have sprung up. But since in the last analysis these tasks of construction correspond to the needs of the country, favourable results may finally be obtained a year or two hence or after a longer period. For the moment there are still gaps and weak points which prevent production from developing in a homogeneous way. For certain products and resources the most essential reserves are lacking, and this renders very problematical the immediate readjustment of these new imbalances. And here lies the core of our present difficulties.

That is why when we make our arrangements for next year's plan it is absolutely essential first of all to make a serious examination of the situation, one which is based on realistic, firm and stable foundations. Where certain points are concerned in the work of construction of 1958 and 1959, points which it seems really impossible to tackle properly, we must take radical measures and interrupt their execution temporarily. In order to obtain some things, we must accept having to renounce others. Without this, the serious imbalances are going to stay with us, and in certain spheres it will be difficult to regain the initiative; this in turn will disrupt the rhythm of the Great Leap Forward and the project of catching up with and overtaking England in four years. And the various difficulties will paralyse the power to take decisions, whatever arrangements the Planning Commission makes.

In 1958 the transformation of the villages into communes was a phenomenon of the greatest significance. Not only was this going to free our country's peasants from poverty once and for all, it also constituted the correct path from socialism to communism. Of course there was a period of confusion where the problems of ownership were concerned, and there were gaps and errors in the work itself. All these things were serious, but the successive conferences of Wuchang, Chengchow and Shanghai made fundamental readjustments, so that these symptoms of disorder are now a thing of the past, while there is a gradual re-establishment of the orthodox path of remuneration according to the labour supplied.

The Great Leap Forward of 1958 solved the problem of unemployment. In a country as densely populated as ours, and with such a backward economy, the rapid solution of this problem is no small matter, it is a considerable achievement.

In the mass mobilisation for the manufacture of steel, the spread of small improvised blast furnaces involved a wastage of resources (raw materials, investments and workforce), and this has naturally been a considerable loss. But we managed to forge an experiment at a nation-wide level, we trained a good number of technicians and the great majority of cadres were tempered and toughened by this movement; of course, this training cost us a lot (two billion yuan), but in a sense it won't be completely useless.

Simply by examining some of the points made above, we can state that the results are considerable but also that they carry a large number of harsh lessons of experience which it would be useful and necessary to analyse thoroughly.

B. *How can we draw the conclusions from these lessons of experience?* The comrades participating in the present conference are in the process of re-examining the lessons of experience acquired on the job, and they have already got together a large number of useful ideas. The current debates will be extremely advantageous for the work of our party. They will enable us to regain the initiative in several spheres and to grasp the principles of socialist economics better, so that the imbalances which have appeared constantly so far can be rectified, while the concept of positive equilibrium will at last be correctly understood. In my opinion, some of the deficiencies and errors which appeared during the Great Leap Forward of 1958 were inevitable. As with all the movements which our party has directed for more than thirty years, considerable results are necessarily accompanied by deficiencies: they are two sides of the same coin. At the moment the main contradiction which we are faced with in our task springs from the tension created in all spheres by the phenomenon of imbalance. By its very nature, the development of this situation is already affecting relationships between peasants and workers and between the various layers of the urban population. As a result, the problem now is of a political nature, and will affect our ability to mobilise the masses into continuing the Great Leap Forward.

In the past, the deficiencies and errors which appeared in our work had multiple causes. Among the subjective factors we must place our lack of familiarity with the work of socialist construction, the incomplete nature of our experience, our superficial understanding of the balanced and planned development of socialism, and the insufficiently thorough and concrete application of the policy of "walking on two legs". When it comes to making decisions in the sphere of socialist construction, we are as a whole still far from possessing the sureness of touch which we possess in the political sphere (when it comes, for example, to bombarding Quemoy or pacifying the Tibetan rebellion). And as far as the objective factors are concerned, our country is in a state of destitution; there is still a large part of the population which does not eat enough to satisfy its hunger, and last year the distribution of cotton cloth was only eighteen feet per person, enough to make a shirt and two pairs of trousers. Our country's backwardness arouses urgent demands for change from the populace. To this we must add the favourable developments in the internal and the international situations. All these factors made us rush the Great Leap Forward. And the idea of taking advantage of a good opportunity to meet the aspirations of the masses, to accelerate our work of construction and to transform the destitute and backward state of our country as quickly as possible, in such a way as to create an international situation that was even more favourable: this was a rigorously correct and necessary idea.

Several problems have appeared in our way of thinking and our working methods, and they deserve to be mentioned. They are mainly as follows.

1. *Resorting increasingly to empty boasting.* Last year during the Peitaiho conference, the statistics for food production were overestimated; since these false premises had given us the illusion that the problem of food production had already been solved, we then tried to tackle industry. But where the development of the iron and steel industries was concerned, we had only a dangerously partial knowledge of the problems; not one person made a serious analysis of the equipment necessary for smelting the steel or crushing the minerals, and no one studied the problem of fuel, raw materials and transport capacity, or the problem of increasing the workforce, or the buying power or management of the market. In short, the project lacked even a rudimentary balance, and reflected a total absence of realism; at the source of it all we find this habit of making empty boasts which has invaded all the regions of the country and all sectors of activity. The newspapers and journals describe truly incredible miracles, and this threatens

the prestige of our party. To read the reports which flowed from all sides at the time, one would have believed that the advent of communism was just around the corner, and this went to the heads of a large number of comrades. Alongside all the boasting about food and textile production and the campaign for iron and steel production, wastage and the blind use of limited resources are spreading. The autumn harvest was a slapdash affair; without taking into account the question of the expenses of exploitation, we began to live at a level which the resources of the country in no way justified. The most serious thing was that for a considerable length of time it was difficult to get any exact knowledge of the situation; and until the Wuchang conference, and then in January of this year the conference of provincial and municipal secretaries, the whole reality of the situation had never been completely exposed. These crude boastful habits have social roots and would repay serious analysis; they are connected with this habit we have of assigning norms for all tasks, but without following them up with concrete steps for their execution. Last year the Chairman indeed gave the whole party instructions to combine a "zeal which shakes the heavens" with a scientific spirit, and to observe the policy of "walking on two legs"; but in fact it seems that these precepts have still not been understood by the majority of leading comrades, including myself.

2. *The petty-bourgeois hot-headedness which too easily inclines us towards leftist errors.* In 1958, during the Great Leap Forward, many other comrades and myself allowed ourselves to be intoxicated by the results of the Great Leap and by the fervour of the mass movement. The leftist tendencies grew considerably. In our impatience to find a short cut to communism, our desire to forge ahead put everything else into the background, and we forgot the mass line and the pragmatic style which had traditionally been typical of our party. In our way of thinking we began to confuse strategy with concrete executive measures, long-term policy with short-term dispositions, the sum and the parts, the whole collectivity and particular collectivities. Thus the slogans launched by Chairman Mao, "sow less to harvest more" and "catch up with England in fifteen years", applied only to strategy and long-term policy. We sinned by failing to reflect; we did not pay enough attention to the specific conditions of the moment. Instead of setting our tasks on a positive, firm and solid footing, instead of raising the norms gradually, we suddenly fixed a target of a year or even a few months for tasks which would normally

demand several years or even ten years or more. And that is how we came unstuck from reality and alienated ourselves from the support of the masses. For example, we prematurely dropped the principle of exchange at par, and we prematurely promised the notion of free food. In regions where the harvest seemed to be good, we temporarily abandoned the normal sales outlets and began to gorge ourselves. Certain techniques were inadvisably made general without having been tested first; we rashly did away with economic laws and scientific principles. There you have more examples of this leftist tendency. In the opinion of some comrades, giving "priority to politics" is a universal panacea. They forget that to give "prioriy to politics" also means to raise the consciousness of labour, to guarantee the quantity and quality of production, to give free play to the positive energy and creative genius of the masses, and thus to accelerate the socialist construction of our economy. "Priority to politics" cannot be substituted for economic laws, and above all it cannot replace specific measures for executing economic tasks. To the principle of "priority to politics" must be added really effective measures concerning our economic tasks; these two aspects must be the object of equal attention, and neither should be given the advantage to the detriment of the other. As the historic experience of our party teaches us, the rectification of these leftist tendencies can prove tougher than the fight against conservative and rightist thought. Over the last six months of last year, there seems to have been an atmosphere in which everybody's attention was fixated on conservative and rightist thought, and this meant that the problem of subjectivism was neglected.

Since last winter, with the Chengchow conference and all the measures which stemmed from it, several of the leftist tendencies have been rectified, and this constitutes a great victory. This victory has served as a lesson to the members of the whole party, without affecting their positive energy. Now, as regards the country's internal situation, we can basically see our way clear. Especially since the recent series of conferences, most of the comrades in the party have basically come to share the same point of view. Our current task is to unify the party as a whole, and to continue to work keenly. It seems to me that it would be a good idea to draw up a systematic balance-sheet of all the results and lessons which we have had since the middle of last year, in order to enlighten the comrades better in the party as a whole. The aim of such an undertaking would be solely to establish a clear distinction between truth and error, to raise the ideological level, and in no way to identify the individuals responsible, which could only threaten our unity and our work. As regards the problems which are due to our lack of experience with the laws of socialist construction, some have been solved as the result of experiences and re-evaluations that have taken place since the middle of last year; as regards others, we still need a certain period of study and of feeling our way before we can master the answers. As regards ideological problems or those concerned with our way of working, present experience has entailed a harsh lesson which has already somewhat woken us up. But while it is really a question of making radical amendments, it will still be necessary to make a stubborn effort. As the Chairman indicated during the present conference, "the results are considerable, the problems are numerous; we have acquired a rich experience, we have a bright future." In order to regain the initiative, our party must unite; once it shows itself able to fight with spirit, the requisite conditions for continuing the Great Leap Forward will exist. This year, next year and for the coming four years of the new plan, it will be necessary to round off the victory. The aim of catching up with England in fifteen years can essentially be resolved in the next four years, and where certain products are concerned we can certainly surpass England: such are our considerable results, and such is our bright future.

Please accept my respectful greetings.

P'eng Teh-huai
14 July 1959.

2

Letter of apology from P'eng Teh-huai to Mao Tse-tung after his disgrace (9 September 1959)

Chairman,
The eighth plenary session of the eighth central committee and
the enlarged conference of the military commission have radically exposed and denounced my mistakes, and have thus eliminated a secret evil, a source of division within the party. This is a
great victory for the party, and at the same time it has given me
a final opportunity to repair my errors. I must thank you sin-
cerely, as well as many other comrades, for the patience with
which you have educated and helped me. The historic and
systematic denunciation of my mistakes, from which the party has
just been freed, was absolutely necessary. This was the only way
in which it was possible to make me really aware of the extraordinarily harmful nature of my mistakes and to neutralise their
detestable influence in the party. I have now been able to measure
the depth to which my bourgeois vision of the world and my
bourgeois way of approaching things were rooted, as well as the
extraordinary degree of gravity which my individualism has
reached. Now I am more aware that it is the party and the
people who formed me, at the cost of considerable sacrifices; and
if my mistakes had not been radically exposed and denounced in
time, what a terrifying danger they could ultimately have constituted! In the past, under the devilish influence of my bourgeois
ideas, I always considered the sincere denunciations which you
had the kindness to make against me to be personal attacks. And
throughout all these struggles, which were connected with the
problems of this mistaken line, I never drew any lesson or benefit,
and my sick obstinacy in making errors refused to be cured. For
more than thirty years I have shown myself to be unworthy of
your teaching and your patience, and you now see me overwhelmed with regret and confused beyond words. I have offended
against the party, I have offended against the people and I have
offended against you yourself. Henceforth I must make the

greatest possible efforts to examine the depths of my mistakes and to study marxist theory zealously so as to reform myself ideologically and to guarantee that in my old age I no longer do anything that might harm the party or the people. With this aim in view I beg the central committee, once the enlarged conference of the military commission is over, to authorise me to apply myself to study, or to authorise me to leave Peking and go to a people's commune where I can study and join in manual labour at the same time. In this way, by sharing the collective life of the working people, I will be able to renew my character and reform myself ideologically. I beg you to be kind enough to examine this suggestion and to let me know your decision.

Respectfully yours,
P'eng Teh-huai
9 September 1959.

3

"Hai Jui reprimands the emperor"

(Article by Wu Han from the *People's Daily*, published on 16 June 1959 under the pseudonym "Liu Mien-chih")

Under the old régime the emperor enjoyed absolute inviolability, even his name was taboo; all the characters used in the writing of his name had to be written with one of the strokes missing. Whoever neglected to do this and carelessly wrote the taboo character in full found he had committed a crime, and he would be brought to trial and condemned to a spell in prison. As for reprimanding the emperor, that was certainly something rarely heard of! Hai Jui was one of those rare individuals who really dared to reprimand the emperor, and who did so with ferocious vigour. The strongest passage in his reprimand was phrased as follows:

> "The people are now overwhelmed with taxes which are quite out of the ordinary; it is like this throughout the country. You spend considerable sums on religion and superstition, and these expenses simply get worse day by day. The population is reduced to naked poverty, and its extreme hardship has lasted for more than ten years. Throughout the empire the people have been making a pun, calling the reign of Chia-ching 'a close shave' (*chieh-ching*), since every family is in fact shorn to its last penny."

Not only had Chia-ching, over the several decades of his reign, never been taken to task so directly and boldy, but throughout the history of the dynasties it would be difficult to find a similar example. Every word scored a bull's eye; Chia-ching was outraged and beside himself with fury, he spat fire.

At the time, Chia-ching had already been on the throne for quite a long time. He neglected affairs of state, and no longer bothered to hold audiences. He had withdrawn to the Park of the West, and spent his time worshipping spirits, organising religious ceremonies and despatching "green messages". These "green messages" were a kind of letter addressed to the spirits. Editing them was a specially complicated affair, and the ministers Yen Sung and Hsu Chieh owed the imperial favour which they enjoyed to the fact that they were specialists in it. Political life was as corrupt as it could be; those courtiers who dared to utter any advice were either executed, disgraced, jailed or sent to bear arms — and in this climate of terror, no one dared open his mouth any longer. In February of the forty-fifth year of Chia-ching's reign (1566), Hai Jui addressed to the emperor a memorandum on the political situation. Dealing with the problems of the moment, he subjected the emperor to a veritable cross-examination and demanded reforms. He wrote:

"Are you worth more than the Han emperor Wen-ti? Some years ago you certainly carried out a number of useful works. But more recently you have merely dedicated yourself to taoist worship and to the construction of vast palaces. You have not held any audiences for more than twenty years now; you fulfil your official functions at your own whim. You are no longer concerned about seeing your two sons: have you stifled all the paternal feeling in you? You have put your ministers to death for suspicions and slanders: is that the benevolence which a sovereign should show to his courtiers? You remain shut up in the Park of the West, no longer returning to your palace: what have you done to the affections of your wife? All over the empire, the civil servants have become corrupt and the generals cowards. The peasants are rebelling everywhere. All these things existed in the first years of your reign too, but they were not so serious. Now, although Yen Sung has been dismissed as prime minister, no reforms are envisaged, and the empire is far from presenting a rosy picture. In my opinion, you stand well below the Han emperor Wen-ti."

Chia-ching compared himself with Yao — he had given himself the surname of Yao-chai — and here was Hai Jui saying that he was not even worth a Han Wen-ti! How could he have failed to burst at the seams with fury? Hai Jui added:

"You only think about taoist practices, you only care about obtaining the secret of long life: you have lost your common sense. The arbitrary nature of your decisions passes all bounds, and partiality leads your judgement astray. When you think you are right, you reject any criticism and add to your mistakes. All your attention is occupied by this desire to become immortal and obtain the secret of long life. Look at Yao, Shun, Yü, T'ang, the king Wen and the king Wu: are any of them still alive today? The teacher who taught you these recipes for long life, T'ao Chung-wen, is now dead: if he himself couldn't ensure his own immortality, how can you hope to do so yourself? You state that the Sovereign of Heaven has given you the peaches of immortality and the pills of long life. How strange! How were these peaches and pills transmitted to you? Did the Sovereign of Heaven give them to you himself, with his own hand?

You should be aware that there is nothing that is any good to be got from these taoist practices. Pull yourself together! Hold an audience every day, study the affairs of the state and the problems of your subjects, reform radically your mistakes of several decades, and set yourself the task of seeing to the happiness of your people! The main problem at the moment is that the sovereign has abandoned the right road, and his ministers cannot pursue their functions honourably. That is what has to be remedied, for everything else depends on it."

On reading this, Chia-ching could no longer contain his anger. He threw the memorandum to the ground and immediately ordered the arrest of Hai Jui before he could escape. The eunuch Huang Chin then intervened. He said, "From what I have heard, this man has prepared himself for the worst. He has already said goodbye to his wife and entrusted his affairs to the care of a friend; his servants were seized with fear and have all fled. He will not try to escape his fate; he has an unbendable and upright character, and he enjoys a great reputation. In his official functions he has always demonstrated a scrupulous honesty, and would never tamper with resources of the state by so much as a single grain of rice. He is truly an honest civil servant!" Chia-ching realised that Hai Jui did not fear death, and so he was completely bewildered. He picked up the memorandum from the floor, sighing, and was incapable of taking a decision. Several days went by; every time the incident came back to him he flew into a rage, banged the table and nagged at his entourage. One day he struck a palace maidservant in anger, who on the quiet mumbled, weeping: "The emperor has been reprimanded by Hai Jui, and now he takes his anger out on us." Chia-ching sent off more emissaries to enquire whether Hai Jui had not been acting at the instigation of accomplices. But Hai Jui's colleagues, fearing that they would be compromised, studiously avoided him. Hai Jui was not in the least affected by all this, and waited at home for them to come and arrest him.

At certain moments Chia-ching could not help exclaiming: "This man is truly of the same temper as Pi Kan; but I am not as perverted as King Chou-hsin."* He called Hai Jui by the names of animals; neither in conversation nor in the notes which he wrote in the margin of Hai Jui's dossier did he call him by his name. Sick and exasperated, he told his minister Hsu Chieh of his intention to abdicate in favour of the crown prince. "Everything that Hai Jui has said is true. But I have been sick for so long: how could I have held audiences and carried out affairs of state?" And he added: "All this is my fault. If I had been looked after better, my health wouldn't be in such a state today. And if I had still been capable of holding audiences and administering the affairs of the empire, I would never have exposed myself to the attacks of this man." In the end, he gave the order to throw Hai Jui in prison, and to establish who was really behind all this. The penal commission recommended the death penalty for Hai Jui, but Chia-ching could not summon up the resolution to sign the warrant. Two months later, Chia-ching died. His successor freed Hai Jui and reinstated him in his former post as vice-president of the Population Board.

Hai Jui's reprimand to the emperor aroused unanimous sympathy and approval. His reputation could only grow. In the fourteenth year of Wan-li's reign (1586), Hai Jui was slandered in front of the emperor. At once the young graduates Ku Yun-ch'eng, P'eng Tsun-ku, and Chu Shou-hsien defended him and sought imperial clemency on his behalf. In their petition they said, among other things: "The name of Hai Jui has been familiar to us from our youth; he was already a hero of our time. He will forever remain an object of admiration for men, for his worth cannot be equalled." Such was the opinion which the young men of his time had of him.

Hai Jui was loved by the masses at the time, and the people sang his praises.

He opposed corruption, he opposed luxury and waste, he encouraged frugality, chastised the arrogant and soothed the wretched. He undertook the fair distribution of lands; he imposed the same law for everyone and abrogated the old privileges,

---

* Pi Kan had dared to criticise Chou-hsin, the last king of the Shang dynasty; on the king's orders, Pi Kan had his heart torn from his body.

and he carried out great irrigation projects. All these initiatives were taken in the interests of the peasants, and they too loved him and sang his praises. Where the city-dwellers were concerned, and above all the traders, he reduced taxes and did away with requisitions; these measures helped to lighten the burden on urban industry and commerce, and the city-dwellers too venerated him and sang his praises. Besides this, he paid quite special attention to affairs of justice. In trials where human lives were at stake he studied each dossier in detail. He took advantage of his post as prefect and then as a provincial governor to judge each case personally, and to settle all the old dossiers which had accumulated. He acquitted large numbers of people who had been unjustly accused, and ended up being a saviour-figure for all the oppressed, the humiliated and the victims of injustice. His name was on everyone's lips, he was blessed, his effigy was made the object of a cult, and he was celebrated in songs and hymns. When he died the population of Nanking suspended all its activity: as the boat which was carrying his remains was crossing the river, a multitude in mourning, massed on both banks, offered funeral libations and wept. Episodes from his life, particularly anecdotes about his judicial decisions, are still popular today, even among the masses.

Under the old régime Hai Jui was the very image of the honest and incorruptible civil servant. He opposed evil and wicked people, he supported good and honest people. In the interests of the people, he resolutely fought to the finish against all obscurantist forces of reaction. There are two aspects of his character which we can still draw inspiration from today: first of all he always made a clear distinction between truth and error, and secondly he maintained his will to fight right to the end against retrograde forces. Obviously Hai Jui lived under the old régime, three or four centuries ago, and his criteria of value were therefore not entirely identifiable with our own today; but the striking way in which he adopted a position, as well as his ardent fighting spirit, well deserve our imitation.

Fragments from the deposition of P'eng Teh-huai during his trial (28 December 1966-5 January 1967)

Before the Liberation, during the seventh party congress, I said: "Mao Tse-tung's thought is 99.9% correct and 0.1% faulty."

During the first years after the Liberation I was mainly inspired by the Soviet model. On the initiative of Ho Lung (and with my own active participation) priority was given to the question of materials; even military equipment was entirely sovietised. Subsequently we abandoned this policy because it was unpopular, and the Chairman criticised it. In Korea I had a blow-up with Kim Il-sung; the Chairman criticised me, and said that it was chauvinism. But hasn't Kim Il-sung now turned to revisionism?

In 1956, during the eighth congress, I proposed that we suppress the reference to Mao Tse-tung's thought in the party constitution. This motion was immediately seconded by Liu Shao-ch'i, who said: "We would do better to cut out this reference." I am against the superstitious cult of personality.

In 1958 I found myself awfully busy, leaping from one end of the country to the other all the time. Doing what? 1958 was the year of the Great Leap Forward, industry and agriculture were in mid-flight. . . . I had my doubts about our ability to produce the quantities projected, but I said nothing at the time.

After the Peitaiho conference, I went to Lanchow in the North-West. In the train from Chengchow we held our own conference, against "communisation". When I went to the enlarged conference of the politbureau at Wuhan, I took advantage of it to go on to Hunan, and there I made enquiries. Not only had production not risen, it had dropped! I composed a poem on the spot:

We have sowed the grain, the leaves on the sweet potatoes
are already withering,
The young people and the strong men have all left to
forge steel,

> Only women and children are left to gather the harvest,
> What will we live on next year?
> In the interests of the people, let's sound the alarm!

I could keep quiet no longer. I was resolved to act like Hai Jui. Subsequently I went to Kiangsi and Anhwei to gather information; I decided to speak out at the Lushan conference.

Concerning the Lushan conference: on the evening of 13 July 1958 I wrote a letter to the Chairman. On the following day it was printed and distributed to all the comrades at the conference. The contents of the letter were essentially as follows:

1. The Great Leap Forward of 1958 was a mixture of failures and victories; on balance, the failures weighed heavier. The real increases in production were lower than the results officially announced.

2. The serious problem at that time was a problem of imbalance; each day scores of millions of people were no longer doing anything but making steel. One had to put a brake on these excesses.

3. Lack of honesty: reports were falsified. Throughout the country, in every sphere of activity, the same reports were drawn up.

4. Petty-bourgeois hot-headedness, and authoritarianism divorced from the masses; we had forgotten the mass line we had cultivated for so many years. Subjectivism, the blind use of resources, waste.

My motives in writing this letter were based on good intentions; my language had the roughness of Chang Fei, without his subtlety.

The Chairman received my letter on the seventeenth. On the twenty-third, he spoke for forty minutes on my problem. His attack lay essentially in phrases such as the following. "P'eng Teh-huai's letter is of a general character; it is an attack against our general line; it supports the people's communes for the sake of form only." "P'eng Teh-huai is subtle; we have a habit of saying 'there are good things and there are bad things', but he says 'there are bad things and there are good things': the bad comes first." "He claims that the mobilisation of tens of millions of men for steel manufacturing is petty-bourgeois triumphalism, and that the habit of making empty boasts is rife in all the sectors of the country's activity; in fact he does not want the people's communes." "If the Liberation Army sides with P'eng Teh-huai, I have no alternative but to start the guerrilla all over again."

In my estimation these remarks of the Chairman are extreme. As for myself, I stick to my position. The Chairman claims that my letter was a "preparation for rebellion", "the act of an ambitious man", "the act of a hypocrite": that's more than I can take! Dismiss me from my posts, I don't see any objection: but I still stick to my own views. Without any official posts I can only feel freer. If I no longer involve myself in this business, there are others who are better qualified than I am: let's make way for them. After the Lushan conference, the Hai Jui whom I dreamed of playing found himself defeated. . . .

5

Cross-examination of P'u An-hsiu (the wife of P'eng Teh-huai) during the trial of P'eng

Investigator's commentary:
P'u An-hsiu, the stinking partner of P'eng Teh-Huai, is in league with P'eng. She actively participated in the anti-party clique of the bandit P'eng. After the disgrace of the bandit P'eng, P'u pretended in 1962 to divorce him, in order to give the impression that she was disowning him, but in fact she was doing her best to protect him in his difficult situation. Today the witch P'u An-hsiu still refuses to unmask the bandit P'eng and strives to resist. She is trying her best to cover up the heinous crimes of the bandit P'eng. We reproduce here the record of her cross-examination, so that it will serve to damn her.

My name is P'u An-hsiu. I married P'eng Teh-huai at Yenan in 1938. I do not know about his activities, I am not aware of anything.

After 1953 I frequently heard him complain: "I'm getting old, the Chairman doesn't like me, he has no consideration for me. The new generation is beginning to rise, and I don't want to stand in their way. I overthrew Chiang Kai-shek, I beat the imperialists: I have fulfilled all the vows of my existence, I can go back to the village and cultivate my garden, and if the Chairman doesn't like me, so much the worse!"

Often when the central party authorities were being photographed, if Chairman Mao was present P'eng did not want to go. At conferences of the central party organs which took place in the afternoon, he no longer wanted to go. In the Peking suburbs there is a superbly equipped place where the higher authorities and Chairman Mao can relax. Often on Sundays I suggested that he should go there to relax, but he never wanted to. He would say: "That place serves as a residence for the Chairman. If you want to go there, go; I'm not going. That residence is run in a much too sumptuous way."

In 1958 P'eng Teh-huai returned to Hunan on an inspection tour. When he came back to Peking he told me how at his family's place even the saucepans had been melted down to help manufacture steel, which made it very difficult to cook. He said that he was not happy with these mass movements; he was grumbling and sighing.

In 1958 P'eng Teh-huai told me: "Chairman Mao gave me a knock, and I gave him one back. If he can shout at me, why can't I shout at him?"

In 1959, after the Lushan conference, he said: "No more official posts, I'm free!" He added: "If I had been against Chairman Mao in the past, I could have opposed him successfully. Why should I have waited till the Liberation?" Then he said: "I have eaten the bread of democratic revolution, but now I am of no more use," and he bought a series of technical books on agriculture, got himself a fishpond and a patch of ground, and began to raise fish and cultivate his allotment.

All along he continued to believe that the Great Leap Forward had got completely out of hand, that he had been proved right and that the central committee and Chairman Mao were wrong; he used to say that it was a question of the political line.

In 1962 he made another plea for his dossier to be re-examined; he stated once more that he had been right.

Subsequently he was reinstated to a third-rank post; I went to visit him. He told me that Chairman Mao had granted him an audience and had advised him to work conscientiously and to rid himself of all his old ideas. But he himself did not want to accept this reinstatement, he thought only about going back to the village to cultivate his allotment. In the past, Chu Teh, Ho Lung, Huang K'e-ch'eng, Chang Wen-t'ien and XXX, XXX and XXX [names censored in the original text] used to drop round frequently, uninvited, to chat with P'eng.

6

Author's note on the historical importance of Sun Yat-sen

The personality, thought and actions of Sun are a fundamental key to the understanding of modern China and her revolution. This is universally accepted in China. Sun is the *only* Chinese political figure of the twentieth century who has succeeded in gaining the unanimous respect of posterity, and the historical impact which he has had on the Chinese people as a whole is so important that even the adventurers who subsequently came to power, from Chiang to Mao, have always felt obliged to legitimise their own authority by claiming to be his spiritual heir. By contrast, the willingness which Westerners have always displayed (and still display today) to ignore, minimise and ridicule Sun's role is all the more striking. It is fashionable among contemporary sinologists to treat Sun with a sort of amused contempt or patronising indulgence. The examples abound — see, for example, a work such as H. McAleavy's *The Modern History of China* (London, 1967): Sun is described there as the "rather ineffectual patron saint of Chinese nationalism" who "throughout his life was never to display much familiarity with the realities of Chinese society." His motives are interpreted as aberrant or mean. Thus in 1917, when he was trying to form a coalition against the government of Tuan Ch'i-jui:

> "The truth was that Sun Yat-sen by now was moved above all by resentment at his exclusion from the councils of Peking and was willing to go to almost any lengths to force his way back on the stage. If Tuan Ch'i-jui could get loans, why should a true patriot not enjoy the same benefits? The idea appeared so reasonable that with all the dignity of his new office behind him, he was soon hawking round economic concessions in the hope of finding a Japanese or American buyer, but in neither country were men of affairs so naive to imagine that he had anything of value to sell."

And when, in the middle of all this, an expert historian — who has found out how to use his long stay in China to rid himself of this Western arrogance and to look at Chinese problems from a Chinese intellectual's point of view — dares, against the tide, to sound another note and render Sun the importance which is due to him (W. Franke: *A Century of Chinese Revolution*), he is immediately taken to task:

"Some of Franke's judgements now seem badly dated. *Particularly annoying is the prominent place given to Sun Yat-sen.* Franke views Sun as 'idealistic and unselfish' and the leader of the Chinese revolution in the early decades of the century. In fact he can just as accurately be viewed as a naive and ineffectual politico, as willing as anybody to play warlord games and grant concessions to foreigners. That he sat out the actual revolution of 1911 in the United States casts doubts on his leadership role, and the revolution would certainly have failed if not for the opportunistic switch of Yuan Shih-k'ai to the revolutionary side. Nor are Sun's 'Three People's Principles' worth the emphasis given them. They were for the most part politically unworkable and of minor intellectual value. Fortunately [*sic*!] several Western scholars are now working on Chinese intellectual and political developments of the period, and the next three or four years will see a more complete and balanced picture emerge." (C. Snyder in *Far Eastern Economic Review* no. 10, 6 March 1971)

It is symptomatic, where Sun Yat-sen is concerned, that since Sharman's competent but rudimentary and dated (1934) study, *no serious work* has ben published or undertaken in the West,* while anachronistic curiosities like Yuan Shih-k'ai, or today trivial and ephemeral clowns such as Madame Mao or Ch'en Po-ta supply fashionable subjects for doctoral theses. This says much about the ignorance in which the West is kept concerning the great *living* currents of contemporary Chinese history. On this subject, in spite of the prodigious inflation in modern Chinese studies which we can observe today, no advance has been made from the prejudices and blind self-satisfaction which prevailed at the turn of the century. From now on, we can be sure that the people who will soon rise up in China to continue and complete the long and twice-betrayed revolution will once more be

---

* H. Z. Schiffrin's study (*Sun Yat-sen and the Origins of the Chinese Revolution*) goes only as far as 1905.

alone in their task, alone as Sun was in his time. From the West they can expect nothing but incomprehension and hostility.

7

Author's note on the T'ien-an Men incident and the Li Yi-che manifesto (April 1976)

At the end of 1974, three young revolutionaries posted on the walls of a busy street of Kwangchow a long and powerful political manifesto which, before it could be suppressed by the authorities, was immediately reproduced and disseminated by way of Chinese-style *samizdat*, and rocked the whole country. Had Western observers paid more attention at the time to this historic document — a spontaneous expression of the masses — instead of focusing on the permanent power-struggle waged between a handful of top bureaucrats, the T'ien-an Men demonstrations of April 1976 would not in that case have taken them so much by surprise.

This manifesto was entitled "On socialist democracy and legality" and signed "Li Yi-che" — pen-name of its three authors, *Li* Cheng-t'ien, Ch'en *Yi*-yang and Huang Hsi-*che*. It constitutes one of the most sophisticated and penetrating analyses of the Chinese political scene ever attempted from inside China. It takes as its starting point the "criticism of Lin Piao", which had been the theme of a huge campaign for the previous few years. The authors observe that the campaign had so far remained largely sterile and empty, since it concentrated on flogging a dead horse: what is the use of merely denouncing an *individual*? What matters, in fact, is not the person of Lin Piao, but the "Lin Piao system", the mechanism by which such a traitor could be propelled to the top, be proclaimed the "closest comrade-in-arms and successor of Chairman Mao", and wield practically absolute power in China for nearly four years (1968-1971). The "victory" of the "Cultural Revolution", as the authors see, must be a myth, since Lin Piao, having usurped power halfway through it, then proceeded to crush all revolutionary activity in order to stage his own apotheosis: the ninth party congress (1969) which anointed him in the exalted dignity of heir-designate and even went to such ludicrous lengths as to enshrine his new status in the revised party constitution. In other words, for four years, China had been under the rule of a fascist military adventurer! What such rule entailed, the manifesto continues, eight hundred million witnesses can testify: bloody suppression of the masses (the Lin Piao military repression in Kwangtung province alone, they state, had 40,000 victims), the imposition of a new "religion" with a ritualistic blind devotion to the Supreme Leader, arbitrary dogmas requiring unconditional obedience, and substitution of a feudal rule-of-ideology for the socialist rule-of-law. What is frightening, continue the authors of the manifesto, is that the downfall of Lin Piao has not led to the end of the "Lin Piao system" — the system which brought him to power *continues to operate as before.* Witness: all the successive political campaigns which have rocked the Chinese scene in the last few years, and in particular the "anti-restoration" movement (which at that time was already aiming at Teng Hsiao-p'ing and was eventually to culminate in his second downfall), were dealing with events and directed against personalities belonging to the post-Lin Piao era: *they never attempted to challenge seriously any of the institutions or personalities established during Lin's heyday* (1968-1971).

It is precisely this "social-fascist dictatorship of a feudal type" that presents the greatest danger for the Chinese proletariat. As the authors recall such an eventuality had already been foreseen by Mao Tse-tung ten years previously: "should such a restoration ever happen in our country, it will not amount to a simple dictatorship of the bourgeoisie, but it will be a reactionary-*fascist* type of dictatorship". Furthermore Mao predicted that after the victory of the revolution, the class struggle would remain a permanent reality inside the socialist régime. The danger of a bourgeois restoration no longer comes of course from the wretched descendants of the former bourgeoisie, who are utterly discredited, powerless, bypassed by history, and constitute but a tiny minority of pathetic scarecrows; the USSR, they point out, is under a bourgeois-revisionist régime, yet Brezhnev did not invite White Russians and former landowners to come back and share his cake! The danger of a bourgeois restoration comes from the *new* bourgeoisie. Here Li Yi-che's analysis is remarkably similar to that of Djilas, and this should not surprise us: like causes produce like effects, and in the framework of bureaucratic totalitarianism, variations are necessarily limited. Within the limits of a socialist economy, the new ruling class has managed to privately appropriate and embezzle the wealth of the community: this is achieved by inflating and expanding its special status, by increasing its various political, economic and social privileges, by making these privileges quasi-hereditary, and by consolidating and protecting them through a system of sectarian oligarchical cliques able to suppress whatever criticism might arise from among the masses.

Confronting the abuses of this "new ruling class" and the menace of a "social-fascist dictatorship", the proletariat has but one weapon: the Cultural Revolution. The original purpose of the Cultural Revolution had been not so much to overthrow Liu Shao-ch'i, as to train the masses in the actual exercise of democracy. The emancipation of the people can be achieved only by the people itself. For a brief period at the beginning of the Cultural Revolution, the masses were able to control their own destiny. *For the first time since the foundation of the People's Republic all the rights and liberties guaranteed to citizens by the constitution were fully put into effect*: freedom of opinion, of the press, of meetings, of association, of movement. But it did not last long: Lin Piao's usurpation brought all this to a brutal halt in 1968. What is needed now — and here the authors of the manifesto address themselves most emphatically to the fourth people's congress, whose convocation was then imminent — is to set a new constitutional basis for the régime, which would ensure "socialist democracy and legality". Such demands for "democracy" were usually seen in the past as an indication of reactionary leanings: in the fifties, in fact, when the freshly dispossessed bourgeoisie could still entertain a dream of restoration, democratic slogans were used by rightists as a smokescreen behind which to attempt their comeback. But in the sixties and today the old bourgeoisie no longer exists; on the contrary it is the new bourgeoisie, the ruling bureaucracy, which — enjoying all the advantages of democracy — constantly denies them to the masses of the people. The new constitution should enable the masses to exert constant control over the State apparatus, the masses should have the right to revoke at any time any party or government leader who loses their trust. The human rights and civic freedoms which in the past, though guaranteed by the 1954 constitution, were constantly violated (arbitrary arrests, trials on trumped-up charges, torture, executions for political crimes) should be reaffirmed and effectively enforced. Most important of all is the freedom of opinion: without free criticism from the people, there can be no true political life, no participation of the masses, no socialist democracy. The authors movingly conclude: "We are young men, we may still lack theoretical knowledge, yet we are not entirely without experience; we are not afraid of the tiger; we know the beast: it has already bitten us once, but did not succeed in swallowing us" (Li Cheng-t'ien, the main editor of the manifesto, had been one of the leaders of a leftist revolutionary group during the "Cultural Revolution", and was jailed for more than a year at the time of the Lin Piao military repression), and they express their faith in the ability of the masses to ultimately get rid of the "Lin Piao system" which continues to rule China under another name.

One month after the appearance of this manifesto, the answer of the maoist establishment was expressed in the convening of the fourth people's congress and the adoption of a new constitution. This new constitution gave official sanction to the dramatic turn towards a reinforced totalitarianism: most of the human rights and civic freedoms guaranteed by the 1954 constitution were abolished and, most important of all, a new article was added allowing the Public Security (i.e. the political police) to make arrests without the authorisation of a People's Court or a People's Prosecutor: in other words, the arbitrary power of the police has been enshrined in the constitution!

It is in this light that we must look at the events of April 1976 in Peking. From what we know at this stage, a huge crowd gathered spontaneously chanting slogans and expressing its devotion to the memory of Chou En-lai — who, it is to be recalled, in his last years had become more and more conscious of the necessity to substitute a code of laws for the increasingly erratic and subjective ideological rule of the "Supreme Leader" — and freely venting their hatred for the Public Security organs. According to one report, attempts were even made to set on fire one building of the Security. The second day, the huge T'ien-an Men square was cordoned off by the Security men and the army in order to prevent further spontaneous demonstrations, and to wash and scrape away all the inscriptions left by the demonstrators, thus in effect robbing them of this basic right — guaranteed by the constitution! — of posting "big character inscriptions", which was in fact the sole democratic weapon left to them.

Then came the announcement that Hua Kuo-feng had been officially confirmed as Premier. Hua Kuo-feng . . . *who happened to be the head of Public Security*! No one could be better qualified for the role of leader in a "social-fascist dictatorship of feudal type"! Predictably enough, huge state-managed demonstrations of dutiful schoolchildren, mobilised civil servants and factory workers marching in good order, mouthing ready-made slogans, are now being organised everywhere in the country to celebrate the promotion of the new Lin Piao.

In the short perspective, the situation looks utterly depressing. Yet, in the long run, we would perhaps be foolish to despair. If one has faith in the people's ability to finally overcome, no people could better justify such faith than the Chinese, since no other people on this planet has succeeded in constantly maintaining against tremendous odds a more durable and richer set of human values in the obstinate fight which we call civilisation.

8

Biographical sketches

These notes, written in 1970, reflect the situation of each indivi-dual at the time of the ninth party congress. Their ultimate fate (up to 1977) is indicated in italics at the end of each sketch.

Chang Ch'un-ch'iao, a prudent extremist

It was the "Cultural Revolution" that fetched Chang out of obscurity and catapulted him to the top (for how long?). We do not know his date of birth: he must be a little over fifty now. Probably from Shanghai, he had various jobs in journalism in the city after 1950, and in 1963 became the director of the propa-ganda department of the municipal party committee. Thanks to the "Cultural Revolution" he became first of all chairman of the Shanghai Revolutionary Committee (February 1967), then a mem-ber of the politbureau of the ninth central committee (1969) — a dangerous promotion. His sole chance of survival is the fact that since February 1967 he has disowned and discouraged any attempt at *unilateral* seizures of power on the part of the "revolu-tionary rebels", and has stated that the *army* must play the dominant role. In many respects, Chang Ch'un-ch'iao remains an unknown. He has the typical physical appearance of a Shanghai intellectual, the fine delicate features of an urban man of letters. *Disgraced (1976).*

Chang Wen-t'ien, the translator of Bergson and Oscar Wilde who dared to defy Mao

Born in 1900, from a well-off Shanghai family. At the age of twenty he left to study in Japan, and then in the USA (at the University of California). On his return he worked in publishing (the Chung Hua Book Company of Shanghai), taught in a secondary school and began to make translations (Bergson, Oscar Wilde, Turgenev, Tolstoy and D'Annunzio). He joined the communist party in 1925 at the recommendation of Ch'en Yün, and went to Moscow to study between 1926 and 1930. He returned to China in the company of the famous group of "28 Bolsheviks" which also contained Wang Ming, Ch'in Pang-hsien etc. and was led by Pavel Mif. He held important posts in organisation and propaganda, and after the Liberation in foreign affairs: he was appointed permanent representative to the UN in 1950 ("pending the acceptance of credentials"); ambassador to Moscow (1951-5); Chou En-lai's companion at the Geneva Conference (1954); Vice-minister of Foreign Affairs (1954) and deputy member of the Politbureau (1956). He was implicated in P'eng Teh-huai's "rebellion" at the Lushan conference (1959), and disgraced. In 1962 he was vegetating as a "special researcher" at the Economic Research Institute of the Peking Academy of Sciences. But even this obscure position did not mean that he was protected against the fury of the "Cultural Revolution", which put him back in the dock in 1967. Chang Wen-t'ien had a brilliant mind; he belonged to that race of intellectuals and academics — now almost completely extinct — which laid the foundations of the leadership of the Chinese Communist Party. This cosmopolitan, urban élite has now been almost completely replaced by an uneducated soldiery.

Ch'en Po-ta, the eternal secretary

Born in 1904 in Fukien. A zealous, colourless recording machine, Mao's secretary since 1937. Chief editor of *Red Flag* since 1958. In the abundant collection of his theoretical writings it is difficult to find one original thought, one idea which is his own. A man of great self-denial, he has always been happy to merely be Mao's penholder. A strict worker, indefatigable and taciturn, he neither smokes nor drinks, but his virtues and his devotion have not been very well rewarded. He is now being indicted for having written an article in . . . 1936 (an article which his own master inspired), on the famous quarrel over "the literature of national defence" and "the literature of the masses". Behind this pretext, which has nothing to do with the real problem, the real target is the leading spokesman of "Cultural Revolution" activism. *Disgraced.*

Ch'en Yi, the impromptu diplomat

Born in Szechuan in 1901, of a mandarin family. Left for France in 1919 with the famous students' and workers' movement;

expelled from France in 1921 for his participation in the Chinese student agitation at Lyon. Back in China, joined the communist party in 1923. Took part in the Northern expedition and in the Nanchang uprising of 1927, then joined Mao as a guerrilla in the Ching-kang mountains (1928). It was Ch'en Yi who carried out the great purge of Fu-t'ien in 1930, which eliminated Mao's opponents and made him the unchallenged leader of the party. Covered the retreat of the Long March with heroic rearguard fighting in Kiangsi-Fukien. During the war he was in charge of military operations in Kiangsu, the largest communist base in enemy territory. He distinguished himself as a strategist again during the civil war of 1947-8. Known abroad mainly as Minister of Foreign Affairs (since 1958), he was in fact a complete novice at this diplomatic role. It should not be forgotten that he was one of the most illustrious and talented military chiefs of the Red Army (he was made a marshal in 1955), and that the attacks made against him by the Red Guards during the "Cultural Revolution" were particularly badly received by the army. A close collaborator of Chou En-lai (he was the latter's assistant at the Whampoa Military Academy in 1925, in the political department), he was semi-disgraced on the outbreak of the "Cultural Revolution" and lost both his ministerial post and his seat on the politbureau, although he retained his place on the central committee. *Rehabilitated, died (1972).*

Ch'i Pen-yü, the biter bit

Ch'i Pen-yü was an unknown until he appeared on the political scene in 1963 with an article denouncing Lo Ehr-kang (the famous historian, a specialist on the Taiping), whose crime had been to find positive qualities in Li Hsiu-ch'eng, a Taiping leader who had published a confession after he was captured. It very soon became clear that this discussion was in no way an academic one (Ch'i was incapable in any case of moving at the same scholarly and historical level as Lo Ehr-kang), and that the discussion (which had Mao's blessing) centred obscurely on a political topic which had in fact a burning currency. The real meaning of this campaign did not become clear until the "Cultural Revolution" arrived: the historical pretext was in fact being used to attack those militants who had been arrested in in the "white zones" by the Kuomintang and had signed confessions on the instructions of Liu Shao-ch'i, Po Yi-p'o and An Tzu-wen. The "Cultural Revolution" suddenly brought Ch'i

Pen-yü to the centre of the stage: it was he who wrote the very first, resounding attack against Liu Shao-ch'i, the famous article "Patriotism or Treason" (*People's Daily*, 1 April 1967). He enjoyed this unexpected glory only for a brief period. Less than a year later, he was ignominiously rejected by his masters: he was a tool they no longer had a use for.

Chiang Ch'ing, Madame Mao

Alias Li Chin, alias Lan P'ing, alias Li Yun-ho: her original name was Luan Shu-meng. Born in 1913 or 1914 in Shantung, while still a child she joined a group of actors from Tsinan. When she was sixteen she entered the Tsinan Academy of Dramatic Arts; the Academy's director, Chao T'ai-mou, made her his mistress. Chao was appointed as a professor at Tsingtao national university and took Chiang Ch'ing along with him, employing her in the university library. Shortly afterwards, Chao married Yü San, a somewhat fashionable actress, and Chiang Ch'ing became the mistress of her brother, Yü Ch'i-wei (alias Huang Ching), who was an underground communist cadre. A little while later, Chiang Ch'ing got to know T'ang Na (the pseudonym of Ma Chi-liang), a Shanghai film critic whom she married in 1934. Between 1934 and 1937 Chiang Ch'ing vegetated under the name of Lan P'ing, as a film actress in Shanghai; she was only given bit parts which were badly paid. In 1937 she left T'ang Na and set out for Yenan in the company of her old lover, Yü Ch'i-wei. In the depths of such a rough and primitive area a Shanghai actress, fifth-rate or not, got the success which passed her by in the big city. Mao soon noticed her, and staked his claim: Yü Ch'i-wei respectfully withdrew, in order to leave the way free for the supreme leader. But when Mao talked about marrying Chiang Ch'ing, Ho Tzu-chen — Mao's second wife — alerted the party's old guard, who sympathised with her opposition to such a marriage. Ho Tzu-chen was herself a genuine revolutionary who had gone all through the Long March with her husband. And Mao's wish to ditch his companion from the heroic period and replace her with an adventuress who had just arrived from the Shanghai film studio caused a scandal among the leading élite of the party, who were afraid that this whim would seriously damage Mao's prestige. Since Mao persisted in his wish, a compromise was reached in the end: he would marry Chiang Ch'ing, but she would keep strictly to the background and would not take part in public life. Chiang Ch'ing observed this restriction with all the impatience of a woman who, with a feel for the stage and a taste for the spotlight, had succeeded in reaching the top of the tree in one leap. In 1950 she was finally given a bone to chew: she was nominated a member of the directing committee of the film industry, which was dependent on the Ministry of Culture. But her colleagues let her know that she was only there by virtue of a private favour, and greeted all her interventions in an offhand way. (They would repent this when the "Cultural Revolution" came: Chiang Ch'ing was to get rid of all the heads of this committee — Hsia Yen, T'ien Han etc. — as well as every influential personality in the cinema and the theatre.) Her enforced restriction was all the more irksome when, at the beginning of the 1960s, she could see Wang Kuang-mei (the wife of Liu Shao-ch'i) starring in public life. The venomous denunciations of Wang Kuang-mei which were made during the "Cultural Revolution" carried a very feminine trademark: she was accused, among other things, of being too elegantly dressed during the voyage she made to Indonesia with Liu Shao-ch'i. While she was waiting, in 1964, Chiang Ch'ing was granted a modest degree of compensation by being elected to the National Assembly at the same time as her rival. Her first real opportunity to display her political activism came in the summer of 1964, during the reform of the opera; but once again she came up against a wall of hostility from the party authorities. The "Cultural Revolution" at last enabled her to hoist herself into the spotlight: the predominant role which she was able to play at various points during this adventure is an indication — and by no means a minor one — of the degree of decadence to which maoist power had sunk. Chinese communism, entirely to its credit, has always given women a big place: Teng Ying-ch'ao (Chou En-lai's wife), Ts'ai Ch'ang (Li Fu-ch'un's wife) and many others have long revolutionary careers behind them, owing their position not to the influence of their husbands but to their own outstanding abilities. Chiang Ch'ing, on the contrary, owes her political credit entirely to her private relationship with Mao. Nothing in her past activities nor in her personality justifies the privileged position which she has today on the national scene. In the twilight of old age, when their jealous suspicion is easily aggravated, despots get rid of competent ministers and people of any character, and rely only on their favourites, concubines, eunuchs and valets. The "Cultural Revolution" dealt a heavy blow at the party's leading élite, replacing it with this mediocre actress as well as a private secretary (Ch'en Po-ta), a policeman (K'ang Sheng) and a colourless general, an ambitious sycophant accompanied by yet another wife (Lin Piao and Yeh Ch'ün): a curious reminder of the classic picture of dynasties in decline. The remarkable fact is not that Chiang Ch'ing regards the old revolutionaries with such hatred and contempt (one might expect that), but that despite her use of all the propaganda resources she has not succeeded in registering her image among the masses, even though their opinion is so easy to manipulate. It can be predicted even now that once Mao disappears, Chiang Ch'ing is the very first person whose power will be threatened. *Disgraced (1976).*

Ho Lung, the colourful adventurer

Born in Hunan in 1896. A career soldier, he joined the communist party in 1926, and was one of the main architects of the Nanchang uprising. Ho Lung is a character out of a novel: his origins were among adventurers and bandits, and he had scarcely any education (his scholastic career was cut short at the age of thirteen, after he had beaten up his teacher). He was a truculent hero in the tradition of the *Water Margin* bandits, and his political consciousness was restricted, like theirs, to a vague ideal of justice and a fierce loyalty to his brothers-in-arms. His prestige and popularity in the army were considerable; his positions in the party hierarchy (member of the politbureau and secretary of the South-Western bureau, which gave him a particularly strong grip over Szechuan) and in the military hierarchy (one of the country's ten marshals) were no less important. When he was denounced by the Red Guards and purged as a "counter-revolutionary revisionist" in January 1967, it caused as violent a disturbance in the army as the purge of P'eng Teh-huai in 1959. *Rehabilitated, died (date unknown).*

Hsiao Hua, the general who dared to defy Chiang Ch'ing

Born in 1915 in Kiangsi. A career soldier who served under Lin Piao from 1929 onwards. After the Liberation he was made director of the political department of the People's Liberation Army, with the rank of general. During the "Cultural Revolution" he violently rebuffed Chiang Ch'ing by preventing her from supervising the "Cultural Revolution" in the army; the Red Guards sacked his house in January 1967, in order to avenge Chiang Ch'ing. Lin Piao's influence was not enough to keep him afloat, and he was finally eliminated in January 1968. *Rehabilitated.*

Hsieh Fu-chih, the tough cop

Born in Hupeh in 1897 (other sources make him ten years younger). Had a military training. Minister of Security from 1959 onwards; commander and political commissar of the security forces. During the "Cultural Revolution" he presented himself as a maoist radical — which is why, in July 1967, the Wuhan mutineers arrested him along with Wang Li. Hsieh runs the Peking Revolutionary Committee, but he seems to have suffered an inexplicable eclipse recently; this is undoubtedly connected with the current purge of the main protagonists of the "Cultural Revolution". It is difficult to foresee what Hsieh's fate will be: he is an old fox with much experience, in the past he has demonstrated a remarkable capacity for survival — and what's more, he has a grip on the police. *Died (1972).*

Hsü Shih-yu, the old trooper

Born in 1906 in Hunan according to some people, in Hupeh according to others, from a peasant family. Studied Chinese boxing at the famous Shaolin temple, then served a term under the famous "warlord" Wu P'ei-fu. He still has something of the "warlord" style: a soldier from top to toe, he does not bother with political trickery — and this led him to commit several resounding gaffes during the "Cultural Revolution". He was commander of the Nanking military region, and this powerful territorial base enabled him to greet the instructions of the Cultural Revolution Group with defiant insolence, and to eat Red Guards for breakfast without the slightest punishment. But the Group succeeded in imposing Chang Ch'un-ch'iao on him as political commissar of the region. It remains to be seen who will get rid of whom: the way things are going at the moment, I would certainly not put my money on Chang Ch'un-ch'iao.

Huang Yung-sheng, the old soldier who owes his position to seniority

Born in Kiangsi (or Hupeh?) in 1906 or 1908. From 1927 onwards he could be found at Mao Tse-tung's side; he fired the first shots with the small guerrilla band in the Ching-kang mountains. Army life was his only school and his only horizon; he gradually got promoted, for being a conscientious soldier. He was commander of the Canton military region when the "Cultural Revolution" caught him off guard. Not very well acquainted with the subtleties of politics, he instinctively lined up with the traditional order, i.e. the bureaucratic apparatus, and began to smash the Red Guards. He was denounced by the revolutionary rebels and recalled to Peking in 1967, to the great joy of his opponents. However, their triumph was short-lived; in the autumn of the same year he returned to Canton with the blessing of Chou En-lai, and in February 1968 became the leader of the new Kwangtung Revolutionary Committee. His promotion did not stop there. A little while later, he was made chief of the general staff of the People's Liberation Army in Peking. *Disgraced (1971)*.

K'ang Sheng, the secret agent sent by Stalin

His real name is Chao Jung; he was born in 1903 in Shantung (Madame Mao's province) into a landowning family. He studied at Shanghai University; in 1927, alongside Ku Shun-chang, he organised the Shanghai workers' insurrection. A close associate of Po Ku on the 1931 politbureau. During two successive stays in Moscow (1932-3 and 1935-7) as a delegate to the Comintern he was in close association with Wang Ming. (Wang Ming and Po Ku were two of Mao's keenest opponents.) In 1937 Stalin sent him to Yenan together with Wang Ming and Ch'en Yün. From this point onwards he took over the secret services, a department which is still the occult source of his power. Educated by the Russians and chosen by Stalin, like Fouché he seems inclined to serve several different masters: it was his obsequious initiative that caused Liu Shao-ch'i's theoretical tract "The Spiritual Formation of the Communist" to be republished in 1962, and at the beginning of 1966 he was a member of the "group of five" which P'eng Chen organised in order to torpedo the "Cultural Revolution". (It is difficult to determine whether his role in this group's activities was that of an eventual turncoat or of someone who was an informer from the beginning.) K'ang Sheng is a riddle, but he is extremely capable; he wields considerable influence, but it is difficult to anticipate how he will use it. He has the impenetrable facial features of a tough, dour cop, but also some unlikely talents: he is an original and delicate amateur painter (in the style of Pa-ta Shan-jen), and his calligraphy is remarkably elegant. *Died (1975)*.

Li Fu-ch'un Chou En-lai's faithful collaborator

Born in Hunan in 1900; studied in France between 1919 and 1924, with the help of the famous "students' and workers' movement" to which Chou En-lai also belonged. During his stay in France he married Ts'ai Ch'ang and joined the communist party. On his return to China he took part in the Long March. His job was chiefly to organise economic affairs; after the Liberation he was put at the head of the Planning Commission. As Vice-chairman of the State Council he is a close collaborator of Chou En-lai's: the attacks made on him several times during the "Cultural Revolution" and the loss of his seat on the polit-bureau were, at the time, setbacks for Chou himself. But he was never in lasting danger; Li has maintained his position on the central committee, and now it is his former adversaries who are badly placed.

Li Hsien-nien, the guerrilla turned technocrat

Born in 1905 in Hupeh. An apprentice carpenter, he left his village in the wake of the armies during the Northern Expedition, and joined the communist party in 1927. Until 1935, when he joined hands with Mao Tse-tung, he led guerrilla activities in Hupeh, Szechuan and Shensi. He was a very popular commander among his troops, and served first under Hsü Hsiang-ch'ien and then under Liu Po-ch'eng. After the Liberation he suddenly dropped his military career to become a technocrat. As Minister of Finance after 1954 and Vice-chairman of the State Council, he was incorporated in Chou En-lai's team of pragmatic adminis-trators, and became one of the people chiefly responsible for the Chinese economy. In this position he demonstrated little receptiveness to Mao Tse-tung's ideas, but his natural prudence always prevented him from showing his full hostility. His attitude is typified by the reply he gave to a Red Guard tribunal which interrogated him about his position during the Lushan confer-ence: "The first day I displayed my agreement with P'eng Teh-huai's views but later, on the second day, I opposed them." This ambiguity, in addition to the fact that he owed his promotion initially to the Liu Shao-ch'i clique, made things considerably difficult for him during the "Cultural Revolution". He was denounced along with T'an Chen-lin, Ch'en Yün, etc. His even-tual survival — he has even kept his place on the politbureau — has undoubtedly been due less to Chou En-lai's influence (which was limited — he did not succeed in saving Ch'en Yi, Li Fu-ch'un or Ch'en Yün) than to the excellent connections which Li has maintained in the army, and perhaps even to the support of Lin Piao, whose subordinate he was for a long time.

Liu Po-ch'eng, the patriarch

Born in 1892 in Szechuan, from a family in genteel poverty. Liu had the benefit of an excellent classical education. A career soldier, he took part in the 1911 campaign against the Manchu dynasty's troops, during which he lost an eye. He was one of the organisers of the Nanchang uprising in 1927, and subsequently took refuge in the USSR, studying at a Moscow military academy. On his return to China in 1930 he became one of the leading figures in the Red Army, and he had a mounting series of spectacular achievements: the seizure of Tsunyi, the crossing of the Tatu, etc. After the Liberation, he was put in charge of organising and supervising the military academies of the whole country, and was promoted to the position of marshal in 1955. He was devoid of political ambitions, and got through the "Cultural Revolution" without doing too badly. He is in poor health (he cannot move unaided), but nevertheless has considerable prestige among his numerous former subordinates, who now form a powerful military mafia at the top of the apparatus.

Lo Jui-ch'ing, the architect or the victim of a coup d'état?

Born in Szechuan in 1904, from a family of rich landowners. Studied at the Huang-p'u (Whampoa) military academy and joined the communist party in 1926. He took part in the Nanchang uprising and then took refuge in the USSR, where he received a theoretical and practical training in secret police activities; he subsequently studied in France for a time, at a party school set up by the Comintern. On his return to China he joined the underground in the Ching-kang mountains and took part at Mao's side in the Long March, as chief of Security. After the Liberation he was appointed Minister of Security and at the same time commander and political commissar of the security forces, until 1959. From 1959 until his arrest at the beginning of 1966, he was a Vice-chairman of the State Council, Vice-minister of Defence and Chief of the General Staff (with the rank of general). He was arrested at the beginning of 1966 on some obscure accusation about conspiring to carry out a coup d'état; he tried to commit suicide by jumping out of a window, but only succeeded in breaking his legs. Hauled up on trial in front of two mass rallies in December 1966, and then again in June 1967. *Rehabilitated.*

P'eng Chen, the man who tried to sabotage the "Cultural Revolution"

Born in Shensi in 1902, from a poor family. Joined the League of Communist Youth in 1922. Organised workers' and students' movements; was arrested in 1929, released in 1935. During the war he directed the guerrillas behind the enemy lines in Shansi-Chahar. When K'ang Sheng lost his job as director of the party school in Yenan in 1941 (for boycotting the thought of Mao Tse-tung!) and was replaced by Mao himself, P'eng was named deputy director. After the Liberation P'eng became a member of the politbureau, secretary of the party committee of Peking municipality, and mayor of Peking. Since 1935 he has had a close relationship with Liu Shao-ch'i, and became one of his best lieutenants. He had considerable influence in the cultural sphere, and this expressed itself through two of his former subordinates, Lu Ting-yi and Chou Yang (respectively director and deputy director of the Propaganda Department — they were both purged during the "Cultural Revolution"). P'eng presided over a bold team of anti-maoists in Peking (Wu Han and Teng T'o), and tried to derail the "Cultural Revolution" from the beginning. Removed in August 1966, he was purged with special ferocity, and in December of that year he was exposed to the fury of a Red Guard rally.

T'ao Chu, betrayed by his own ambition

Born in 1905 in Hunan. Joined the communist party in 1926, took part in the Northern Expedition in Yeh T'ing's army; took part in the Nanchang uprising, then in the Canton uprising, in which he played an important role. Arrested by the Kuomintang in 1933 and condemned to life imprisonment, but released in 1937. During the war he led the guerrillas in Hupeh. After the Liberation he made himself noticed in Kwangsi-Kwangtung by the implacable ferocity with which he carried through the agrarian reform. He was rewarded for his zeal: in the end he monopolised virtually all political, military and administrative power in these two southern provinces. This power eventually caused worries. At the beginning of the "Cultural Revolution" Mao, rather than set this weighty figure against him, dangled in front of him the bait of a glorious promotion: he made him director of the Propaganda Department and placed him on the standing committee of the politbureau, where he got to fourth position in the supreme hierarchy (August 1966). By going to Peking, Tao was of course forced to abandon the cover of his private fortress: for Mao, it had all been a ploy to isolate him and, several months later, to get rid of him.

Teng T'o, the conscience and the dignity of an intellectual

Born in 1911 in Shantung. Active in the clandestine communist networks of the "white" zones before the war, he was imprisoned by the Kuomintang. During the war, he reached the frontier region of Shansi-Chahar (a guerrilla zone run by P'eng Chen) and became director of the region's daily paper. After the Liberation he was named chief editor of the *People's Daily*, a post which he occupied from 1953 to 1959. From 1959 until his disgrace in 1966 he was secretary to the secretariat of the Peking municipal committee of the party, and chief editor of *Ch'ien-hsien* (its journal). Teng T'o is an enormously cultured man who is equally at home in marxist philosophy or in the history of classical China. He is well served by his brilliant writing talents, and excels in short satirical or polemical essays which recall the magnificent tradition of Lu Hsun. The writings published at the beginning of the 1960s in *Peking wan-pao*, *Peking jih-pao* and *Ch'ien-hsien* (which were collected and published under the title *Evening Conversations at Yenshan*) constitute what is so far the boldest and most perspicacious denunciation of maoism ever made in China. Teng T'o owed his freedom of action essentially to the protection of P'eng Chen. As a prelude to the elimination of P'eng, Teng was purged in May 1966. It is not known what became of him subsequently.

Tung Pi-wu, a relic from the past

Born in 1886 in Hupeh, Tung is a venerable and historic monument. In 1901 he obtained the *hsiu-ts'ai* degree in the mandarin examinations of the old Ch'ing empire. In 1910, in Japan, he joined Sun Yat-sen's clandestine revolutionary party, and later took part in the 1911 revolution (in Hupei). In 1915 he was arrested during a plot against Yüan Shih-k'ai. A founding member of the Chinese Communist Party in Shanghai, 1921. After the White Terror of 1927 he took refuge in Moscow, where he stayed for five years. He took part in the Long March. During the war, he was the communist party's delegate to the nationalist government at Chungking. He took part in the Chungking negotiations in 1945, as well as in the San Francisco conference of the same year, which created the United Nations Organisation. In 1959 he was elected Vice-chairman of the People's Republic, a position which he has held until now. He was quite badly treated during the "Cultural Revolution" (his second son, Tung Lei-hsün, was arrested in Canton in 1967 for "counter-revolutionary activities"); he was eventually fished out of trouble but relieved of his protocol posts (accepting letters of accreditation from new ambassadors in the absence of the Chairman, etc.), and seems to have lost all political influence. *Rehabilitated and reactivated, died (1975).*

Wang Li, *sic transit . . .*

Born in 1918 in Kiangsu, from a landowning family. He was a Kuomintang militant at first, but joined the communist party in 1939. He was employed on propaganda activities, and after the Liberation became deputy director of the *Red Flag.* During the "Cultural Revolution" he distinguished himself by his fervour and his radicalism; he functioned as director of the Propaganda Department after T'ao Chu was purged. He was sent to Wuhan in July 1967 with Hsieh Fu-chih to sort out some local problems, and was seized and badly beaten by local mutineers: on his return to Peking he was given a triumphant welcome. Bent on continuing his career as a martyr, he demanded that those who were guilty should be punished: this upset the military, and in order not to hurt their feelings Wang Li was sacrificed forthwith. In October 1967 he was deprived of all his posts, dragged through the mud and swept aside.

Wang Tung-hsing, "the gorilla"

His date of birth is unknown, as are his biographical details. Like K'ang Sheng he is a policeman, and has the taste for secrecy and obscurity which is common to their profession. In contrast to K'ang Sheng, however, he is unequivocally faithful to Mao, and was his "gorilla" for a long time. Deputy Minister of Security from 1955 to 1958 and from 1962 to the present.

Wu Fa-hsien, the corpulent commissar

Born in 1914 in Kiangsi. A soldier from a very early age, Wu spent his entire career in the army as a political commissar. He was promoted to commander-in-chief of the airforce, and has for a long time had solid connections with Lin Piao. Wu is easily identifiable on official photographs: he is monstrously fat, and his face is so blubbery that it is difficult to see his eyes. *Disgraced.*

Wu Han, the first victim of the "Cultural Revolution"

Born in 1909 in Chekiang, from a poor family. He revealed his talents while working to pay his way through Tsinghua University (history); he was put in charge of a course at the same university as soon as he had graduated. During the war he was professor of history at Yunnan University, and after the victory he returned to teach at Tsinghua. During this whole period he was secretly a member of the communist party, and was very active in its underground networks. From the Liberation until his disgrace in 1966, he was deputy mayor of Peking. Like Teng T'o, with whom he was closely connected, he enjoyed the protection of P'eng Chen, the mayor of Peking. A specialist in Ming history, he wrote several scholarly works on this period (a biography of Chu Yuan-chang, studies on Hai Jui etc.). He subsequently used his studies on Hai Jui to put before a wider public a bold political allegory on the unjust dismissal of P'eng Teh-huai, as well as a critique of Mao's autocratic methods (the article in the *People's Daily* "Hai Jui reprimands the emperor", and above all the Peking classical opera *The Dismissal of Hai Jui*). It was the denunciation of this opera by Yao Wen-yuan (acting on Mao's personal instructions) in November 1965 that marked the beginning of the "Cultural Revolution". *Committed suicide.*

Yao Wen-yuan, the model pupil

Like Chang Ch'un-ch'iao (whose assistant and junior he is), Yao's star rose with the "Cultural Revolution". His father, Yao P'eng-tzu, was a minor writer active among left-wing literary circles in Shanghai (and in Szechuan during the war). Yao is probably a little over forty now. We do not know very much about his past record; in 1951 he was a member of the central committee of the Youth League in Shanghai. He was a literary critic and then a member of the editorial board of a Shanghai literary and artistic journal; he distinguished himself politically for the first time in 1955 as one of the young cubs in the pack which the great huntsman Chou Yang let loose against his unfortunate quarry, Hu Feng. From that moment on, Yao had found his vocation: he was to specialise in the denunciation of writers and intellectuals, and busied himself fixing Ting Ling, Feng Hsueh-feng, Pa Jen, Chou Ku-ch'eng and many others. This great fondness for witch-hunting got him promoted to the editorial committee of *Liberation Daily*, the paper of the Shanghai party's municipal committee, as well as bringing him to the attention of Chang Ch'un-ch'iao, who was then director of the propaganda department of the same committee. He was hated in literary circles (the famous dramatist Hsia Yen and the great novelist Pa Chin did not hide their contempt for him); his indifference to ethical principles and aesthetic values, and his talent for using "the thought of Mao Tse-tung" to expose the crimes of any writer named to him as a target, made him Mao's ideal auxiliary when the "Cultural Revolution" was being launched. He was given the honour of lighting the touchpaper, with his famous article of November 1965 in *Wenhui pao*; under cover of an attack against Wu Han's essay, the article was in fact aimed at P'eng Chen. It was written on the initiative and instructions of Mao, and was revised and corrected by Chiang Ch'ing; it was followed by another commissioned article which was theoretically directed against Teng T'o, but which in fact was designed to close the trap sprung on P'eng Chen. Yao proved himself on various missions to be a keen and efficient tout for Mao and Chiang Ch'ing; he was rewarded with high office, becoming first the adjutant of Chang Ch'un-ch'iao at the head of the Shanghai Revolutionary Committee and then the youngest member of the politbureau. This latter promotion is really surprising, in view of his lack of experience or of any particular talents (his articles are merely indigestible and dogmatic occasional pieces, dictated by his employers); but it can perhaps be explained precisely by this unconditional docility of his, which is the sole virtue that the ageing Mao now demands of his collaborators. And according to an (unverifiable) rumour, he married either Mao's niece or his stepdaughter; this would obviously explain the exceptional favours which he has enjoyed. His appearance is disconcerting: he reminds one of a village idiot, with his cap crammed over his forehead and his silly smile. He looks like a simple cretin rather than a professional polemicist. *Disgraced (1976).*

Yeh Chien-ying, a marshal and a diplomat

Born in Kwangtung in 1899 (or in 1896 or 1903, according to other sources). Received a traditional education; went with his father to Singapore and subsequently to Vietnam. In 1919 he went to the military academy in Yunnan. In 1923 he accompanied Sun Yat-sen on the punitive Kweilin expedition. He took part in the Northern Expedition, serving under Chang Fa-k'ui. In 1927 he took part in the Nanchang uprising and then took refuge in Hong Kong along with Chou En-lai, whom he looked after during his illness. Together with Yeh T'ing he organised the "Canton Commune" uprising (December 1927). He went to Moscow in 1928 to study military science, then travelled to Germany and Paris. On returning to Moscow he studied to be a theatre director: this was a talent which he was able to use when he went back to China in 1931, where he organised a drama group in the Kiangsi soviet. He drew up the strategic plans for the Long March, during which he took Mao's side in the dispute with Chang Kuot'ao (1935). He played some part in the preparations for the Sian incident. During the war he organised the infiltration of the communists into the Kuomintang armies; this enabled him to deploy his talents as a politician and diplomat which, according to eye-witnesses, were worthy of a Chou En-lai. He assisted Mao at the peace negotiations with the Kuomintang in 1945, and in 1955 he was appointed a marshal (China only has ten). In August 1965, sensing that the wind was going to change, he published an article about the military operations of 1948-9, which attributed their entire success to the leadership of Mao Tse-tung alone. This article, which indicates his subtle political instinct, enabled him in the end to survive the "Cultural Revolution" triumphantly, in spite of some delicate moments. He is the father-in-law of the famous pianist Liu Shih-k'un, who was less fortunate: the Red Guards broke his fingers, accusing him of playing too much Western classical music.

Yeh Ch'ün, a lady of elegance

Just about all we know of her is that she is Lin Piao's wife. The fact that this sole qualification has now got her into the politbureau is an eloquent testimony to the régime's decadence. Since 1968 she has had an official post in an administrative department of the Military Commission; on official occasions she wears military uniform. In complete contrast to Chiang Ch'ing, she is a woman of extraordinarily distinguished, thoroughbred appearance; all her movements are marked by a kind of aristocratic, nonchalant elegance. A strange companion for Lin Piao. *Disgraced, died (1971).*

Notes

1. See *Mao Tse-tung hsuan-chi* ("Selected Works of Mao Tse-tung"), vol. 3, p. 1101.
2. Edgar Snow, *Red Star over China*, p. 150 (New York, 1938).
3. *Mao chu-hsi yü-lu* ("Thoughts of Mao"), p. 33.
4. *Mao Tse-tung hsuan-chi*, vol. 2, pp. 507-24 (Peking, 1952).
5. Charles de Gaulle, *Mémoires d'espoir*, vol. 2 (Paris, 1971).
6. Stuart Schram, *Mao Tse-tung*, p. 299 (Harmondsworth, 1966).
7. Quoted in *Ming pao* (a Hong Kong independent daily), 18 August 1967.
8. Text reproduced in *Ming pao*, 5 July 1968.
9. *Ching-kang-shan pao* (newspaper of the Red Guards at Tsinghua University), 18 April 1967. Reproduced in English in *Survey of China Mainland Press*, no. 3946, and in *Current Background*, no. 834.
10. See "The ins and outs of the counter-revolutionary Ch'ang Kuan-lou affair: let us angrily unmask the abominable criminal activities of the counter-revolutionary putschist group of the ex-Peking municipal committee", in *Tung-fang hung*, newspaper of the Red Guards at Peking Mining Institute), 20 April 1967. Reprinted in Ting Wang, *Teng T'o hsuan-chi* ("Writings of Teng T'o"), pp. 548-66 (Hong Kong, 1969).
11. Huang Chen-hsia, *Chung-kung chün-jen chih* ("Mao's Generals"), pp. 207-18 (Hong Kong, 1968).
12. *People's Daily*, 17 August 1967. See also *China News Analysis*, no. 685, 17 November 1967.
13. See Ting Wang, *P'eng Teh-huai wen-t'i chuan-chi* ("Documents on the P'eng Teh-huai question"), vol. 3, pp. 19-25 (Hong Kong, 1969).
14. See Charles Neuhauser, "The Chinese Communist Party in the 1960s: prelude to the Cultural Revolution", in *China Quarterly*, no. 32, October-December 1967.
15. *People's Daily*, 18 May 1965, quoted in B. Bridgham, "Mao's Cultural Revolution: origins and development", in *China Quarterly*, no. 29, January-March 1967.
16. John Gittings, *The Role of the Chinese Army*, p. 256 (Oxford 1967), quoted in Neuhauser, op. cit.
17. Ch'i Pen-yü, "Critique of the reactionary capitalist position of the *Ch'ien-hsien* and the *Peking jih-pao*", in *Red Flag*, 11 March 1966.
18. See *Chinese Communist Party Documents of the Great Proletarian Cultural Revolution*, pp. 3-12 (Hong Kong, 1968).
19. Eventually published in the *People's Daily*, 17 May 1967.

Index

Li Ching-ch'üan, 67, 135
Li Fu-ch'un, 62, 118, 126, 133, 158, 159, 179, 185, 244, 247-8
Li Hsien-nien, 26, 62, 69, 179, 182, 183, 185, 248
Li Hsiu-ch'eng, 242
Li Hsueh-feng, 69, 90, 109, 127, 182, 184
Li Li-san, 82
Li Teh-sheng, 184
Li Tsai-han, 205
Li Tso-p'eng, 182, 183, 184
Li Tsung-jen, 165-6
Li Yi-che, 235-9
Li Yü, 16
Li Yuan, 127
Liang Hsing-ch'u, 67
Liang Jen-k'ui, 110
Lieh Tzu, 14
Lin Chieh, 85, 89, 113, 158
Lin Piao, 23, 36, 37-40, 44, 47, 49, 50, 51, 52, 58, 61, 62, 63, 66, 76, 77, 80, 83, 87, 89, 93-5, 106, 110, 116, 117, 118, 119, 120, 121, 122, 126, 127, 130, 133, 134, 147, 148, 149, 150, 156, 162, 167, 179, 180, 181, 182, 183, 184, 185, 186, 190, 196, 197, 202, 203, 205, 206, 235-8, 245, 248, 252, 255
Liu Chi-fa, 111
Liu Chien-hsün, 108
Liu Feng, 110
Liu Hao-t'ien, 182
Liu Hsien-ch'üan, 84, 182
Liu Ke-p'ing, 182
Liu Lan-t'ao, 135
Liu Ning-yi, 69
Liu Pang, 15
Liu Po-ch'eng, 77, 80, 179, 183, 248, 249
Liu Po-yü, 63
Liu Shao-ch'i, 22, 24-9, 31, 32, 33, 36, 38, 39, 43, 50, 51, 52, 64-5, 72, 81, 95, 97-8, 99-105, 107, 108, 109, 113, 117, 119, 122, 124, 146, 150, 151, 160, 171, 178, 186, 198, 202, 203, 204, 205, 227, 237, 242, 243, 244, 247, 248, 250
Liu Shih-k'un, 255
Liu Tien-ch'en, 109
Liu Tzu-hou, 109
Liu Ya-tzu, 15
Lo Chia-lun, 17
Lo Ehr-kang, 242
Lo Jui-ch'ing, 32, 47, 49, 52, 60, 93, 102, 117, 118, 119, 120, 249
Lu Hsün, 86, 251
Lu Ting-yi, 32, 33, 50, 51, 77, 98, 102, 144, 250
Ludwig II of Bavaria, 16
Lushan Conference, 22-4, 30-31, 40, 84, 126, 207, 213, 228, 229, 231, 241, 248

Ma Hui, 109
McAleavy, H., 232
Malraux, André, 16
Mao Tse-tung:
  poet and artist, 15
  Mao and Chinese tradition, 16, 19, 145
  hostility towards intellectuals, 17, 96-7
  Great Leap Forward, 20-22
  Mao and Liu Shao-ch'i, 24, 97-8, 100-105, 152
  "A new stage", 25
  Lushan Conference, 22-31
    under attack, 34-5
  Mao and Lin Piao, 37-40, 93-5
  attempts to return to power, 40-5
  launching the "Cultural Revolution", 45-9
  cult of Mao, 70, 75-6, 130-31, 149, 168, 196, 227
  on education, 96-7, 144-5, 161
  as emperor, 99, 148-9
  on the "Cultural Revolution", 134-41
  Selected Works, 165, 169
  mummified, 207-10